Impacts and Challenges of Cloud Business Intelligence

Shadi Aljawarneh
Jordan University of Science and Technology, Jordan

Manisha Malhotra
Chandigarh University, India

A volume in the Advances in
Systems Analysis, Software
Engineering, and High Performance
Computing (ASASEHPC) Book Series

Published in the United States of America by
    IGI Global
    Business Science Reference (an imprint of IGI Global)
    701 E. Chocolate Avenue
    Hershey PA, USA 17033
    Tel: 717-533-8845
    Fax: 717-533-8661
    E-mail: cust@igi-global.com
    Web site: http://www.igi-global.com

Library of Congress Cataloging-in-Publication Data

Names: Aljawarneh, Shadi, editor. | Malhotra, Manisha, 1987- editor.
Title: Impacts and challenges of cloud business intelligence / Shadi
  Aljawarneh and Manisha Malhotra, editors.
Description: Hershey, PA : Business Science Reference, [2021] | Includes
  bibliographical references and index. | Summary: "This book provides
  research on business intelligence in cloud computing and explores its
  applications in conjunction with other tools"-- Provided by publisher.
Identifiers: LCCN 2020005665 (print) | LCCN 2020005666 (ebook) | ISBN
  9781799850403 (hardcover) | ISBN 9781799854470 (paperback) | ISBN
  9781799850410 (ebook)
Subjects: LCSH: Information technology--Management. | Cloud computing. |
  Business intelligence.
Classification: LCC HD30.2 .I477 2021 (print) | LCC HD30.2 (ebook) | DDC
  658.4/72--dc23
LC record available at https://lccn.loc.gov/2020005665
LC ebook record available at https://lccn.loc.gov/2020005666

This book is published in the IGI Global book series Advances in Systems Analysis, Software Engineering, and High Performance Computing (ASASEHPC) (ISSN: 2327-3453; eISSN: 2327-3461)

British Cataloguing in Publication Data
A Cataloguing in Publication record for this book is available from the British Library.

All work contributed to this book is new, previously-unpublished material.
The views expressed in this book are those of the authors, but not necessarily of the publisher.

For electronic access to this publication, please contact: eresources@igi-global.com.

Advances in Systems Analysis, Software Engineering, and High Performance Computing (ASASEHPC) Book Series

ISSN:2327-3453
EISSN:2327-3461

Editor-in-Chief: Vijayan Sugumaran, Oakland University, USA

MISSION

The theory and practice of computing applications and distributed systems has emerged as one of the key areas of research driving innovations in business, engineering, and science. The fields of software engineering, systems analysis, and high performance computing offer a wide range of applications and solutions in solving computational problems for any modern organization.

The **Advances in Systems Analysis, Software Engineering, and High Performance Computing (ASASEHPC) Book Series** brings together research in the areas of distributed computing, systems and software engineering, high performance computing, and service science. This collection of publications is useful for academics, researchers, and practitioners seeking the latest practices and knowledge in this field.

COVERAGE

- Parallel Architectures
- Engineering Environments
- Virtual Data Systems
- Computer System Analysis
- Performance Modelling
- Distributed Cloud Computing
- Computer Networking
- Computer Graphics
- Human-Computer Interaction
- Software Engineering

IGI Global is currently accepting manuscripts for publication within this series. To submit a proposal for a volume in this series, please contact our Acquisition Editors at Acquisitions@igi-global.com or visit: http://www.igi-global.com/publish/.

Titles in this Series

For a list of additional titles in this series, please visit:
http://www.igi-global.com/book-series/advances-systems-analysis-software-engineering/73689

Handbook of Research on Modeling, Analysis, and Control of Complex Systems
Ahmad Taher Azar (Prince Sultan University, Saudi Arabia) and Nashwa Ahmad Kamal
(Cairo University, Egypt)
Engineering Science Reference • © 2021 • 480pp • H/C (ISBN: 9781799857884) • US
$295.00

Artificial Intelligence Paradigms for Smart Cyber-Physical Systems
Ashish Kumar Luhach (The PNG University of Technology, Papua New Guinea) and Atilla
Elçi (Hasan Kalyoncu University, Turkey)
Engineering Science Reference • © 2021 • 392pp • H/C (ISBN: 9781799851011) • US
$225.00

Advancements in Model-Driven Architecture in Software Engineering
Yassine Rhazali (Moulay Ismail University of Meknes, Morocco)
Engineering Science Reference • © 2021 • 287pp • H/C (ISBN: 9781799836612) • US
$215.00

Cloud-Based Big Data Analytics in Vehicular Ad-Hoc Networks
Ram Shringar Rao (Ambedkar Institute of Advanced Communication Technologies and
Research, India) Nanhay Singh (Ambedkar Institute of Advanced Communication Technologies
and Research, India) Omprakash Kaiwartya (School of Science and Technology, Nottingham
Trent University, UK) and Sanjoy Das (Indira Gandhi National Tribal University, India)
Engineering Science Reference • © 2021 • 312pp • H/C (ISBN: 9781799827641) • US
$245.00

*Formal and Adaptive Methods for Automation of Parallel Programs Construction Emerging
Research and Opportunities*
Anatoliy Doroshenko (Institute of Software Systems, Ukraine) and Olena Yatsenko (Institute
of Software Systems, Ukraine)
Engineering Science Reference • © 2021 • 279pp • H/C (ISBN: 9781522593843) • US
$195.00

For an entire list of titles in this series, please visit:
http://www.igi-global.com/book-series/advances-systems-analysis-software-engineering/73689

701 East Chocolate Avenue, Hershey, PA 17033, USA
Tel: 717-533-8845 x100 • Fax: 717-533-8661
E-Mail: cust@igi-global.com • www.igi-global.com

Table of Contents

Section 1
Impact of Cloud Business Intelligence

Section 2
Cloud Governance and Big Data: A Case Study

Section 3
Metaheuristic Approach and Cloud Security

Section 4
Energy and Scheduling Optimization

Detailed Table of Contents

Section 1
Impact of Cloud Business Intelligence

Chapter 1

> *Inderbir Kaur Sandhu, GSSDGS Khalsa College, Patiala, India*
> *Manisha Malhotra, Chandigarh University, India*
> *Praneet Rangi Randhawa, DAV College, Chandigarh, India*

One of the dynamic and emerging technologies is cloud computing, which provides
a supporting spectrum for applications, especially in the education sector. The
increasing use of this versatile technology is due to its low cost, resource pooling,
and rapid elasticity features. These amazing features act as an innovative driver of
success for the organization. The deployment of cloud is done in various applications
of enterprise resource planning (ERP), customer relationship management (CRM)
applications, supply chain management applications (SCM), medical applications,
education sector, and mobile applications. But the two major challenge for the
successful deployment of the cloud is the trust of the customer and the secure
network of the cloud for the integrity of the customer data. This chapter tries to
explore the various concepts of cloud computing technology from technical and
service point-of-view. Various opportunities using cloud computing are underlined.
Along with that, the emphasis is on the major two challenges of cloud computing
in terms of trust and security

Chapter 2

Pooja Thakur, Chandigarh University, India
Manisha Malhotra, Chandigarh University, India

The outburst of COVID-19 has affected the whole world. COVID-19 is the seventh member of the coronavirus family. There is no vaccine for the diseases, and due to this, the whole world has taken the step of social distancing that leads to lockdown. Due to the implementation of lockdown, normal working of all organizations converted to work from home. During such situation, organizations are opting to provide smooth working for the operations of business. Before the pandemic situation, each organization was concentrating on maximizing profit. But today they are opting the practices such as cloud computing, business intelligence, neural network, IoT, and many more so that business work can be done. During this pandemic situation, cloud business intelligence plays an important role for the smooth working of business. The contribution of this chapter is to show how cloud business intelligence is used to fulfill the need of the business ecosystem.

Chapter 3

Meenakshi Garg, Government Bikram College of Commerce, India
Gaurav Dhiman, Government Bikram College of Commerce, India

In recent years, cloud computing technology has gained a great deal of interest from both academia and industry. Cloud computing's success benefited from its ability to offer global IT services such as core infrastructure, platforms, and applications to cloud customers around the web. It also promises on-demand offerings and new ways of pricing packages. However, cloud job scheduling is still NP-complete and has become more difficult due to certain factors such as resource dynamics and on-demand customer application requirements. To fill this void, this chapter presents the seagull optimization algorithm (SOA) for scheduling work in the cloud world. The efficiency of the SOA approach is compared to that of state-of-the-art job scheduling algorithms by having them all implemented in the CloudSim toolkit.

Chapter 4

Shivani Jaswal, Chandigarh University, India

Cloud Computing has emerged as an expression that has described various other computing concepts that involve computers that are interconnected virtually. It is so prominent that it has modified the architecture by incorporating new design principles. Also, the present economic crisis, which is being experienced by most of the world, has oriented us towards cloud computing and its efficient services.

Here, business intelligence plays a pivotal role in extraction of valuable information and identifying hidden patterns of data. Also, any organization in striving stage can also act smartly with the use of various business intelligence solutions. Various benefits are also offered by the BI solutions such as working together as a team and identifying various resolutions. The contribution of this chapter is to show how the cloud computing environment has been merged with business intelligence to fulfil the future need of uplifting of economy.

Section 2
Cloud Governance and Big Data: A Case Study

Chapter 5

    Anustup Mukherjee, Chandigarh University, India
    Harjeet Kaur, Chandigarh University, India

Artificial intelligence within the area of computer vision is creating a replacement genre in detection industry. Here, AI is using the power of computer vision in creating advanced educational software LMS that detects student emotions during online classes, interviews, and judges their understanding and concentration level. It also generates automated content in step with their needs. This LMS cannot only judge audio, video, and image of a student; it also judges the voice tone. Through this judgement, the AI model understands how much a student is learning, effectivity, intellect, and drawbacks. In this chapter, the power of deep learning models VGG Net and Alex Net in LMS computer vision are used. This LMS architecture will be able to work like a virtual teacher that will be taking a parental guide to students.

Chapter 6

    Samia Chehbi Gamoura, Strasbourg University, France
    Manisha Malhotra, Chandigarh University, India

With the advent of big data in supply chain information systems (SCIS), data compliance and consistency are becoming vital. Today, SC stakeholders need to pay more attention to data governance, which requires changing traditional management methods. These can be achieved by mastering a single repository through what is usually named master data management (MDM). However, accomplishing this objective is particularly challenging in the complex logistics networks of supply chains (SC). The volatile nature of the logistics flows that increase exponentially because of the facilitation of exchanges' interoperability in the information systems. In this chapter, the authors propose an MDM-based framework for the supply chain information systems as an enabler for strong collaboration and compliance. For proof of concept, a case study of a French hypermarket is examined through benchmarking scenarios. The outcomes of the case validate our approach as a hands-on solution when applied correctly. Finally, the chapter discusses the key findings and the limitations of our framework.

Chapter 7

Sunny Sharma, Chandigarh University, India
Manisha Malhotra, Chandigarh University, India

Web usage mining is the use of data mining techniques to analyze user behavior in order to better serve the needs of the user. This process of personalization uses a set of techniques and methods for discovering the linking structure of information on the web. The goal of web personalization is to improve the user experience by mining the meaningful information and presented the retrieved information in a way the user intends. The arrival of big data instigated novel issues to the personalization community. This chapter provides an overview of personalization, big data, and identifies challenges related to web personalization with respect to big data. It also presents some approaches and models to fill the gap between big data and web personalization. Further, this research brings additional opportunities to web personalization from the perspective of big data.

Chapter 8

Meenakshi Garg, Government Bikram College of Commerce, India
Amandeep Kaur, Sri Guru Granth Sahib World University, India
Gaurav Dhiman, Government Bikram College of Commerce, India

In cloud computing systems, current works do not challenge the database failure rates and recovery techniques. In this chapter, priority-based resource allocation and scheduling technique is proposed by using the metaheuristic optimization approach spotted hyena optimizer (SHO). Initially, the emperor penguins predict the workload of user server and resource requirements. The expected completion time of each server is estimated with this predicted workload. Then the resources activities are classified based on the criteria of the deadline and the asset. Further, the employed servers are classified based on the workload and the estimated completed time. The proposed approach is compared with existing resource utilization techniques in terms of percentage of resource allocation, missed deadlines, and average server workload.

Section 3
Metaheuristic Approach and Cloud Security

Chapter 9

Amandeep Kaur, Sri Guru Granth Sahib World University, India
Gaurav Dhiman, Government Bikram College of Commerce, India
Meenakshi Garg, Government Bikram College of Commerce, India

Cloud computing provides internet users with quick and efficient tools to access and share the data. One of the most important research problems that need to be addressed is the effective performance of cloud-based task scheduling. Different cloud-based task scheduling algorithms based on metaheuristic optimization techniques like genetic algorithm (GA) and particle swarm optimization (PSO) scheduling algorithms are demonstrated and analyzed. In this chapter, cloud computing based on the spotted hyena optimizer (SHO) is proposed with a novel task scheduling technique. SHO algorithm is population-based and inspired by nature's spotted hyenas to achieve global optimization over a given search space. The findings show that the suggested solution performs better than other competitor algorithms.

Chapter 10

Yogesh Madhukar Ghorpade, Bharathiar University, India
R. Kamatchi Iyer, ISME School of Management and Entrepreneurship,
India

The cost-effective methodology and its implementation are the primary approaches towards cost computing to bring effectiveness with the proper requirements and provide the proper solution. This chapter focuses on the discussion about the cost-effective method using cloud infrastructure model for building and management of on-premise with the off-premise cloud service provider in business analytics. This chapter also elaborates the methodology undertaken and design considerations for implementation of cloud infrastructure with non-virtualized and on-premise infrastructure environment. The experiment using YGCIS (YG-cloud infrastructure solution) methodology is built for business analytics platform where infrastructure and its resources play a vital role. The cost-effective approach for total cost ownership (TCO) is implemented using YGCCS (YG-cost computing solution) framework. Thus, the solution obtained after implementing the above frameworks increases ROI % and reduces the TCO, impacting the business analytics needs.

Chapter 11

Prathap R., Vellore Institute of Technology, Vellore, India
Mohanasundaram R., Vellore Institute of Technology, Vellore, India

In the information technology sector, cloud computing plays an important role. Information was externalized in the cloud in the IT sector and part of data as a software. These offer utilities such as storage, software as a service, and application as a service and some web models, such as the deployment models, in four forms. The third-party wanted the data to be outsourced. In this chapter, the authors research and analyze technologies and frameworks for cloud computing. In cloud services, security problems are important. Therefore, the authors discuss safety problems and the concerns found in this chapter.

Section 4
Energy and Scheduling Optimization

Chapter 12

Ahan Chatterjee, The Neotia University, India

Cloud computing is the growing field in the industry, and every scale industry needs it now. The high scale usage of cloud has resulted in huge power consumption, and this power consumption has led to increase of carbon footprint affecting our mother nature. Thus, we need to optimize the power usage in the cloud servers. Various models are used to tackle this situation, of which one is a model based on link load. It minimized the bit energy consumption of network usage which includes energy efficiency routing and load balancing. Over this, multi-constraint rerouting is also adapted. Other power models which have been adapted are virtualization framework using multi-tenancy-oriented data center. It works by accommodating heterogeneous networks among virtual machines in virtual private cloud. Another strategy that is adopted is cloud partitioning concept using game theory. Other methods that are adopted are load spreading algorithm by shortest path bridging, load balancing by speed scaling, load balancing using graph constraint, and insert ranking method.

Chapter 13

Lokesh Pawar, Chandigarh University, India
Gaurav Bathla, Chandigarh University, India

Migrating applications on the cloud storage from the systems physically available on the premises is a difficult task. There are a lot of research articles providing solutions for the current problem of migration of applications by software industry. The chapter is shedding light on how to migrate the application efficiently using mathematical approach. The dependency of migration is directly proportional to the size of the data and the speed of the network. There are a number of storage options available on cloud for easy accessibility, cache-ability, and consistency. This chapter focuses on difficult migration of an application.

Chapter 14

Cloud business intelligence can solve numerous management issues that are faced by many businesses. If it is used in a correct manner, it can substitute seamless utilization of crucial information in the growth of business. In the self-hosted environment, business intelligence will face resource crisis situation on the never-ending expansion of warehouses and OLAP's demands on the primary network. Today, cloud computing has instigated optimism for the prospects of future business intelligence. But thing to focus here is, how will business intelligence be implemented on cloud platform, and further, how will the traffic be managed and what will the demand profile look like? Moreover, in today's world, data generated on a daily basis from many different sources are numerous and valuable information for making effective decisions. This chapter focuses and tries to attempt these questions related to taking business intelligence to the cloud.

Preface

Cloud basically stands for **C**ommon **L**ocation-independent **O**nline Utility service, available on-**D**emand. It's a pool of virtualized computer resources which supports large variety of different workloads, including batch-style back-end jobs and interactive, user-facing applications. Cloud computing thus offers computing technologies being offered at cloud. Cloud computing offer lots of advantages over traditional computing such as online resources, offline access, flexibility, and savings. It is distributed into three segments namely, applications, platforms and infrastructure. Majorly, the definition of cloud computing specifically revolves round the terms like scalability, pay-per use model, and virtualization. In fact, enablers supporting cloud computing are interoperability, portability, integration of components, ease of deployment, pay as per use, economic, rapid provisioning and elasticity and so on. Because of the appealing features mentioned above, cloud computing is becoming a temptation for all business organizations. Due to dynamic nature of cloud computing it is quite easy to increase the capacity of hardware or software, even without investing on purchases of it. From last few years, cloud computing has become a promising business concept. All existing business applications are complicated in nature and much too expensive. To run these applications there is a need of data centers having supporting staff and infrastructure like bandwidth, networks and server etc. along with a dedicate team for its execution. For deploying such kind of applications, organizations have to invest large amount of funds which makes it difficult for small businesses to establish themselves. Therefore cloud computing provides a simple alternative to start IT based business organization with much less initial investment.

OBJECTIVE OF THE BOOK

The purpose of this book is to present the concept of cloud computing and explore the various shortcomings of cloud. The background of assorted issues that arises in the field of cloud computing is to be discussed. It also highlights the comparison among the existing techniques of various problems. Furthermore, the future work will be provided to pursue the research in the same field. The main aim of this book is to provide the information to research community, students, practitioners, and academician also in the form of various aspects.

ORGANIZATION OF THE BOOK

This book contains 14 chapters arranged in different four sections. Section 1 comprises of four chapters which highlights the impact of business intelligence in Cloud computing. It also elaborates the impact of Covid-19 on it. Section 2 describes the four chapters which explains the concept of cloud governance and a case study of a hypermarket. Section 3 throws highlights on scheduling and security of cloud computing in three chapters. Finally section 4 divides into three chapters which describes an optimized energy efficiency algorithms. The summary of book organization is as follows:

SECTION 1: IMPACT OF CLOUD BUSINESS INTELLIGENCE (CHAPTERS 1-4)

This section highlights the impact of business intelligence on cloud computing. It also describes the impact of COVID-19 on it along with its future.

Chapter 1: This chapter presents economic crisis which is being experience by the maximum parts of the world has oriented towards cloud computing and its efficient services. Business intelligence plays a pivotal role in extraction of valuable information and hidden patterns of data can also be identified. Various benefits are also offered by the BI solutions such as working together as a team and identifying various resolutions. The contribution of this chapter is to represent the how the cloud computing environment has been merged with Business Intelligence to fulfill the future need for upliftment of economy.

Chapter 2: This chapter focuses on the discussion about the cost-effective method using cloud infrastructure model for building and management of on-premise with the off-premise cloud service provider in business analytics. It also elaborates about methodology undertaken and design considerations for implementation of cloud infrastructure with non-virtualized and on-premise infrastructure environment.

Chapter 3: This chapter focuses and tries to attempt these questions related to taking business intelligence to the cloud. Cloud Business Intelligence can solve numerous management issues that are faced by many businesses now a day. If it is used in a correct manner, it can substitute seamless utilization of crucial information in the growth of business. In the self-hosted environment, business intelligence will face resource crisis situation on the never ending expansion of warehouses and OLAP's demands on the primary network. Today cloud computing has instigated optimism for the prospects of future business intelligence. But thing to focus here is, how business intelligence will be implemented on cloud platform and further how will the traffic will be managed and demand profile will looks like

Chapter 4: This chapter represents how cloud business intelligence is used to fulfill the need of business ecosystem. The outburst of COVID-19 has affected the whole universe. COVID-19 is the 7th member of the coronavirus family. There is no vaccine for the dieses, due to this reason whole universe take the step of social distancing that leads to lockdown. Due to the implementation of lockdown, normal working of all organization converted to the work from home. During such situation organizations are opting the way by using which they can provide the smooth working for the operations of business. Before the pandemic situation, each organization was concentrating on maximizing profit. But now a day they are opting the practices such as Cloud Computing, business intelligence, neural network, IOT and many more so that business work come on track. During this pandemic situation Cloud business intelligence play important role for the smooth working of business.

SECTION 2: CLOUD GOVERNANCE AND BIG DATA – A CASE STUDY (CHAPTERS 5-8)

This section throws a light on cloud governance and explained the effect of big data with a case study of hypermarket Carrefour through benchmarking scenario.

Chapter 5: This chapter proposes an MDM-based framework for the Supply Chain Information Systems as an enabler for strong collaboration and compliance. For proof of concept, a case study of a French hypermarket is examined through benchmarking scenarios. The outcomes of the case validate our approach as a hands-on solution when applied correctly.

Chapter 6: This chapter used the power of Deep Learning models VGG Net and Alex Net in LMS computer vision. The LMS architecture will be able to work like a virtual teacher, that will be taking a parental guide to students. Artificial Intelligence within the area of computer vision is creating a replacement genre in Detection Industry. Here AI is using power of computer vision in creating advanced educational software LMS, that detects students emotions during online classes, interviews and judges their understanding and concentration level additionally also generate automated contents in step with their needs . This LMS cannot only judge audio, video and image of a student it also judge the voice tone. Through this judgment the AI model understand, how much a student is learning, its effectively, intellect & drawbacks.

Chapter 7: This chapter provides an overview of personalization, big data and identifies challenges related to web personalization with respect to big data. It also presents some approaches and models to fill the gap between big data and web personalization. Further, this research brings additional opportunities to Web personalization from the perspective of big data. Web usage mining is the use of data mining techniques to analyze user's behavior in order to better serve the needs of user. This process of personalization uses a set of techniques and methods for discovering the linking structure of information on the web. The goal of web personalization is to improve the user experience by mining the meaningful information and presented the retrieved information in a way the user intends. The arrival of big data instigated novel issues to the personalization community.

Chapter 8: The present article is putting light on how to migrate the application efficiently using mathematical approach. The dependency of migration is directly proportional to size of the data and speed of the network. There are number of storage options available on cloud for easy accessibility, cache-ability and consistency. This article focuses on difficult migration of an application. Migrating applications on the cloud storage from the systems physically available on the premises is a difficult task. There are a lot of research articles providing solution for the current problem of migration of applications by software industry.

SECTION 3: METAHEURISTIC APPROACH AND CLOUD SECURITY (CHAPTERS 9-11)

This section depicts the metaheuristic approach for scheduling and security in cloud computing.

Chapter 9: In this chapter, priority-based resource allocation and scheduling technique is proposed by using the metaheuristic optimization approach "Spotted Hyena Optimizer (SHO)". Initially, the emperor penguins predict the workload of user server and resource requirements. The expected completion time of each server is estimated with this predicted workload. Then the resources activities are classified based on the criteria of the deadline and the asset. Further, the employed servers are classified based on the work load and the estimated completed time. The proposed approach is compared with existing resource utilization techniques in terms of percentage of resource allocation, missed deadlines, and average server workload.

Chapter 10: In the information technology sector, cloud computing plays an important role. Information was externalized in the cloud in the IT sector. And part of data as a software. This knowledge transfer of services through the Cloud, cloud computing. These offer utilities such as storage, software as a service, and application as a service and some web models, such as the Deployment models, in four forms. The third-party wanted the data to be outsourced. In this chapter, authors do research and analyze technologies and frameworks for cloud computing. In cloud services, security problems are important. Therefore, we discuss safety problems and the concerns found in this paper.

Chapter 11: The deployment of Cloud is done in various applications of enterprise resource planning (ERP), customer relationship management (CRM) applications, supply chain management applications (SCM), medical applications, education sector, and mobile applications. But the two major challenges for the successful deployment of the cloud is the trust of the customer and the secure network of the cloud for the integrity of the customer's data. This chapter tries to explore the various concepts of Cloud computing technology from technical and service point-of-view. Various opportunities using cloud computing are underlined. Along with that, the emphasis is on the major two challenges of cloud computing in terms of trust and security.

SECTION 4: ENERGY AND SCHEDULING OPTIMIZATION (CHAPTERS 12-14)

This section describes the optimization techniques on energy efficiency in cloud computing.

Chapter 12: Cloud Computing is the up growing field in the industry, every scale industry needs it now. And the high scale usage of this cloud has resulted in huge power consumption, and this power consumption has led to increase of carbon footprint affecting our mother nature. Thus we need to optimize the power usage in the cloud servers. Various model is used to tackle this situation, of is model based on link load. It minimized the bit energy consumption of network usage which includes energy efficiency routing and load balancing. Over this multi constraint rerouting is also adapted. Other power model which has been adapted is virtualization framework using multi tenancy oriented data center. It works by accommodating heterogeneous network among virtual machine in virtual private cloud. Another strategy which is adopted is cloud partitioning concept using game theory. Other methods which are adopted are load spreading algorithm by shortest path bridging, load balancing by speed scaling is also used, load balancing using graph constraint and insert ranking method.

Chapter 13: Cloud computing provides Internet users with quick and efficient tools to access and share the data. One of the most important research problems that need to be addressed is the effective performance of cloud-based task scheduling. Different cloud-based task scheduling algorithms based on metaheuristic optimization techniques like Genetic Algorithm (GA) and Particle Swarm Optimization (PSO) scheduling algorithms are demonstrated and analyzed. In this paper, cloud computing based on the Spotted Hyena Optimizer (SHO) is proposed with a novel task scheduling technique. SHO algorithm is population-based and inspired by nature's spotted hyenas to achieve global optimization over a given search space. The findings show that the suggested solution performs better than other competitor algorithms.

Chapter 14: In recent years, cloud computing technology has gained a great deal of interest from both academia and industry. Cloud computing 's success benefited from its ability to offer global IT services such as core infrastructure, platforms, and applications to cloud customers around the web. It also promises on-demand offerings and new ways of pricing packages. However, cloud job scheduling is still NP-complete and has become more difficult due to certain factors such as resource dynamics and on-demand customer application requirements. To fill this void, this chapter presents the seagull optimization algorithm (SOA) for scheduling work in the cloud world. The efficiency of the SOA approach is compared to that of state-of-the-art job scheduling algorithms by having them all implemented in the CloudSim toolkit.

This book is expected to assist academician, IT professionals, researchers, industry people, advanced level students, government officials who are working in the field cloud computing. The book is expected to serve as a reference for the postgraduate students as it offers the requisite knowledge for understanding the security, scalability issues along with different solutions. This book is based on a research studies carried out by experienced academicians and is expected to shed new insights for researchers; academicians, students and improves understanding of cloud computing.

Shadi Aljawarneh
Jordan University of Science and Technology, Jordan

Preface

Manisha Malhotra
Chandigarh University, India

Acknowledgment

"A great book should leave you with many experiences, and slightly exhausted at the end. You live several lives while reading." – William Styron

Writing of a book is a rigorous task that contains lots of attention and dedication. Firstly we would like to pay our sincere gratitude to God for making things possible at the right time always. A word of special thanks to our family members for their constant support.

We would like to acknowledge the help of all the people involved in this book and, more specifically, to the authors and reviewers that took part in the review process. Without their support, this book would not have become a reality.

First, we extend our sincere thanks to each one of the authors for their contributions. Our sincere gratitude goes to the chapter's authors who contributed their time and expertise to this book.

Second, we wish to acknowledge the valuable contributions of the reviewers regarding the improvement of quality, coherence, and content presentation of chapters. Most of the authors also served as referees; we highly appreciate their double task.

We are very grateful to IGI Publishing team for giving this opportunity and believe in us. We extent our heartiest thanks and appreciate the team for providing constant technical and moral support and resources time to time. Without them this project cannot be completed.

Last but not the least we are thankful to our reader for choosing this book. We wish it would be an abundant resource for you in its domain.

Acknowledgment

"A great book should leave you with many experiences, and slightly exhausted at the end. You live several lives while reading." – William Styron

Shadi Aljawarneh
Jordan University of Science and Technology, Jordan

Manisha Malhotra
Chandigarh University, India

Section 1
Impact of Cloud Business Intelligence

Chapter 1
A Review of Trust and Security Concerns in Cloud Computing Adoption Intention in the Higher Education Sector:
Research in Progress

Inderbir Kaur Sandhu
GSSDGS Khalsa College, Patiala, India

Manisha Malhotra
(iD) https://orcid.org/0000-0002-9056-9473
Chandigarh University, India

Praneet Rangi Randhawa
(iD) https://orcid.org/0000-0003-2482-6985
DAV College, Chandigarh, India

ABSTRACT

One of the dynamic and emerging technologies is cloud computing, which provides a supporting spectrum for applications, especially in the education sector. The increasing use of this versatile technology is due to its low cost, resource pooling, and rapid elasticity features. These amazing features act as an innovative driver of success for the organization. The deployment of cloud is done in various applications of enterprise resource planning (ERP), customer relationship management (CRM)

DOI: 10.4018/978-1-7998-5040-3.ch001

applications, supply chain management applications (SCM), medical applications, education sector, and mobile applications. But the two major challenge for the successful deployment of the cloud is the trust of the customer and the secure network of the cloud for the integrity of the customer data. This chapter tries to explore the various concepts of cloud computing technology from technical and service point-of-view. Various opportunities using cloud computing are underlined. Along with that, the emphasis is on the major two challenges of cloud computing in terms of trust and security

INTRODUCTION

With the advent of technology, Cloud Computing proved itself as a success to reduce the computational cost, to improve application hosting and delivery of content. It is a practical approach which transforms the data center to a highly reliable and effective network. Forrester defines cloud computing as: "A pool of abstracted, highly scalable, and managed to compute infrastructure capable of hosting end-customer applications and billed by consumption."

Apart from various benefits of Cloud computing technology, there are various challenges of cloud computing technology. Among them, the trust of the customer in the cloud environment and the secure network are the two major challenges.

The previous studies emphasized on the challenges faced by lack of trust and security. But no study till now identify the affect of trust and security factors on the behaviour intention of the student to adopt the cloud computing concept in his learning process and hence the research gap exits (Al-Shargabi et al, 2020; Aljawarneh, 2012; Aljawarneh et al, 2017; Chehbi-Gamoura et al, 2018; Esposito et al, 2018; Jaswal et al, 2019; Kalpana et al, 2018; Lizcano et al, 2020; Malhotra et al, 2019; Mohammed et al, 2019; Mouchili et al, 2018; Singh,2011).

Research Question: To study the relationship and impact of trust and security factors towards the behaviour of the student to adopt cloud computing concept in his learning process.

CLOUD COMPUTING MODELS

Figure 1. Need of Cloud

Three categories of cloud models are specified as:

1. **Software as a Service (SaaS):** Highly scalable internet-based applications which provide services to the users. Examples are Google, Salesforce, Microsoft.
2. **Platform as a Service (Paas):** a platform which provides the facility to design, develop and build the application. Examples are the Azure Service platform, force.com.
3. **Infrastructure as a Service (Iaas):** IaaS provides basic storage and computing capabilities as standardized services over the network. Examples are Amazon web services, Go Grid.

CLOUD DEPLOYMENT MODELS

- **Public Cloud:** The most popular deployment model is Public Cloud. This service is meant for everyone and is usually free of cost.
- **Private Cloud:** The other routinely deployment model is Private Clouds. A Private Cloud is best suited where the data and customer is concerned with a certain level of security and normally used in an organization.

- **Hybrid Cloud:** The Hybrid Cloud came out after the merging of Private and Public Cloud or combination of different clouds. Hybrid cloud setup is mostly used for large organizations. Sensitive and Crucial data is usually preferred hosted in a Private Cloud.
- **Community Cloud:** This cloud is between people who have the same concerns like security, application types and performance demands or between the people having the same interest or same community.

Figure 2. Cloud Structure

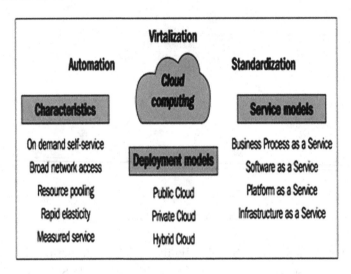

CHARACTERISTICS OF CLOUD

Cloud technology is the fast-growing technology which is proving itself in all fields due to its amazing features. These are:

- On-demand capabilities
- Rapid elasticity
- Measured service
- Resource pooling
- Broad network access

SCOPE OF STUDY

This research study is a literature review that analyses the Cloud Computing concept in various areas especially in the Higher Education sector with special focus on the two challenges of Cloud computing concept in terms of Trust and Security. The study reviews the existing literature in the international as well as in the Indian context.

LITERATURE REVIEW

The study tries to discuss the various concerns related to the prominent factors of trust and security in the adoption of cloud computing in various areas, especially in the higher education sector.

Trust

Earlier trust was referred to as the "belief that a party's word or promise is reliable and that a party will fulfill his/her obligations in an exchange relationship" (Schurr & Ozanne, 1985, p. 940). Trust is considered high if it is having a higher degree of commitment, agreement, loyalty and positive attitude towards the user.

Trust is also defined as "the belief that the other party will behave in a socially responsible manner, and, by so doing, will fulfill the trusting party's expectations without taking advantage of its vulnerabilities".

(P. A. Pavlou, 2003, p. 106).(Khan & Malluhi, 2010; Ko et al., 2011; Quynh et al., 2014;Schyff et al.,2014), in their studies discussed the various parameters of trust as loss of data Control, prevention, ownership, accountability, reputation, audit ability, transparency, personal perception, structural assurance, and security. In this study, trust refers to students' belief, confidence, and reliance on cloud computing applications and their providers. It is found that when students perceived or identified the cloud environment as secure, confidential, and trustworthy, they will surely adopt them and hence, trust has an impact on students' perceived usefulness of the cloud environment and intention to adopt the cloud computing applications in their educational sector.

(Sato et al, 2010; Guo et al, 2011) in their study mentioned the need of trust factor in cloud computing. They mentioned trust models and trust evaluation systems such as ETEC which discussed the various types of trust as direct trust (time-variant), recommendation trust(space-variant), internal trust and contracted trust to solve the security problems of the cloud environment.

(Ko et al, 2011; Daniel O & Elijah I.O, 2016) emphasized on the need of trust issues to be solved in the adoption of cloud services in public and private universities in Kenya. They proposed a conceptual framework and a detective trust framework which emphasis on trust, security, integrity, and accountability of data storing feature in cloud. They added that the trust factor played an important role in the adoption intention of Cloud computing.

(Abbadi & Alawneh, 2012; Abbadi, 2013) in their study proposed a foundation framework for depicting the need for the trust for adopting cloud computing and addressing and identifying various trust challenges. Further, a concept of Cloud Provenance is discussed which is the key requirement to establish the base for implementing trust within the cloud.

(Manuel P., 2013) proposed a QoS based trust model which considers past credentials and present capabilities of the cloud service provider. It includes reliability, availability, turns around time and data integrity.

(Sidhu, J. and Singh, S(2014; Sajjad.H,2013), in their study, mentioned that the trust is built by taking the views by service providers and peers groups. The generation of service level agreement (SLA) is there with the generation of Compliance report.

Further, studies also depict a strong relationship and implementation of trust factor in any technology adoption. (Gefen et al.,2003; P. A. Pavlou, 2003; Wu, Zhao, Zhu, Tan, and Zheng, 2011) in their studies depicted the relationship of trust and TAM in social interaction and online activities. Gefen worked on influenced of trust factor on perceived usefulness and intention to use Business-to-Consumer (B2C) website. P. A. Pavlou (2003) integrated trust and perceived risk into TAM to predict consumer e-Commerce acceptance while Wu, Zhao, Zhu, Tan, and Zheng (2011) conducted a meta-analysis of the impact of trust on perceived usefulness, perceived ease of use, attitude, and behavioral intention in TAM structure.

Mostly studies supported the major significance of trust in technology adoption.

Security

This is another one of the major issues that hinder the adoption of cloud computing technology. (Alshamaila, Papagiannidis, & Li, 2013; Coursaris, van Osch, & Sung, 2013; E. Park & Kim, 2014; A. Verma & Kaushal, 2011). User's data is always at high risk of various security threats like data loss, data theft, criminal activity and unauthorized access(Pramod et al., 2013). Security has a high impact on the behavioral intentions of users for adopting cloud computing applications. More the secure environment more is the trust of the user to use the cloud computing applications.

(S. Subashini et al, 2010; V.Krishna et al, 2011; K.Sachdeva, 2011; Philipp et al, 2011), in their study mentioned that major concern regarding security is data maintenance. The studies depicted the various security framework and risk-based security platform used for accessing and storing the essential information regarding money and assets of the industry and hence ensured the privacy of the individual and industry. The models worked on automatic analysis and evaluation of risk in the cloud arena.

In the study of (M.Firdhous et al, 2011; Farhad Soleimanian et al, 2012; Sajjad.H,2013), it is mentioned that security concerns must be taken seriously while implementing the cloud computing environment in a public network as data security is one of the main factors in system cloud computing.

Also, the study of (M. Monsef et al, 2011; D. Zissis et al, 2012;Sajjad.H,2013) emphasized on the great need of a suitable degree of both security and trust in the environment of Cloud computing so that user can easily trust the network while using it.

(Grossman,R..L,2009;Wang,C,et.al.,2010;Marston.S, et al.,2011)discussed the need for strong security for the data. They mentioned that data breeching is also one of the reasons of lack of security and hence leads to loss of trust in the cloud especially in higher education institutions where the data is big in volume and is confidential in nature.

Another study is given by(Zhou et al.,2010)depicted that privacy and security are the two major barriers for a user to adapt to the cloud computing concept. The security and privacy concerns are mentioned in terms of aspects like availability, confidentiality, audit, control and data integrity. Also, privacy issues occur if there are multi located data storage and services in the cloud.

CONCEPTUAL FRAMEWORK

Based on the literature survey, a model is proposed as following:

Figure 3. Conceptual framework for Cloud Applications adoption

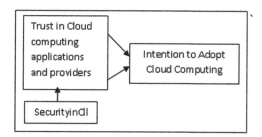

The literature survey depicts that both trust and security factors have an impact on the behavioural intentions of students to adopt cloud computing applications in their education. Also, the study shows that security has an impact on the trust of the user.

CONCLUSION

Although the cloud computing concept is evolving to its fullest in all aspects, yet there is a need to study the various factors affecting the adoption intention of the cloud in the education sector. Especially in the higher education sector, cloud computing adoption is highly affected by the two prominent factors of trust and security. (Sajjad.H,2013)mentioned that cloud providers and the government should take the necessary measures and enough trust to enhance the cloud computing adoption intention among users. So there is a great need to study these two factors in the adoption area of cloud computing in the educational sector. Also, there is a wide scope of study in accessing the behavioural intentions to adopt cloud computing applications in various other areas apart from education related to trust and security

FUTURE WORK

The study recommends further research to do quantitative research to get:

1. The credible results of trust and security factors on the adoption intentions of the students in the higher education sector based on the above-proposed model.
2. Study on various other implementation challenges while adopting cloud services in the higher education sector.

REFERENCES

Abbadi, I. M. (2013). A framework for establishing trust in Cloud Provenance. *International Journal of Information Security*, *11*(2), 111–128. doi:10.100710207-012-0179-0

Abbadi, I. M., & Alawneh, M. (2012). A framework for establishing trust in the cloud. *Computers & Electrical Engineering*, *38*(5), 1073–1087. doi:10.1016/j.compeleceng.2012.06.006

Al-Shargabi, B., Al-Jawarneh, S., & Hayajneh, S. M. (2020). A cloudlet based security and trust model for e-government web services. *Journal of Theoretical and Applied Information Technology*, *98*(1), 27–37.

Aljawarneh, S. (Ed.). (2012). *Cloud computing advancements in design, implementation, and technologies*. IGI Global.

Aljawarneh, S., & Malhotra, M. (Eds.). (2017). *Critical Research on Scalability and Security Issues in Virtual Cloud Environments*. IGI Global.

Alshamaila, Y., Papagiannidis, S., & Li, F. (2013). Cloud computing adoption by SMEs in the northeast of England: A multi-perspective framework. *Journal of Enterprise Information Management, 26*(3), 250–275. doi:10.1108/17410391311325225

Chehbi-Gamoura, S., Derrouiche, R., Malhotra, M., & Koruca, H. I. (2018, June). Adaptive management approach for more availability of big data business analytics. In *Proceedings of the Fourth International Conference on Engineering & MIS 2018* (pp. 1-8). 10.1145/3234698.3234758

Coursaris, C. K., van Osch, W., & Sung, J. (2013). *A "cloud lifestyle": The diffusion of cloud computing applications and the effect of demographic and lifestyle clusters*. Paper presented at the 2013 46th Hawaii International Conference on System Sciences.

Esposito, C., Su, X., Aljawarneh, S. A., & Choi, C. (2018). Securing collaborative deep learning in industrial applications within adversarial scenarios. *IEEE Transactions on Industrial Informatics, 14*(11), 4972–4981. doi:10.1109/TII.2018.2853676

Firdhous, Ghazali, & Hassan. (2011). *Trust and Trust Management in Cloud Computing -A Survey*. Inter Networks Research group, University Utara Malaysia, Technical Report.

Grossman, R.L. (2009). The Case for Cloud computing. *IT Professionals, 11*(2), 23-27.

Guo, Q., Sun, D., Chang, G., Sun, L., & Wang, X. (n.d.). Modeling and evaluation of trust in cloud computing environments. *Third International Conference on Advanced Computer Control*, 112-116.

Jaswal, S., & Malhotra, M. (2019, December). A detailed analysis of trust models in cloud environment. In *Proceedings of the Second International Conference on Data Science, E-Learning and Information Systems* (pp. 1-5). 10.1145/3368691.3368740

Kalpana, G., Kumar, P. V., Aljawarneh, S., & Krishnaiah, R. V. (2018). Shifted adaption homomorphism encryption for mobile and cloud learning. *Computers & Electrical Engineering, 65*, 178–195. doi:10.1016/j.compeleceng.2017.05.022

Khan, K. M., & Malluhi, Q. (2010). Establishing trust in cloud computing. *IT Professional, 12*(5), 20–27. doi:10.1109/MITP.2010.128

Ko, R., Jagadpramana, P., Mowbray, M., Pearson, S., Kirchberg, M., Liang, Q., & Lee, B. S. (2011), Trust cloud: a framework for accountability and trust in cloud computing. *World Congress on services*, 584-588.

Krishna Reddy, V., & Reddy, L. S. (2011). Security architecture of Cloud Computing. *International Journal of Engineering Science and Technology*, *3*(9), 7149–7155.

Lizcano, D., Lara, J. A., White, B., & Aljawarneh, S. (2020). Blockchain-based approach to create a model of trust in open and ubiquitous higher education. *Journal of Computing in Higher Education*, *32*(1), 109–134. doi:10.100712528-019-09209-y

Malhotra, M., & Singh, A. (2019). Role of Agents to Enhance the Security and Scalability in Cloud Environment. In Cloud Security: Concepts, Methodologies, Tools, and Applications (pp. 552-573). IGI Global. doi:10.4018/978-1-5225-8176-5.ch028

Manuel, P. (2013). A trust model of cloud computing based on the quality of service. *Annals of Operations Research*, *2013*, 1–12.

Marston, S., Li, Z., Bandyopadhyay, S., Zhang, J., & Ghalsasi, A. (2011). Cloud computing-The Business Perspective. *Decision Support Systems*, *51*(1), 176–189. doi:10.1016/j.dss.2010.12.006

Mohammed, T. A., Ghareeb, A., Al-bayaty, H., & Aljawarneh, S. (2019, December). Big data challenges and achievements: applications on smart cities and energy sector. In *Proceedings of the Second International Conference on Data Science, E-Learning and Information Systems* (pp. 1-5). 10.1145/3368691.3368717

Monsef, M., & Gidado, N. (2011). *Trust and privacy concern in Cloud, European cup*. IT Security for the Next Generation.

Mouchili, M. N., Aljawarneh, S., & Tchouati, W. (2018, October). Smart city data analysis. In *Proceedings of the First International Conference on Data Science, E-learning and Information Systems* (pp. 1-6). Academic Press.

Onyango & Omwenga. (2016). Using Cloud computing in Higher Education: A Strategy to address trust issues in adoption of Cloud services in Kenyan public and private universities. *International Journal of Applied Information Systems, 11*(7).

Park, E., & Kim, K. J. (2014). An integrated adoption model of mobile cloud services: Exploration of key determinants and extension of technology acceptance model. *Telematics and Informatics*, *31*(3), 376–385. doi:10.1016/j.tele.2013.11.008

Pavlou, P. A. (2003). Consumer acceptance of electronic commerce: Integrating trust and risk with the technology acceptance model. *International Journal of Electronic Commerce*, *7*(3), 101–134. doi:10.1080/10864415.2003.11044275

Pramod, N., Muppalla, A. K., & Srinivasa, K. (2013). Limitations and challenges in cloud-based applications development. In Z. Mahmood & S. Saeed (Eds.), *Software Engineering Frameworks for the Cloud Computing Paradigm* (pp. 55–75). Springer. doi:10.1007/978-1-4471-5031-2_3

Quynh, N. L. T., Heales, J., & Xu, D. (2014). *Examining significant factors and risks affecting the willingness to adopt a cloud-based CRM*. Paper presented at the 1st International Conference on HCI in Business, Crete, Greece. 10.1007/978-3-319-07293-7_4

Sachdeva, K. (2011), *Cloud computing: Security Risk Analysis and Recommendations* (Master Thesis). University of Texas, Austin, TX.

Sajjad, H. (2013). Cloud computing technology: Security and Trust challenges. *International Journal of Security, Privacy and Trust Management, 2*(5).

Sato, H., Kanai, A., & Tanimoto, S. (2010). A cloud trust model in a security-aware cloud. *10th IEEE/IPSJ International Symposium on the application and the internet, IEEE*, 121-124.

Schurr, P. H., & Ozanne, J. L. (1985). Influences on exchange processes: Buyers' preconceptions of a seller's trustworthiness and bargaining toughness. *The Journal of Consumer Research, 4*(11), 939–953. doi:10.1086/209028

Schyff, K. (2014). Higher education cloud computing in South Africa: Towards understanding trust and adoption issues. *SACJ, 55*, 40–54.

Sidhu, J., & Singh, S. (2014). Compliance based trustworthiness calculation mechanism in a cloud environment. *Procedia Computer Science, 37*, 439–446. doi:10.1016/j.procs.2014.08.066

Singh, A., Juneja, D., & Malhotra, M. (2017). A novel agent based autonomous and service composition framework for cost optimization of resource provisioning in cloud computing. *Journal of King Saud University-Computer and Information Sciences, 29*(1), 19–28. doi:10.1016/j.jksuci.2015.09.001

Soleimanian, F., & Hashemi, S. (2012). Security Challenges in Cloud computing with more emphasis on Trust and Privacy. *International Journal of Scientific and Technology Research, 1*(6), 49–54.

Subashini, S., & Kavitha, V. (2010). A survey on security issues in service delivery models of cloud computing. *Network and Computer Applications, 34*, 1–11.

Verma, A., & Kaushal, S. (2011). Cloud computing security issues and challenges: A survey. Paper presented at the International Conference on Advances in Computing and Communications, Kochi, India. 10.1007/978-3-642-22726-4_46

Wang, C., Ren, K., Lou, W., & Li, J. (2010). *Towards publicly auditable secure cloud data storage services* (Vol. 24). IEEE.

Zech, P. (2011). Risk-based Security Testing in Cloud Computing Environments. *Fourth IEEE International Conference on Software Testing Verification and Validation*, 411-414. 10.1109/ICST.2011.23

Zhou, M., Zhang, R., Xie, W., Qian, W., & Zhou, A. (2010). Security and privacy in Cloud Computing: A Survey. *Sixth International Conference on Semantics, Knowledge, and Grids, IEEE-2010*. 10.1109/SKG.2010.19

Zissis, D., & Lekkas, D. (2012). Addressing Cloud computing security issues. *Future Generation Computer Systems*, *28*(3), 583–592. doi:10.1016/j.future.2010.12.006

Chapter 2
Impact of COVID–19 on Cloud Business Intelligence

Pooja Thakur
Chandigarh University, India

Manisha Malhotra
(iD) https://orcid.org/0000-0002-9056-9473
Chandigarh University, India

ABSTRACT

The outburst of COVID-19 has affected the whole world. COVID-19 is the seventh member of the coronavirus family. There is no vaccine for the diseases, and due to this, the whole world has taken the step of social distancing that leads to lockdown. Due to the implementation of lockdown, normal working of all organizations converted to work from home. During such situation, organizations are opting to provide smooth working for the operations of business. Before the pandemic situation, each organization was concentrating on maximizing profit. But today they are opting the practices such as cloud computing, business intelligence, neural network, IoT, and many more so that business work can be done. During this pandemic situation, cloud business intelligence plays an important role for the smooth working of business. The contribution of this chapter is to show how cloud business intelligence is used to fulfill the need of the business ecosystem.

DOI: 10.4018/978-1-7998-5040-3.ch002

INTRODUCTION

The epidemic of COVID-19 has affected all industries, as well as consumer behavior. For economies and cultures, it has a huge effect. With the indefinite closure of workplaces, educational institutions and industrial facilities, the postponement of major sports and activities, and the introduction of work-from-home and social distancing policies globally, corporations are increasingly making efforts to introduce technology that support them through this difficult period. Analytics experts, BI professionals, and advanced analytics experts have been called upon to assist managers in making business decisions to adapt to the COVID-19 spread's new challenges. Due to the lockdowns imposed worldwide, Business Intelligence solutions and services providers are experiencing a slowdown in their growth.

Businesses have also begun to make attempts to return to the normal and encounter various client and organizational challenges. Some of the main challenges faced by companies are meeting consumer requirements in the terms of process optimization and also growing security issues for the connected networks, rising networking problems, and decreasing industrial and manufacturing operations. New practices such as work-from-home and social distancing, as well as the development of digital infrastructures for large-scale technology deployments, have resulted from the need for remote health monitoring of patients and assets and smart payment technologies. In addition, the implementation of lockdowns has led to an increased focus on solutions focused on the cloud. With a growing emphasis on fitness, there has been an increase in demand for wearable devices related to health and business.

Under such circumstances, solution is based on Cloud Computing known as Cloud BI. According to the new report of PMMI, BI currently using 67% of cloud computing. Cloud computing enables manufacturers to access production data and controls, remotely and in real time. By continuously uploading data to the cloud, manufacturers can obtain a comprehensive view of their operations, monitoring where products are, controlling what production lines are doing, and analyzing gathered data, without the need to be physically present at the site of production. Edge computing enables many of the same advantages of cloud computing, but without the option of remote access to data.

DEFINITION

COVID-19

COVID-19 is a disease caused by a new strain of coronavirus. 'CO' stands for corona, 'VI' for virus, and 'D' for disease. Formerly, this disease was referred to as '2019 novel coronavirus' or '2019-nCoV.' The COVID-19 virus is a new virus linked to the same family of viruses as Severe Acute Respiratory Syndrome (SARS) and some types of common cold.

Cloud Computing

Cloud computing is a construct that allows applications to be hosted on either a private or a public cloud. The software for these cloud applications are used out of the box as it is and minimum changes are required to get it working. The cloud provider does all the patching and upgrades as well as keeping the infrastructure running (Al-Shargabi et al, 2020; Aljawarneh, 2012; Aljawarneh et al, 2017; Chehbi-Gamoura et al, 2018; Esposito et al, 2018; Jaswal et al, 2019; Kalpana et al, 2018; Lizcano et al, 2020; Malhotra et al, 2019; Mohammed et al, 2019; Mouchili et al, 2018; Singh,2011).

According to Gartner definition, Cloud Computing is a computing style in which massively scalable IT-enabled capabilities are offered to external customers using Internet technology as a service (Bohn, R. B et al., 2011).

According to Quoting Chan, Cloud Computing can be described as a general, location-independent, online utility that is available on demand. This approach emphasizes the fact that on multiple applications and clients, any common resource is statistically multiplied. Thus, he can access the data in the cloud no matter where the customer is physically located. The feature on demand means that resources must be distributed dynamically. (Ghilic-Micu, B et al., 2011).

Most important developments for the growth of IT provision, management and security within an enterprise is Cloud Computing. There has no any universally accepted meaning at present. NIST and CSA describe Cloud Computing as a model that helps in providing access to a shared reserve of configurable computing resources (such as network, server, storage, application, and service) on demand. These may be available quickly and with minimal management effort or service provider involvement (ISACA, A., 2009). Following features are provided by Cloud Computing (Li, H.et al., 2010, Malcolm, 2009, ISACA, A., 2009):

- Approach for services of IT
- virtualization, dynamics and massive infrastructure;
- shared and configurable resources
- Accessibility of resources using internet from any device
- platform used for the support of self-management
- use of model based on services
- pay as per use.

BUSINESS INTELLIGENCE

Business intelligence (BI) is an organization's ability to gather, manage and coordinate information. This creates vast volumes of data that can help to create new possibilities. A sustainable market advantage and long-term stability can be created by recognizing these opportunities and executing an efficient strategy (Berkowitz, J., 2009).

Business intelligence is a broad concept that contain software, infrastructure, instruments, and best practices that make knowledge to be accessed or evaluated to enhance and improve decision and results. (Birst, 2010).

MARKET DYNAMICS DURING COVID-19

The market dynamics during COVID-19 contain the various aspect. These aspects are discussed below (Figure 1):

1. Rising Demands of Virtualization of Data to Increase the Capacity in Taking Business Decision

Today, most organizations are adopting a simplified process that consists of identifying, collecting, maintaining, and sharing a large amount of data. BI solutions are used for this data to have a fast and simplified business decision-making process. The data should be provided with a standard visualization ability, which is used to identify customer preferences and tendencies, extract strategic insights, and help maintain a balance between the demand and supply of new and existing products and services. Companies across verticals adopt data visualization solutions to understand data in an easy manner and derive actionable business insights. Data visualization tools in cloud enable organizations to have a cost-effective and scalable way for data analysis. The data visualization capability helps companies identify business drivers and Key Performance Indicators (KPIs) through BI solutions. It helps eliminate unnecessary data to discover patterns, insights, trends, and usage strategies, which help leverage its growth in the market. The current COVID 19 pandemic also increased the demand for data visualization and dashboards solutions to track the data of worldwide patient data and make decisions based upon the report. Many business intelligence vendors offered dashboards and visualization solutions for tracking the COVID-19 spread. For example, every two weeks, Salesforce Research surveys a representative sample of the general public to understand their changing experiences, preferences and viewpoints as customers and members of the workforce. Explore various topics and filter responses by the respondent's country of residence, generation, income level, and gender. Salesforce developed the COVID-19 economy data track for the traction of various data in the pandemic.

2. Data Integration

Integration is one such factor that defines the clientele and users of software. The end-to-end integration helps professionals to access all the data in an integrated system. However, integration is a major challenge faced by business intelligence and analytics vendors. As the demand for cloud-based business intelligence solutions is high in the market due to enormous advantages offered, cloud deployments pose several challenges such as security and integration issues with on-premises data. The integration of various analytics software, business intelligence, Master Data Management (MDM), big data, and analytics applications is a challenge in this industry.

3. Opportunity

Most businesses are looking at operations, revenues, income, and costs during the current COVID-19 crisis, just as during the 2008 crisis. High-level risks are faced by businesses. due to the rising effects of COVID-19, they are losing revenue. At both a local and global level, leaders need to know what generates their sales. Everywhere, local legislatures are different. For countries within Europe, what may be important to the US (even particular states) may not be relevant. It is therefore important to narrow down the actions of customers and determine what is applicable to the audience. COVID-19 has increased the need for all businesses to put their data to work to speed up the decision-making process. A comprehensive practice in business intelligence can allow companies to identify proper metrics to better survive a crisis, and for many businesses, these times can be a silver lining. Business intelligence allows companies to take a closer look at how they are operating by taking inventory of where they are doing well and where they can improve. The purpose of business intelligence is to leverage data to make decisions that improve and optimize revenue.

IMPACT OF COVID-19 ON BUSINESS ECOSYSTEM

WHO Director-General Dr. Tedros Adhanom Ghebreyesus stated on COVID-19; "We have a long way to go, this pandemic will remain with the human for a longer time. The world cannot go back to the way things were." (World Health Organization, 2020). Most of the business ecosystem depends heavily on in-person interactions or

Figure 1. Market Dynamics

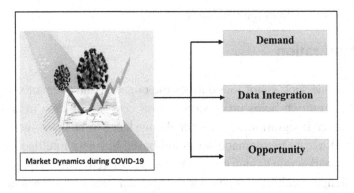

close physical meets at the different business stages, i.e. production, quality analysis, distribution, or sales. Post-implementation of the governments' force lockdown, the industry around the world started encountering significant economic consequences. These vulnerable service providers started realizing a severe problem after the implementation of Social Distancing. But simultaneously overcoming the same through manpower training and delighting the customers in area of after sales service is perquisite. The stock markets reflect the world economy and always respond to the considerable incidents; similar to the previous pandemics. SARS – CoV and MERS - CoV the contagious COVID-19 has created an impact on the global stock markets. COVID- 19 pandemics have conceived the most unprecedented effect on the stock market in a more powerful way than Spanish flu. Within a short period, the cross-country pandemic elicited by the COVID-19 has claimed many lives. The Corona Virus has disrupted the businesses' operation and profitability abruptly. It has also applied severe restrictions to private and business growth. To get the optimum output from the workforce is one of the critical needs of the hour. Due to the massive impact of COVID-19, many people have lost their jobs. The number was approximately 25 million in the USA during the mid of March and April 2020, which is way higher than any other pandemic, including the gigantic recession of 2007-09. There is a significant decrease in labor income across the globe, which has forced governments to unfold the bailout packages. The COVID-19 has amplified the probability of sack or deterioration of employment around all the business domains. The world has been actively budding the measures to support the industries and citizens who have lost their jobs due to the epidemic situation.

BUSINESS INTELLIGENCE MODEL

Model of Business Intelligence permit the consumers of business to conceptualize the rules and operations of business by using concepts that are familiar to them, including: Actor, Directive, Intention, Event, Situation, Indicator, Influence, Process, Resource, and Domain Assumption. These concepts (and their semantics) are synthesized from business and conceptual modeling sources. The more fundamental goal, in the sense of BI, is to provide a business-friendly way to gain the large amounts of data gathered by the business. BIM alone will promote the analysis of the business. The BIM collaborates with advanced technologies for computational data integration.

ROLE OF BI MODELS DURING COVID-19

From February 2020, when the first epidemic cluster of Novel Coronavirus (COVID-19) appeared in Lombardy (4-7), AREU decided to apply BI to the management of the EMS using real-time data. Indeed, BI records the number of requests that are being received from each SOREU and that have been classified as respiratory and/or infectious episodes during the telephonic interview. The BI keeps track of all the requests that reached each SOREU from their designated territory 24 hours a day every day of the week. These data show the number of first aid calls reaching from specific areas of the region for respiratory or infectious health problems. AREU decides to use these figures to estimate where the contagion was occurring and consequently used them to better allocate the resources (vehicles and human resources) in the territory.

Furthermore, BI allows comparing the number of episodes that are being registered with the data of previous days, which is crucial to verify if real-time figures match with the forecast model in each area. Moreover, AREU have been monitoring the pattern of the epidemic over time using the following BI model. The BI model analysis the trend of the number respiratory and/or infectious episodes registered in each pre-set group of municipalities (Li, B. H. et al., 2010). As SARSCoV-2 is still spreading in the region, the BI will be updated and improved daily to ameliorate the EMS.

BI model:

E= number of the respiratory and/or infectious episodes reported the day before
m_preC= mean of the respiratory and/or infectious episodes from 20/01/2020 to 16/02/2020
m_5gg= mean of the respiratory and/or infectious episodes during the previous 5 days
sigma= standard deviation

Rules:

```
grey: "no spread of SARS-CoV-2" if
(E-m_preC)<=(2sigma_m_preC)
red: "increasing trend spread of SARS-CoV-2" if
(E-m_preC)>(2sigma_m_preC) and (E-m_5gg)>=(sigma_m_5gg)
yellow: "stable trend spread of SARS-CoV-2" if
(E-m_preC)>(2sigma_m_preC) and
(-sigma_m_5gg)<=(E-m_5gg)<=(sigma_m_5gg)
green: "decreasing trend spread of SARS-CoV-2" if
(E-m_preC)>(2sigma_m_preC) and (E- m_5gg)<(sigma_m_5gg)
```

ROLE OF CLOUD COMPUTING DURING COVID-19

With the use of Cloud Computing users can increase or decrease the resources demand as per the usages. Resources may be in terms of power consumption and spaces used (Bohn, R. B et al., 2011). Cloud Computing provides various services to the end users that include on demand, access of network, distribution of resources, traffic management (Mell, P et al., 2011). During COVID, cloud providers provides different services to the consumer that typically include software as a service, platform as a services, infrastructure as a service. Also offers different deployment models private, public, hybrid (Bohn, R. B et al., 2011). During COVID, preference is given to the work from home and SAAS (that is web based model for s/w delivery and s/w tools) is used. Users have to pay for the subscription. This reduce the worry of users regarding maintenance and many others (Carroll M. et al., 2011). Cloud platforms are also concerned with protection, safety, enforcement, and legal risks that need to be mitigated by the management of the business and the cloud provider (Subashini et al, 2011, Yang, C. et al,, 2018).

SELF-SERVICE BUSINESS INTELLIGENCE

SSBI is a BI approach that is intended to allow business users to search, capture, store, access, and analyze data without IT experts being involved. Decision-makers can recognize the latest and necessary changes in the settings with the aid of SSBI. Without the involvement of experts, business users may analyze data (Ghilic-Micu et al., 2011). SSBI is described by Imhoff and White as the facilities within the BI environment that enable BI users to become more self-reliant and less dependent on the IT organization." In addition, they highlight the following main objectives of SSBI instruments (Berkowitz, J, 2009):

1.   Data sources are easily accessed by using it.
2.   It provides easy user interface to the consumers.
3.   It provides the support for data analysis
4.   Easy to manage

Figure 2. Cloud Computing with BI

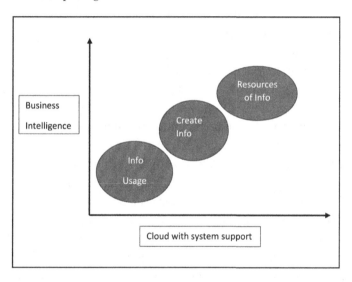

BUSINESS CONTINUITY MANAGEMENT (BCM) PRACTICES DURING THE COVID-19 OUTBREAK

"Business Continuity Management is a universal controlling procedure that categorizes the possible intimidations to a business, and the collisions to its operations threats, if gotten, might elicit". The BCM feeds a structure to activate organizational resilience with an operational retort's competency that upholds its key shareholders' interests, reputation, intellectual properties, and accomplishments. The industries have faced a series of challenges due to the ongoing pandemic, in the form of layoffs, bankruptcies in affected sectors, supply-side issues due to lockdown and demand-side issues due to financial disruptions. In this turbulent environment, organizations implement a full proof strategy and business continuity plan (BCP) to continue critical business operations. An optimum BCP enables an organization to absorb the disruption due to the unfavorable situation and help it return to the normal state as soon as possible. Most of the businesses today expected to be "always-on," the adoption of "Work from Home" kept the promise of 24*7 availability unremitting. For optimum productivity, not only availability at work is essential; the optimum usage of resources is equally important, which made the implementation of BI and analytics solutions a need of the hour. A competent crisis leadership can implement an effective business continuity plan (BCP) to optimize the organization's overall crisis performance. With outbreaks previous to novel coronavirus, the world never had experienced such a significant impact across the countries. In comparison to prior pandemics e.g., SARS and MERS, the coronavirus spread is even across the globe. Information on people's movement, travel restriction, behavior, etc. plays a pivotal role in preventing the range across the community.

The extraordinary impact of COVID-19 across the continents has ignited the need for exceptional digital solutions, contributing significantly to keeping the businesses disruption-free. The governments and businesses utilize social media and other web information to seek pandemic related data known as Infodemiology. Infodemiology refers to "the set of procedures, to study the health data on the internet to determine public health information. Given the continuous mounting cases, businesses have been launching massive business continuity plans (BCP). Tata Consultancy Services (BSE: 532540, NSE: TCS), one of the top employers in 29 countries including the North America, Europe, Asia Pacific, and Middle East, launched Secure Borderless Workspaces™ (SBWS™), model. This model sanctions its employees to work from home with minimal support from their colleagues working from offices. The Work from Home (WFH) is the most forceful change, driven by COVID-19 across the professions. Though some individuals had very minimal or no WFH experience, for example, primary education teachers, etc.; they are also forced by the law of the land, to adopt the work from home arrangements. (Kramer, 2020).

ELEMENTS FOR THE ADOPTIONS OF BUSINESS INTELLIGENCE CLOUD COMPUTING DURING COVID-19

In many companies, the various resources are used in the form of virtualisation, encapsulation and these are provided by cloud (Li, B. H et al., 2010, Sridhar, 2016). During recent COVID pandemic situation, when the resources are cut off, with the help of cloud, enterprises found an alternate for providing resources to the consumers (Li, B. H et al., 2010). For the sharing of information between end users, cloud computing provides cloud edge devices structure to the business. Edge computing receive the data from the edge nodes for the fast processing of data. During pandemic situation end users interact with each other using edge computing. By using this cloud computing structure, business enterprises exchange the real time information on time. To overcome the communication delay, increase the interconnectivity, increase the computing task speed, 5G can be used. A dynamic service selection method can be deployed across multiple manufacturing clouds to effectively deal with uncertainties (Berkowitz, J., 2009).

Table 1 shows the elements corresponding to the adoption of Business Intelligence Cloud Computing (ISACA, A., 2009, Li, H. et al., 2010, Subashini et al., 2011, Sridhar, 2016 et al., 2016, Mell, P et al., 2011, Yang, C et al., 2018).

Table 1. Elements for Adoption of Cloud Computing

Typical Elements Suited for External Clouds	Supplementary Elements of Applications Suited for Software as a Service

• These does not provide advantages for competition.
    • It does not presuppose a critical mission.
    • These are not helpful business applications.
    • It does not include sensitive data and these are not affected by latency.
    • Provides various resources patterns.
	• These are in reengineering stage of their lifecycle.
	    • In contain minimal personalization.
	    • It provides standard industrial workflow.

BI Applications Supplementary Elements	

• It is suited for large organisation critical work.
    • It is created for small organisation and can handle small amount of data.
    • It uses the concept of cloud for the analysis of ad hoc data and this data is received from the multiple sources.
    • It deals with the processing of independent processes and other applications.	

CONCLUSION

Initially the starting point of COVID -19 was China. The first case was found in November,2019. Nowadays, many countries are affected by the COVID. It has significant impact on the business of evet country. Most enterprises are affected as never before. It will take several years for industries as well as the economy of countries to recover from the effects of COVID-19. After lock down, business continuity was the most challenging step for any organization. For this, organization choose the option of work from home and here cloud business intelligence plays an important role. They provide the resources such as data storage, traffic management, virtualization, network, communication etc. to the business and also implement the business intelligence solutions.

REFERENCES

Al-Shargabi, B., Al-Jawarneh, S., & Hayajneh, S. M. (2020). A cloudlet based security and trust model for e-government web services. *Journal of Theoretical and Applied Information Technology*, *98*(1), 27–37.

Aljawarneh, S. (Ed.). (2012). *Cloud computing advancements in design, implementation, and technologies*. IGI Global.

Aljawarneh, S., & Malhotra, M. (Eds.). (2017). *Critical Research on Scalability and Security Issues in Virtual Cloud Environments*. IGI Global.

Berkowitz, J. (2009). *Cloud Computing (Part 1): Advantages, Types and Challenges*. CRM Mastery Weblog.

Birst. (2010). *Why Cloud BI? The 9 Substantial Benefits of Software-as-aService Business Intelligence*. Birst, Inc.

Bohn, R. B., Messina, J., Liu, F., Tong, J., & Mao, J. (2011, July). NIST cloud computing reference architecture. In *2011 IEEE World Congress on Services* (pp. 594-596). IEEE. 10.1109/SERVICES.2011.105

Carroll, M., Van Der Merwe, A., & Kotze, P. (2011, August). Secure cloud computing: Benefits, risks and controls. In *2011 Information Security for South Africa* (pp. 1-9). IEEE.

Chehbi-Gamoura, S., Derrouiche, R., Malhotra, M., & Koruca, H. I. (2018, June). Adaptive management approach for more availability of big data business analytics. In *Proceedings of the Fourth International Conference on Engineering & MIS 2018* (pp. 1-8). 10.1145/3234698.3234758

Esposito, C., Su, X., Aljawarneh, S. A., & Choi, C. (2018). Securing collaborative deep learning in industrial applications within adversarial scenarios. *IEEE Transactions on Industrial Informatics*, *14*(11), 4972–4981. doi:10.1109/TII.2018.2853676

Ghilic-Micu, B., Mircea, M., & Stoica, M. (2011). Main aspects of the adoption of cloud solutions in managing service-oriented organizations-the case of higher education. Academy of Economic Studies. *Ecological Informatics*, *11*(1), 27.

ISACA. (2009). *Cloud Computing: Business Benefits With Security, Governance and Assurance Perspectives*. ISACA.

Jaswal, S., & Malhotra, M. (2019, December). A detailed analysis of trust models in cloud environment. In *Proceedings of the Second International Conference on Data Science, E-Learning and Information Systems* (pp. 1-5). 10.1145/3368691.3368740

Kalpana, G., Kumar, P. V., Aljawarneh, S., & Krishnaiah, R. V. (2018). Shifted adaption homomorphism encryption for mobile and cloud learning. *Computers & Electrical Engineering, 65*, 178–195. doi:10.1016/j.compeleceng.2017.05.022

Li, B. H., Zhang, L., Wang, S. L., Tao, F., Cao, J. W., Jiang, X. D., ... Chai, X. D. (2010). Cloud manufacturing: A new service-oriented networked manufacturing model. *Jisuanji Jicheng Zhizao Xitong, 16*(1), 1–7.

Li, H., Spence, C., Armstrong, R., Godfrey, R., Schneider, R., Smith, J., & White, J. (2010). *Intel Cloud Computing Taxonomy and Ecosystem Analysis*. Printed in USA 0210. KC/KC/PDF, 1-4.

Lizcano, D., Lara, J. A., White, B., & Aljawarneh, S. (2020). Blockchain-based approach to create a model of trust in open and ubiquitous higher education. *Journal of Computing in Higher Education, 32*(1), 109–134. doi:10.100712528-019-09209-y

Malcolm, D. (2009). *The five defining characteristics of cloud computing*. ZDNet.

Malhotra, M., & Singh, A. (2019). Role of Agents to Enhance the Security and Scalability in Cloud Environment. In Cloud Security: Concepts, Methodologies, Tools, and Applications (pp. 552-573). IGI Global. doi:10.4018/978-1-5225-8176-5.ch028

Mell, P., & Grance, T. (2011). *The NIST definition of cloud computing*. NIST.

Mircea, M., Ghilic-Micu, B., & Stoica, M. (2011). Combining business intelligence with cloud computing to delivery agility in actual economy. *Journal of Economic Computation and Economic Cybernetics Studies, 45*(1), 39–54.

Mohammed, T. A., Ghareeb, A., Al-bayaty, H., & Aljawarneh, S. (2019, December). Big data challenges and achievements: applications on smart cities and energy sector. In *Proceedings of the Second International Conference on Data Science, E-Learning and Information Systems* (pp. 1-5). 10.1145/3368691.3368717

Mouchili, M. N., Aljawarneh, S., & Tchouati, W. (2018, October). Smart city data analysis. In *Proceedings of the First International Conference on Data Science, E-learning and Information Systems* (pp. 1-6). Academic Press.

Singh, A., Juneja, D., & Malhotra, M. (2017). A novel agent based autonomous and service composition framework for cost optimization of resource provisioning in cloud computing. *Journal of King Saud University-Computer and Information Sciences, 29*(1), 19–28. doi:10.1016/j.jksuci.2015.09.001

Sridhar, S. (n.d.). *A Study On Various Programming Languages to Keep Pace with Innovation*. Academic Press.

Sridhar, S. (2016). *A study on various software models as inclusive technology for sustainable solutions*. Academic Press.

Sridhar, S. (2016). Cloud computing made easy. *International Journal of Innovative Technology and Research, 4*(2), 2875–2906.

Subashini, S., & Kavitha, V. (2011). A survey on security issues in service delivery models of cloud computing. *Journal of Network and Computer Applications, 34*(1), 1–11. doi:10.1016/j.jnca.2010.07.006

Yang, C., Lan, S., Wang, L., Shen, W., & Huang, G. G. (2020). Big Data Driven Edge-Cloud Collaboration Architecture for Cloud Manufacturing: A Software Defined Perspective. *IEEE Access: Practical Innovations, Open Solutions, 8*, 45938–45950. doi:10.1109/ACCESS.2020.2977846

Yang, C., Shen, W., & Wang, X. (2018). The internet of things in manufacturing: Key issues and potential applications. *IEEE Systems, Man, and Cybernetics Magazine, 4*(1), 6–15. doi:10.1109/MSMC.2017.2702391

Chapter 3
Job Scheduling in Cloud Using Seagull Optimization Algorithm

Meenakshi Garg
Government Bikram College of Commerce, India

Gaurav Dhiman
Government Bikram College of Commerce, India

ABSTRACT

In recent years, cloud computing technology has gained a great deal of interest from both academia and industry. Cloud computing's success benefited from its ability to offer global IT services such as core infrastructure, platforms, and applications to cloud customers around the web. It also promises on-demand offerings and new ways of pricing packages. However, cloud job scheduling is still NP-complete and has become more difficult due to certain factors such as resource dynamics and on-demand customer application requirements. To fill this void, this chapter presents the seagull optimization algorithm (SOA) for scheduling work in the cloud world. The efficiency of the SOA approach is compared to that of state-of-the-art job scheduling algorithms by having them all implemented in the CloudSim toolkit.

INTRODUCTION

Scientific computing is a promising field of study that is usually associated with large-scale computer modelling and usually requires a large amount of simulation Resource computing (Yan et. al, 2014). Scientific applications for example in

DOI: 10.4018/978-1-7998-5040-3.ch003

different fields such as science in computer materials, Physics of high energy, molecular modelling, earth sciences, and the production of massive environmental computing Simulation data sets or extensive experiments on data sets. That is why, Analysis and dissemination among researchers of these data sets / Researchers in a large geographical area requires high computer power, which goes beyond a single machine's capabilities. Ever-growing before, Data developed by and created by scientific applications the sophistication of the applications themselves, Slow to use and run those applications prohibitively Traditional paradigms of computing (Chandrawat et. al, 2017, Al-Shargabi et al, 2020; Aljawarneh, 2012; Aljawarneh et al, 2017; Chehbi-Gamoura et al, 2018; Esposito et al, 2018; Jaswal et al, 2019; Kalpana et al, 2018; Lizcano et al, 2020; Malhotra et al, 2019; Mohammed et al, 2019; Mouchili et al, 2018; Singh,2011).

To deal with the growing complexity and Computational criteria for these broad scientific applications, the cloud computing concept has been implemented. It Provides scalable and elastic computing tools (e.g. Networks CPU, storage, memory...) (Singh & Dhiman, 2017). To deal with the growing complexity and computational criteria for these broad scientific applications. The cloud computing concept has been implemented. It Provides scalable and elastic computing tools (e.g. Quickly accessible CPU, storage, memory, and network supplied and released with minimal administration effort or interaction between service providers (Kaur & Dhiman, 2019), (Singh & Dhiman, 2018). 0these cloud services are feasible be scaled up or down automatically and quickly and delivered on a pay per use basis to the end customers model of payment. Key cloud provider services May be listed as a service (IaaS) infrastructure, Service network (PaaS) and service applications (SaaS). Underneath the cloud stack is the IaaS model. PaaS is the next layer of the stack. PaaS gives you an integrated high level ecosystem for construction, research, implementation and Host software developed by the developer or acquired. SaaS assigned to the top of the stack and distribution of apps Model in which apps or services are supplied Internet to allow end users to access it through a web navigator. This model allows people to use apps online Rather than the one built locally(Singh & Dhiman, 2018). SaaS is now an A Below model distribution for service applications including web mail, Google Docs and apps for social networking. This model encourages people to use web applications instead of locally constructed. Now SaaS is an underneath the service applications model delivery like web mail, Google Social Networking Docs and Games (Dhiman & Kumar, 2018), (Singh & Dhiman, 2018), (Dhiman & Kumar, 2019).

RELATED WORKS

There has recently been considerable concern using metaheuristics to overcome various problems (MHs). They will use previously solve another set of problems with optimization traditional methods that cannot be resolved. Based on these benefits, multiple studies have found that the MH methods give good outcomes for cloud task planning issues. In addition to other conventional approaches, computing (Kennedy & Eberhart, 1995), (Dorigo et. al, 2006), a full review was performed by the writers in (Aleem et. al, 2019), (Babikir et. al, 2019), (Elkadeem et. al, 2019) different metaheuristics for the resolution cloud computing task planning issues.

Guo et al. (Guo et. al, 2012) proposed an approach for task planning according to the algorithm to be updated of PSO Minimize user activity processing costs by embedding Operators for PSO crossover and mutation Procedure. Findings suggested that the PSO was changed offers good performance particularly with a large scale Data set.

Khalili and Babamir have also established a similar approach (Ewees & Elaziz, 2020) using various techniques to change the PSO version Update your weight of inertia. A variant of method was used in one Cloud environment for workload reduction timetable (Heilig et. al, 2018) Depending on the complex shipping queues (TSDQ) Timetable. First approach merged fuzzy logic with first approach the second method combined PSO (TSDQ-FLPSA), PSO (TSDQ-SAPSO) simulated annealing.

(Erol et. al, 2006) introduced the GA for the assignment of tasks to minimize the work time to complete. GA effects are analyzed with simple methods of allocation capacity and make-up. Findings showed that other algorithms are outperformed by GA. The writers in (Dhiman, 2019) has been submitted with a heuristic- modified GA version.

Talatahari et al. (Kaveh & Talatahari, 2010) developed new technologies Operators are using this to increase the GA output Model for improving job scheduling results. In (Hatamlou, 2013), the following authors have given MGGS, an updated GA and greedy tactic mix. The results showed that they were able to find an acceptable solution for the Issue of job planning.

In addition, the optimization of ant colony (ACO) is now one of the most common methods of task planning (Du et. al, 2006). The job scheduling algorithm proposed by (Kaveh & Khayatazad, 2012) ACO-based cloud computing technology Area. The version updated, named the goal of MACOLB is to reduce the make-up time Device load balancing. The firefly algorithm (FA) is also available was used to change the work schedule outcomes. As in (Heilig et. al, 2018), FA as a local search tool is suggested improving the competitive imperialist algorithm (ICA) and This leads to better make-up.

Heidari (Heidari et. al, 2019) proposed the FA to reduce work output time, Comparing first-come results with the first-served results found the FA exceeding the FCFS algorithm. Algorithm. Refer to the FA for more details (Bao et. al, 2019), (Jia et. al, 2019), (Chen et. al, 2020).

ALGORITHM FOR SEAGULL OPTIMIZATION (SOA)

The motivation and mathematical modelling of the proposal in this section detailed discussion of the algorithm.

Paradigm

Seagulls however have a special couple drums just above your eyes, specially built to flush the system's salt through bill openings. In general, in colonies, seagulls live. You use your expertise find and attack the prey, find and attack the prey. Seagulls the most critical thing It's their actions that migrate and strike. The concept of migration seasonal travel from place to place find the richest and most abundant food supply environmental sufficiency.

This is the following behaviour:

- They ride in a group during migration. The first places Seagulls are different to prevent each collision other.
- Seagulls will fly in a group towards the best fittest seagull life, i.e. a seagull of fitness 1 in comparison with others it is poor.
- Other seagulls can upgrade their original by using the fittest seagull positions.

Seagulls are also threatened by migratory birds across the sea from one place to another, they move. You will spiral yourself movement of the natural form during the attack. A model of concept is shown in the Fig. 1. This paper focuses on two natural conduct Seagulls.

Migration

The algorithm simulates how seagulls are collected during migration moving to another place. A seagull at this stage, three requirements should be met:

- Crash avoidance: To prevent neighbourhood collision an extra variable is used (i.e. other seagulls) for the current search agent location calculation.

Figure 1. Seagulls' migrations and assaults

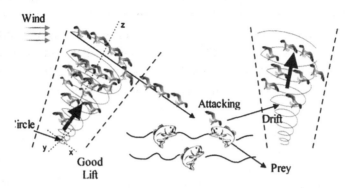

- Movement in the direction of the best neighbour: The neighbours' collision between the search agents.
- Stay near the best quest agent: Search, finally agent can change their position on the best search agent

Operation (Attacking)

The farm aims to take advantage of the past and experience of the method of looking. Seagulls will continually adjust the angle of attack as well as migration speed.

EXPERIMENTAL ENVIRONMENT AND DATASET

To determine the performance of SOA approach established, performance assessments and comparison of other algorithms for scheduling were executed on the simulator CloudSim Toolkit is an open source system with high performance For CC environment modelling and simulation. It Supports cloud component modelling support For example: data centers, hosts, VMs, the cloud Brokers for resources and solutions for capital delivery. On a desktop computer tests were carried out with Intel Core CPU @ 2.40 GHz 4 GB of RAM using CloudSim toolkit 3.0.3 and perform Ubuntu 14.04. The configuration for the employee can be found in Table 1 world of simulation. All studies are carried out Hosted inside a data by 25 VMs on 2 host machines. VM processing power is taken into account.

Both synthetic workload and norm for experiments Traces of workload are used for performance evaluation the methodology suggested by the SOA. The workload synthetic is generated by means of a uniform distribution Small, medium, and large employment equal numbers. We considered that each cloud system job was submitted different processing times and their processing requirements may be important Measured in MI, too. Table 1 sums up the workload used synthetically.

The normal parallel, apart from the synthetic workload workloads consisting of the iPSC/860 NASA Ames and HPC2N (North Core of High-Performance Computing) is Used to assess results. iPSC/860 from NASA Ames and HPC2N set log is one of the most popular and commonly known information technologies.

RESULTS

Result review and experimental discussion of proposed policy for SOA job preparation. To obtain objective results Assess the SOA strategy results, we have It has been validated by five known algorithms. In order to demonstrate SOA's success on SSA, We have compiled solution graphs MFO, PSO, FA and HHO Quality (i.e. makepan) relative to the number of iterations As seen in Figures 2–4, the three datasets. Of the of Synthetic workload convergence curves shown in SOA converges faster than other algorithms as shown in tables 1-3.

Table 1. Best Synthetic values of Makespan for the SOA algorithm and compared algorithms

	Instances	PSO	FA	SSA	MFO	HHO	SOA
Synthetic	100	49.6	50.4.	45.85	45.3	35	33.12
	300	124.5	110.25	100.15	98.33	78.25	64.4
	500	180.62	170.9	160.8	157	112.2	98.74
	700	200.08	200.4.	220.5	100.9	146.29	125.23
	900	300.7	250.3	250.45	254.45	180.6	160.65

CONCLUSION

This chapter proposes an alternative work schedule process for computing in the cloud. The solution proposed is subject to boost the Harris hawks optimizer efficiency (HHO) uses an algorithm for simulated ringing. Since it uses many high operators ability to balance between the search operating and exploring. Motivated by these shifts, The SOA approach is proposed in this study tackling the cloud planning epidemic. Test The output of the experimental sequence of our system are carried out with a large number of instances 200 to 1000 synthetic workload cloudlets and up to 2500 Cloudlets with regular traces for workload. It is, moreover, five popular metaheuristics validated, including MFO, SSA, FA, and PSO. A new bio-inspired

Figure 2. The obtained synthetic values

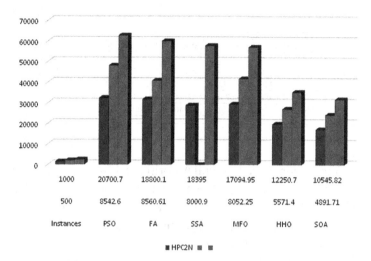

Table 2. Best NASAiPSC values of Makespan for the SOA algorithm and compared algorithms

	Instances	PSO	FA	SSA	MFO	HHO	SOA
NASAiPSC	400.00	81.50	73.95	65.65	65.83	53.65	40.65
	900.00	170.03	155.70	145.40	140.83	100.11	90.05
	1400.00	257.60	240.30	233.41	225.49	155.65	165.11
	1900.00	340.11	330.02	320.85	300.85	200.80	185.11
	2400.00	450.35	441.00	415.73	415.74	260.20	235.45

Figure 3. The obtained NASAiPSC values

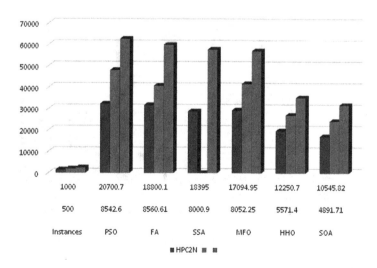

Table 3. Best HPC2N values of Makespan for the SOA algorithm and compared algorithms

	Instances	PSO	FA	SSA	MFO	HHO	SOA
HPC2N	500	8542.6	8560.61	8000.9	8052.25	5571.4	4891.71
	1000	20700.7	18800.1	18395	17094.95	12250.7	10545.82
	1500	32362.6	31725.5	28823.9	29284.8	19730	17105.44
	2000	48034.06	40745.85	42800..7	41631.17	27075.5	24230.55
	2500	62700.8	60020.45	57740.84	57100.45	35227.45	31759.46

algorithm for optimisation named Seagull Algorithm for Optimization (SOA). In this piece, SOA is checked to verify its 44 benchmark tests performance effectiveness. The results show that SOA is highly competitive Results compared to nine common algorithms for optimization. The findings of the unimodal and multimodal research functions indicate SOA algorithm discovery and exploitation power. At the same period, results are benchmarks Tests show that SOA can overcome problems and challenges Real problems were restricted by the high dimensionality bound. Statistical details test to show the statistical importance were conducted over benchmark test functions of the proposed SOA. Moreover, SOA is used by 7 industries in real life (i.e. Optical) Design of buffer, vessel design, design of speed reducer, Welded beam architecture, spring voltage/compression. Moreover, the proposed method is further enhancing to solve the real-life engineering problems (Chandrawat et. al, 2017), (Singh & Dhiman,2017), (Kaur & Dhiman, 2019), (Singh & Dhiman, 2018),

Figure 4. The obtained HPC2N values

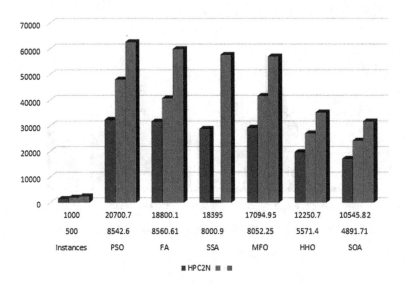

(Singh et. al, 2018), (Dhiman & Kumar, 2018), (Singh & Dhiman, 2018),(Dhiman & Kumar, 2019), (Singh et. al, 2018), (Dhiman & Kumar, 2017), (Dhiman & Kumar, 2018), (Dhiman & Kumar, 2018), (Dhiman & Kumar, 2019), (Dhiman & Kaur, 2019), (Dhiman, 2019), (Dhiman, 2020), (Kaur et. al,2020), (Dhiman, 2019), (Dhiman et. al, 2020).

REFERENCES

Al-Shargabi, B., Al-Jawarneh, S., & Hayajneh, S. M. (2020). A cloudlet based security and trust model for e-government web services. *Journal of Theoretical and Applied Information Technology*, *98*(1), 27–37.

Alba, E., & Dorronsoro, B. (2005). The exploration/exploitation tradeoff in dynamic cellular genetic algorithms. *IEEE Transactions on Evolutionary Computation*, *9*(2), 126–142. doi:10.1109/TEVC.2005.843751

Aleem, S. H. A., Zobaa, A. F., Balci, M. E., & Ismael, S. M. (2019). Harmonic overloading minimization of frequency-dependent components in harmonics polluted distribution systems using harris hawks optimization algorithm. *IEEE Access: Practical Innovations, Open Solutions*, *7*, 100824–100837. doi:10.1109/ ACCESS.2019.2930831

Aljawarneh, S. (Ed.). (2012). *Cloud computing advancements in design, implementation, and technologies*. IGI Global.

Aljawarneh, S., & Malhotra, M. (Eds.). (2017). *Critical Research on Scalability and Security Issues in Virtual Cloud Environments*. IGI Global.

Babikir, H. A., Abd Elaziz, M., Elsheikh, A. H., Showaib, E. A., Elhadary, M., Wu, D., & Liu, Y. (2019). Noise prediction of axial piston pump based on different valve materials using a modified artificial neural network model. *Alexandria Engineering Journal*, *58*(3), 1077–1087. doi:10.1016/j.aej.2019.09.010

Bao, X., Jia, H., & Lang, C. (2019). A novel hybrid harris hawks optimization for color image multilevel thresholding segmentation. *IEEE Access: Practical Innovations, Open Solutions*, *7*, 76529–76546. doi:10.1109/ACCESS.2019.2921545

Chandrawat, R. K., Kumar, R., Garg, B. P., Dhiman, G., & Kumar, S. (2017). An analysis of modeling and optimization production cost through fuzzy linear programming problem with symmetric and right angle triangular fuzzy number. In *Proceedings of Sixth International Conference on Soft Computing for Problem Solving* (pp. 197-211). Springer. 10.1007/978-981-10-3322-3_18

Chehbi-Gamoura, S., Derrouiche, R., Malhotra, M., & Koruca, H. I. (2018, June). Adaptive management approach for more availability of big data business analytics. In *Proceedings of the Fourth International Conference on Engineering & MIS 2018* (pp. 1-8). 10.1145/3234698.3234758

Chen, H., Jiao, S., Wang, M., Heidari, A. A., & Zhao, X. (2020). Parameters identification of photovoltaic cells and modules using diversification-enriched Harris hawks optimization with chaotic drifts. *Journal of Cleaner Production, 244*, 118778. doi:10.1016/j.jclepro.2019.118778

Dhiman, G. (2019). ESA: A hybrid bio-inspired metaheuristic optimization approach for engineering problems. *Engineering with Computers*, 1–31. doi:10.100700366-019-00826-w

Dhiman, G. (2019). *Multi-objective metaheuristic approaches for data clustering in engineering application (s)* (Doctoral dissertation).

Dhiman, G. (2020). MOSHEPO: A hybrid multi-objective approach to solve economic load dispatch and micro grid problems. *Applied Intelligence, 50*(1), 119–137. doi:10.100710489-019-01522-4

Dhiman, G., & Kaur, A. (2019). Stoa: A bio-inspired based optimization algorithm for industrial engineering problems. *Engineering Applications of Artificial Intelligence, 82*, 148–174. doi:10.1016/j.engappai.2019.03.021

Dhiman, G., & Kumar, V. (2017). Spotted hyena optimizer: A novel bio-inspired based metaheuristic technique for engineering applications. *Advances in Engineering Software, 114*, 48–70. doi:10.1016/j.advengsoft.2017.05.014

Dhiman, G., & Kumar, V. (2018). Emperor penguin optimizer: A bio-inspired algorithm for engineering problems. *Knowledge-Based Systems, 159*, 20–50. doi:10.1016/j.knosys.2018.06.001

Dhiman, G., & Kumar, V. (2018). Multi-objective spotted hyena optimizer: A multi-objective optimization algorithm for engineering problems. *Knowledge-Based Systems, 150*, 175–197. doi:10.1016/j.knosys.2018.03.011

Dhiman, G., & Kumar, V. (2018). Multi-objective spotted hyena optimizer: A multi-objective optimization algorithm for engineering problems. *Knowledge-Based Systems, 150*, 175–197. doi:10.1016/j.knosys.2018.03.011

Dhiman, G., & Kumar, V. (2019). KnRVEA: A hybrid evolutionary algorithm based on knee points and reference vector adaptation strategies for many-objective optimization. *Applied Intelligence, 49*(7), 2434–2460. doi:10.100710489-018-1365-1

Dhiman, G., & Kumar, V. (2019). Seagull optimization algorithm: Theory and its applications for large-scale industrial engineering problems. *Knowledge-Based Systems*, *165*, 169–196. doi:10.1016/j.knosys.2018.11.024

Dhiman, G., Soni, M., Pandey, H. M., Slowik, A., & Kaur, H. (2020). A novel hybrid hypervolume indicator and reference vector adaptation strategies based evolutionary algorithm for many-objective optimization. *Engineering with Computers*, 1–19. doi:10.100700366-020-00986-0

Dorigo, M., Birattari, M., & Stutzle, T. (2006). Ant colony optimization. *IEEE Computational Intelligence Magazine*, *1*(4), 28–39. doi:10.1109/CI-M.2006.248054

Du, H., Wu, X., & Zhuang, J. (2006, September). Small-world optimization algorithm for function optimization. In *International conference on natural computation* (pp. 264-273). Springer. 10.1007/11881223_33

Elkadeem, M. R., Abd Elaziz, M., Ullah, Z., Wang, S., & Sharshir, S. W. (2019). Optimal planning of renewable energy-integrated distribution system considering uncertainties. *IEEE Access: Practical Innovations, Open Solutions*, *7*, 164887–164907. doi:10.1109/ACCESS.2019.2947308

Erol, O. K., & Eksin, I. (2006). A new optimization method: Big bang–big crunch. *Advances in Engineering Software*, *37*(2), 106–111. doi:10.1016/j.advengsoft.2005.04.005

Esposito, C., Su, X., Aljawarneh, S. A., & Choi, C. (2018). Securing collaborative deep learning in industrial applications within adversarial scenarios. *IEEE Transactions on Industrial Informatics*, *14*(11), 4972–4981. doi:10.1109/TII.2018.2853676

Ewees, A. A., & Abd Elaziz, M. (2020). Performance analysis of chaotic multi-verse harris hawks optimization: A case study on solving engineering problems. *Engineering Applications of Artificial Intelligence*, *88*, 103370. doi:10.1016/j.engappai.2019.103370

Formato, R. A. (2009). Central force optimization: A new deterministic gradient-like optimization metaheuristic. *Opsearch*, *46*(1), 25–51. doi:10.100712597-009-0003-4

Golilarz, N. A., Gao, H., & Demirel, H. (2019). Satellite image de-noising with harris hawks meta heuristic optimization algorithm and improved adaptive generalized gaussian distribution threshold function. *IEEE Access: Practical Innovations, Open Solutions*, *7*, 57459–57468. doi:10.1109/ACCESS.2019.2914101

Guo, L., Zhao, S., Shen, S., & Jiang, C. (2012). Task scheduling optimization in cloud computing based on heuristic algorithm. *Journal of Networks,* *7*(3), 547.

Hatamlou, A. (2013). Black hole: A new heuristic optimization approach for data clustering. *Information Sciences, 222*, 175–184. doi:10.1016/j.ins.2012.08.023

Heidari, A. A., Mirjalili, S., Faris, H., Aljarah, I., Mafarja, M., & Chen, H. (2019). Harris hawks optimization: Algorithm and applications. *Future Generation Computer Systems, 97*, 849–872. doi:10.1016/j.future.2019.02.028

Heilig, L., Lalla-Ruiz, E., Voß, S., & Buyya, R. (2018). Metaheuristics in cloud computing. *Software, Practice & Experience, 48*(10), 1729–1733. doi:10.1002pe.2628

Jaswal, S., & Malhotra, M. (2019, December). A detailed analysis of trust models in cloud environment. In *Proceedings of the Second International Conference on Data Science, E-Learning and Information Systems* (pp. 1-5). 10.1145/3368691.3368740

Jia, H., Lang, C., Oliva, D., Song, W., & Peng, X. (2019). Dynamic harris hawks optimization with mutation mechanism for satellite image segmentation. *Remote Sensing, 11*(12), 1421. doi:10.3390/rs11121421

Kalpana, G., Kumar, P. V., Aljawarneh, S., & Krishnaiah, R. V. (2018). Shifted adaption homomorphism encryption for mobile and cloud learning. *Computers & Electrical Engineering, 65*, 178–195. doi:10.1016/j.compeleceng.2017.05.022

Kaur, A., & Dhiman, G. (2019). A review on search-based tools and techniques to identify bad code smells in object-oriented systems. In *Harmony search and nature inspired optimization algorithms* (pp. 909–921). Springer. doi:10.1007/978-981-13-0761-4_86

Kaur, S., Awasthi, L. K., Sangal, A. L., & Dhiman, G. (2020). Tunicate Swarm Algorithm: A new bio-inspired based metaheuristic paradigm for global optimization. *Engineering Applications of Artificial Intelligence, 90*, 103541. doi:10.1016/j.engappai.2020.103541

Kaveh, A., & Khayatazad, M. (2012). A new meta-heuristic method: Ray optimization. *Computers & Structures, 112*, 283–294. doi:10.1016/j.compstruc.2012.09.003

Kaveh, A., & Talatahari, S. (2010). A novel heuristic optimization method: Charged system search. *Acta Mechanica, 213*(3), 267–289. doi:10.100700707-009-0270-4

Kennedy, J., & Eberhart, R. (1995, November). Particle swarm optimization. In *Proceedings of ICNN'95-International Conference on Neural Networks* (Vol. 4, pp. 1942-1948). IEEE. 10.1109/ICNN.1995.488968

Kirkpatrick, S., Gelatt, C. D., & Vecchi, M. P. (1983). Optimization by simulated annealing. *Science, 220*(4598), 671-680.

Lizcano, D., Lara, J. A., White, B., & Aljawarneh, S. (2020). Blockchain-based approach to create a model of trust in open and ubiquitous higher education. *Journal of Computing in Higher Education, 32*(1), 109–134. doi:10.100712528-019-09209-y

Lozano, M., & García-Martínez, C. (2010). Hybrid metaheuristics with evolutionary algorithms specializing in intensification and diversification: Overview and progress report. *Computers & Operations Research, 37*(3), 481–497. doi:10.1016/j. cor.2009.02.010

Malhotra, M., & Singh, A. (2019). Role of Agents to Enhance the Security and Scalability in Cloud Environment. In Cloud Security: Concepts, Methodologies, Tools, and Applications (pp. 552-573). IGI Global. doi:10.4018/978-1-5225-8176-5.ch028

Mohammed, T. A., Ghareeb, A., Al-bayaty, H., & Aljawarneh, S. (2019, December). Big data challenges and achievements: applications on smart cities and energy sector. In *Proceedings of the Second International Conference on Data Science, E-Learning and Information Systems* (pp. 1-5). 10.1145/3368691.3368717

Mouchili, M. N., Aljawarneh, S., & Tchouati, W. (2018, October). Smart city data analysis. In *Proceedings of the First International Conference on Data Science, E-learning and Information Systems* (pp. 1-6). Academic Press.

Rashedi, E., Nezamabadi-Pour, H., & Saryazdi, S. (2009). GSA: A gravitational search algorithm. *Information Sciences, 179*(13), 2232–2248. doi:10.1016/j.ins.2009.03.004

Singh, A., Juneja, D., & Malhotra, M. (2017). A novel agent based autonomous and service composition framework for cost optimization of resource provisioning in cloud computing. *Journal of King Saud University-Computer and Information Sciences, 29*(1), 19–28. doi:10.1016/j.jksuci.2015.09.001

Singh, P., & Dhiman, G. (2017, December). A fuzzy-LP approach in time series forecasting. In *International Conference on Pattern Recognition and Machine Intelligence* (pp. 243-253). Springer. 10.1007/978-3-319-69900-4_31

Singh, P., & Dhiman, G. (2018). A hybrid fuzzy time series forecasting model based on granular computing and bio-inspired optimization approaches. *Journal of Computational Science, 27*, 370–385. doi:10.1016/j.jocs.2018.05.008

Singh, P., & Dhiman, G. (2018). Uncertainty representation using fuzzy-entropy approach: Special application in remotely sensed high-resolution satellite images (RSHRSIs). *Applied Soft Computing, 72*, 121–139. doi:10.1016/j.asoc.2018.07.038

Singh, P., Dhiman, G., & Kaur, A. (2018). A quantum approach for time series data based on graph and Schrödinger equations methods. *Modern Physics Letters A, 33*(35), 1850208. doi:10.1142/S0217732318502085

Singh, P., Rabadiya, K., & Dhiman, G. (2018). A four-way decision-making system for the Indian summer monsoon rainfall. *Modern Physics Letters B, 32*(25), 1850304. doi:10.1142/S0217984918503049

Wolpert, D. H., & Macready, W. G. (1997). No free lunch theorems for optimization. *IEEE Transactions on Evolutionary Computation, 1*(1), 67–82. doi:10.1109/4235.585893

Yan, Z., Wang, J., & Li, G. (2014). A collective neurodynamic optimization approach to bound-constrained nonconvex optimization. *Neural Networks, 55*, 20–29. doi:10.1016/j.neunet.2014.03.006 PMID:24705545

Chapter 4
Integrating Business Intelligence With Cloud Computing

Shivani Jaswal
Chandigarh University, India

ABSTRACT

Cloud Computing has emerged as an expression that has described various other computing concepts that involve computers that are interconnected virtually. It is so prominent that it has modified the architecture by incorporating new design principles. Also, the present economic crisis, which is being experienced by most of the world, has oriented us towards cloud computing and its efficient services. Here, business intelligence plays a pivotal role in extraction of valuable information and identifying hidden patterns of data. Also, any organization in striving stage can also act smartly with the use of various business intelligence solutions. Various benefits are also offered by the BI solutions such as working together as a team and identifying various resolutions. The contribution of this chapter is to show how the cloud computing environment has been merged with business intelligence to fulfil the future need of uplifting of economy.

INTRODUCTION

To provide computing at a lower cost has been framed as a big concern for development in IT sector. Grid and Distributed computing deliver efficiency at a high rate by considering the principle of separating and allocating vast processes to various providers. The IT industry has always been looking for that computing

DOI: 10.4018/978-1-7998-5040-3.ch004

model that could provide connectivity from anywhere to computing resources, with infinite number of resources in minimal time and cost at any time. Utility computing (Cloud Computing) uses the "pay as per the use" principle which eliminates the processing cost. This technology of virtualization represents multiple autonomous structures from one physical device to another. The resource can be given without human intervention whenever needed (Al-Shargabi et al, 2020; Aljawarneh, 2012; Aljawarneh et al, 2017; Chehbi-Gamoura et al, 2018; Esposito et al, 2018; Jaswal et al, 2019; Kalpana et al, 2018; Lizcano et al, 2020; Malhotra et al, 2019; Mohammed et al, 2019; Mouchili et al, 2018; Singh,2011).

Business Intelligence is a highly resource-intensive technology that involves parallel processing on a wide scale and immense data warehouse storage capabilities. At periodic intervals, the data warehouses are periodically updated by queries performed on business and transactional databases. A challenge can emerge in the future for businesses to continue adding resources to data warehouses. A fresh hope for potential business intelligence opportunities has been instigated by cloud computing. Business intelligence's mission is to enhance the timeliness and accuracy of information and to help managers to understand their company's role as opposed to competitors. Business intelligence plays an essential role in the extraction of useful data and the identification of secret trends in both internal and external data sources. Most of the organisational information, however, is in unstructured form or in the minds of its workers. At the right time and in a meticulous arrangement, Business Intelligence facilitates the necessary data. It freely provides user-friendly data to users where they can work as a team.

Cloud Computing is based on pay as per use model. It provides various resources through virtualization mode. These resources can be computing power, storage space. This paradigm has helped setting of busines say large scale or middle scale or small scale in the market. Cloud Computing is so prominent in the present era such that it has modified the architecture of working by incorporating new design principles. Also, with this, present economic crisis which is being experience by the maximum parts of the world has oriented towards cloud computing and its efficient services. Cloud computing and business intelligence has been considered as perfect match. Business intelligence is about supplying the right data at the right time to the right users and cloud computing offers a lightweight, scalable way to access BI apps. The benefit of Cloud BI apps is that on various platforms and web browsers they are available. This circumvents conventional software challenges, such as the need for on-site access to the programmes. Enterprises are switching to the cloud and are still benefiting from the advantages, such as reduced costs, faster speed of implementation and ease of usage. Cloud systems now have processing power equal to on-premise applications. They provide consumers with capabilities that were only accessible in locally installed applications up until now. However, when the concept of cloud computing has been merged with Business Intelligence, then the strategies those implemented in the marketplace helps in generating profound benefits i.e. return on investments, cost benefit analysis, easy maintenance etc. In a computer network such as the Internet, Cloud Business Intelligence (BI) applications are hosted. They are used as access to BI-related information such as control panels, KPIs and other market metrics for companies. Enterprises, such as Customer Relationship Management (CRM) apps (Salesforce), online file sharing and storage (Dropbox, Box) and support desk apps (UserVoice), are gradually moving to cloud-based tools. This pattern entails tools for market intelligence accepting the Cloud's agility and usability. As we already know that in an ear, financial or economic crisis takes place. Therefore, Cloud Business Intelligence helps in setting up of strategies and helping an organization to implement those successfully in any business environment.

Cloud business intelligence is the easiest and most cost-efficient way for business intelligence software to be accessed and processed by associations. It is a way of reporting and reviewing the installed solutions to be built and consumes less cost. Cloud delivery allows quick deployment; in days or weeks, most organisations can create an initial BI environment compared to months of conventional BI solutions. Most of the organizations now recognise that traditional on-premise BI 's high expenditures and overall cost of ownership makes these strategies inefficient and unattractive.

In the face of the ongoing global crisis, organisations should assume that their future will become increasingly uncertain. The essence and structure of the new competitive word is causing the crisis to become a characteristic of modern business today, not the state of emergency, in times of confusion, risks and incomplete information (Koral et. al, 2010).

Each company tends to become an intelligent organisation in the current economy and to gain market competitive advantage through the use of fresh and creative BI solutions. Integration of a BI solution requires a significant amount of human and financial resources, which is an objective to accomplish and not a fact for many small and medium-sized organisations. Furthermore, under conditions of recession, corporations must use all the possibilities to optimise productivity and minimise costs. Large investments in conventional BI solutions are often impractical and unattractive under these circumstances, whereas popular Cloud Computing-based solutions have gained popularity (Gurjar et al, 2013).

Cloud applications offer strong and scalable market knowledge, but are quicker, simpler and less expensive than "behind the firewall" custom solutions. Cloud BI 's market advantages are persuasive and true. Various types of services are part of the cloud-based business intelligence network. Any of them are: software-as-a-service (SAAS), infrastructure-as-a-service (IAAS), platform-as-a-service (PAAS). Performance and opportunities of Cloud Computing depends on various organization

Figure 1. Risks and benefits associated with Cloud BI

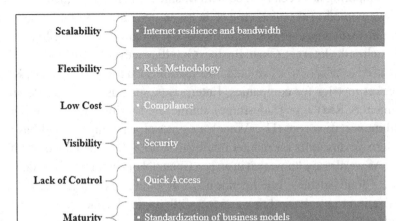

circumstances and its benefits, risks (figure 1) and the same has been outlined in (Berkowitz (2009), Birst (2010), Cattedu (2009), ISACA (2009), Hong (2009)).

The task of a cloud ecosystem marketplace is to manage the relationships between the various parties (service providers and service customers), to improve discovery of product and its cash transactions. The most critical functions of marketplace is to look for goods compositions and selecting best out of them. There have been different techniques of selecting ideas, from consumers', service providers' and overall output scope for provisioning in distributed and service-oriented systems.

Services are known as reusable elements of service-oriented infrastructures, serving business activities. A service can be a web service, independent or connected. This approach can provide a high degree of standardisation and may also disclose interchangeable features of the application that can be easily accessed, customised and consumed by various end users. Menasce et al, (2009) have proposed a selection algorithm that illustrates the optimal solution is being converged by correctly selecting the set of service providers that satisfy the requested QoS parameters. Optimized service selection is formulated in this paper as a problem of nonlinear programming optimization, with the objective of selecting the service from the solution space that minimises the average execution time under the cost constraints provided. A heuristic search algorithm is also presented that performs very close to the optimum, exploring only a small percent of the solution space, though. Both of the above-mentioned approaches to service selection seek to reduce total execution time or expense, while taking into account only two QoS limitations, namely cost and time of execution.

On the other hand, the scheme that selects the service that optimises the Quality of Services provided is proposed by Cardellini et al, (2007) which helps in optimising an acceptable objective function under threshold values of certain interest attributes. In this process, the selection process is carried out per category rather than per request, in order to prevent and handle the overload of possible requests more effectively. The service selection mechanism proposed by Dubey et al, (2010) is based on the maximum use of the utility role of users, subject to its cost limitations. Utility functions derived from distributed autonomous self-optimization systems are used to calculate the level of customer satisfaction in terms of a set of attributes (response time, availability, etc.). Nonetheless, these solutions do not take stakeholder relationships into account.

In a B2B marketplace setting, a supplier selection process carried out in two phases to reduce the impact of knowledge overload, Chamodrakas et al, (2010) proposed a computational complexity. The first step reduces the initialising set of potential solutions according to difficult user constraints and in the second phase the remaining ones are reviewed and evaluated. This solution acknowledges the presence but not the implementation relationships of a large number of consistency parameters. Trummer et al, (2010) also define a two-phase selection algorithm. The first stage lists all possibilities for the requested service to be partitioned, while the second decides the solution by turning the problem into a problem of optimization based on constraints, attempting to reduce the total cost. This mechanism considers various potential dependencies between various components of the given services or applications and/or combinations and constraints, but focuses only on the minimization of overall costs.

A multi-criteria service selection approach has been suggested and formalised by Rehman et al, (2011), leading to the selection of the service collection that best meets the requirements of a customer, according to performance criteria, measurement functions and user priority weights. This method, however, is only successful for service selection among service instances of similar requirements and without performance relationships between them. Graupner et al, (2011) have introduced a company operating environment to support services from the point of view of the service user. This business environment offers capabilities for the classification, collection, contracting, integration and execution of services that can be connected based on the current pattern of XaaS delivery. In conclusion, the above-mentioned mechanisms concentrate primarily on optimising rather than addressing all the requested parameters, a subset of the requested criteria. It is also not necessary to apply them to composite materials. Composite goods and more complex requests tend to need to be managed successfully as the cloud environments grow in order to be able to deliver XaaS. Therefore, cloud markets must also have the required exchange and support mechanisms for these goods, such as enhanced service resolution and selection mechanisms and the association of competitive pricing models.

BUSINESS INTELLIGENCE ARCHITECTURE

The structure of the precious infrastructure needs to be measured to understand the implementation of Cloud BI. This three-layered architecture proposed by Baars et al, (2008) is the basis of the following discussion (Figure 2). The layers are discussed in more detail below.

The Data Layer

For management support, this layer is held responsible for saving various structured and unstructured data. The core component is the data warehouse (DWH) with respect to structured data. In support of executive process, a DWH is widely described as a "subject-oriented view which includes time-variant, and non-volatile data collection." Many current DWH realisations are based on so-called core DWHs. Typically, core DWHs are not considered for direct source for research systems but rather data can be distributed among data marts. It holds extracts of relevant data from the submission. More recently, a step has been taken towards integrating of functioning systems with DWH infrastructures. This is done to hold real time transaction which can be achieved by implementing Operational Data Store (ODS). Active Data Warehousing systems can be built using ODS/DWH architectures.

Here, various tools like ETL (Extract-Transform-Load) tools are required to supply the various data stores. The ETL instrument facilitates data extraction and conversion from heterogeneous source systems. This transformation involves extracting and filtering syntactic errors, matching and aggregating and enriching data from various sources. Document Management Systems (DMS) and Content Management Systems (CMS) are integrated into the data layer (Baars et al, (2008) for storing and administrating unstructured data.

The Logic Layer

The analysis of structured and unstructured content is provided by logic layer that helps in facilitating the distribution of required information among various users. In BI environments, monitoring, data mining, and OLAP tools are the most popular tools. In report-oriented formats, quantitative data is generated by including numbers, graphs or other reporting tools. OLAP denotes an idea of aggregated quantitative market data for interactive and multidimensional analysis. Based on statistical approaches such

Figure 2. Architecture of Business Intelligence
(Spruit et al, (2010))

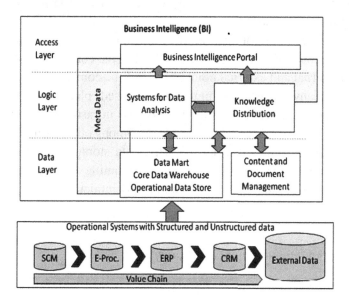

as correlation analysis, grouping, or clustering, data mining techniques enable the detection of hidden trends in large quantities of structured data. The word Advanced Analytics also applies to data mining and related model-based tools.

The Access Layer

The Access Layer enables the user, within the limits of specified user roles and user rights, to correctly use all relevant Logic Layer functions in an integrated way.

STAGES OF INTEGRATION OF CLOUD COMPUTING WITH BUSINESS INTELLIGENCE

1. **INITIATION:** It involves the identification and arrangement of the various hierarchies of business and its priorities, the assessment of the cost required to use the Cloud solution based on Business Intelligence, the creation of the team involved in this work, several deadlines and implementation and maintenance of resources. In addition to this, the team must be identified who will help in conducting the proper management of work and resources and must remain active in the next following phases. IT staff as well as company chiefs must

be part of the Cloud BI strategy work team. For each cloud project, they will interact with stakeholders (both internal and external) about priorities, development and costs.

2. **ANALYSIS**: The current opportunities and potential requirements of a Cloud BI solution must also be defined at the level of the company. Therefore, both from an internal and external point of view of the company, the present stage of the company must be examined and assessed, placing the focus on the value of the company, on substantial business infrastructure and processes. Business infrastructure assessment requires, among other items, their analysis of application management and security, data storage, data discovery and classification (Verizon (2009)). Cloud Computing can be considered an extension of SOA at the level of the enterprise (Linthicum et al, (2009)) (Figure 3).

Figure 3. Stages of integration of Cloud Computing with BI

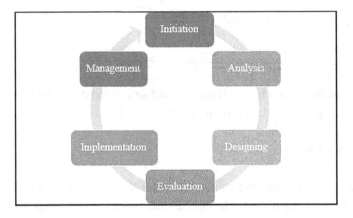

3. **DESIGNING:** The main objective of this phase is to define, when it makes sense, a method for replicating old available solutions. The pivotal elements are also required to be defined (Winian et al, (2009)). Here, the final product will be a cloud BI solution which will have operations required for Cloud Computing and Business Intelligence. The following steps can be used to develop the Cloud BI solution: a) Mapping of BI specifications as per the models of Cloud Computing. To take advantage of both solutions, the secret of successful Cloud BI strategy is to achieve the right connection between the cloud and internal development (Knight et al, (2009)). The cloud transition can be done progressively and the models of software distribution can coexist over a specific time (Figure 4). Taking into consideration the fact that most

companies use Cloud Computing hybrid models, keep pivotal elements of their in-house systems under direct control and outsource the less responsive components, strategic studies on integration / migration decisions need to be carried out in order to select the implementation solution. (b) Identification and assessment of various plans to validate the advantages of the Cloud BI solution. c) Finding out the cloud BI service provider that can implement technical and business aspects. This can be achieved on the basis of information from search engines, consultation from firms etc.

4. **EVALUATION**: The relationship between the several forces present in BI and Cloud Computing can acquire new heights and polarizations due to the notable changes in the market of technology created by globalisation and the new economy. As a result, the assessment of provided solutions/ providers must be carried out on the basis of the most current sources (providers, consulting companies, the latest articles), the rest of the information sources reflecting the reasons for obtaining a global picture of the Cloud BI sector.

5. **IMPLEMENTATION**: By performing various types of data transmissions and processes through the cloud, the proper implementation solution can be achieved (figure 7). Also, continuous evaluations are also required to be performed. It includes various factors for risk management and testing solutions for better performance and management.

With the use of well- defined strategies as well as models, data migration, services and processes migration to the cloud can be achieved. Each migration model includes various specified objectives. By considering parameters such as data accuracy, migration speed, non-cooperation time involved and minimal cost, data migration can be achieved . For the migration of application those are critical in nature, human resources for the proper management is required (Verizon (2009)).

6. **MANAGEMENT:** An appropriate model must be considered for taking various factors into account such as continuous evaluations, risk management etc. It is also required for quality management system. The quality is however measured by including processes and services. In this, URLs are being monitored with the help of maintaining log files, management and evaluation of various contracts involved (Ghilic et al, (2008)).

CLOUD BUSINESS INTELLIGENCE FRAMEWORK

In regards to the defining Cloud Business Intelligence, it is an umbrella that consists of service providers and other contract related issues". It is also required to be test

Figure 4. Cloud Business Intelligence framework
(Spruit et al, (2010))

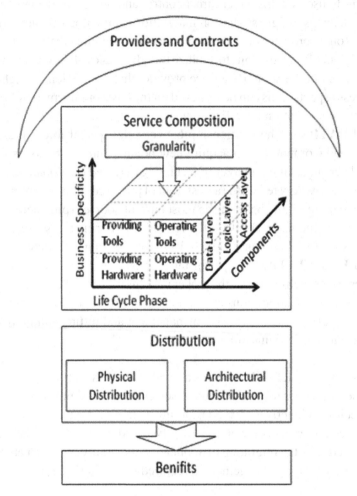

whether the service provider is trustworthy or not. Also, with this, agreement promises various other features of cloud such as high availability, scalability, consistency and reliability. This is required to be fulfilled as the discussion ongoing over the cloud environment is highly sensible (Mcknight (2005)).

The "composition of the service" is considered as the next building block in the framework. This can be achieved by implementing granularity on the layer having tools i.e. web services, processes etc and also by considering BI services along with its life-cycle phase.

If the service category is implicitly part of the structure of the service, delivery is the second distinguishing feature of the cloud as shown in figure 4. In BI, this basically has two sides: the spatial distribution and the distribution of architecture. Finally, the intended advantages have to be commented on. This can be passed on to rationals for outsourcing focused on conventional cost or to harnessing the Cloud approach's qualitative characteristics (introducing consistency, scalability, efficiency, or additional functionality). There can even be insightful advantages (through the provider's add-on data integration services) or even transformative results (by incorporating additional capabilities).

THE BENEFITS OF CLOUD COMPUTING FOR BUSINESS INTELLIGENCE

Various benefits have been identified when integration of Cloud Computing with Business Intelligence takes place. It can be related to generating of faster response to user's query, decreased costs and data sharing. These benefits have been elaborated below:

- **MINIMAL COSTS:** Under the philosophy of cloud computing, enterprises do not need to spend huge sums of money to purchase hardware, applications, licences and expertise to bring this platform of business intelligence. They will just have to negotiate with a supplier of cloud storage to pay for the services they need. It is needless to compensate for the time that the programme is not used by any user and the device resources stay inactive.

- **DUPLICATE SITES:** One of the biggest challenges of business intelligence practitioners is to keep the longest possible schedule of solutions open. Getting several sites that indicate replication is one way to do this. This attribute is accomplished because most cloud service services have locations globally distributed.

- **SCALABILITY OF RESOURCES:** During the day, business analytics applications do not have the same burden of commitment. This method causes certain servers to be inactive at some points in time, while others can hit their peaks in loading, memory use or I / O operations. You can scale in and scale out seamlessly and easily using cloud computing tools. For e.g. the solution could use computing power from application servers during the ETL process yesterday evening and analytical processes could use memory in the daytime.

- **IMPROVING ON-DEMAND PERFORMANCE:** One of the most common issues found in business intelligence applications is where consumers need to extend their data warehousing because the migration to the modern world requires high investment in new infrastructure, storage, licences and human effort. Under a possible hypothesis, by taking advantage of current hardware and software infrastructure, this issue can be solved almost instantaneously and transparently for consumers.

- **FASTER DEVELOPMENT:** The framework can be up and running in just minutes, ready to customise applications and begin populating the data warehouse instead of taking a long-time planning and upgrading the necessary hardware and software.
- **MAINTENANCE:** The Cloud Storage Company conducts much of the maintenance needed for hardware and applications, such as firmware upgrades and promotion. Furthermore, because these applications are accessed via internet browsers, maintenance on client computers is significantly reduced (Baars et al, (2010).

CONCLUSION

Cloud has undoubtedly emerged as a future scope for Business Intelligence with uncountable benefits such as cost benefits analyses, implementation in flexibility and in speed of implementation of any strategies based on Business intelligence. In this way, the field of business intelligence has been influenced and convinced by appropriate management of projects that provides an endless pool of several IT resources such as space for storage, computing power, memory space for various business intelligence infrastructures. Along with cloud, Business Intelligence has been emerged to increase the productivity and efficiency of business strategies and software. By combining large volume and mission critical enterprise systems, BI on the Cloud provides tremendous possibilities for eliminating obstacles to decision making. A Cloud BI solution may also be a viable approach to the problems of the financial crisis. Via such a solution, small, medium or large economic entities will take advantage of business prospects that would not be available under normal circumstances.

In addition, taking into account the Cloud Computing features viewpoint, implementing a business-level Cloud BI approach will reflect the premises of enterprises transferring to a superior type of knowledge society, the virtual enterprise. The proposed Cloud BI approach can also be a response to adapting organisations to the new economic and social environments by exchanging capital and increasing the speed of consumer integration, by increasing the speed of business processes and incorporating conventional BI solutions. Last but not least, another point in favour of the viability of a Cloud BI approach is the estimation of the economic utility of the suggested solution by the cost-performance relationship dependent on the ROI indicator.

A further statement in support of the notion that information and communication systems make their impact known in all aspects of social and economic life is present in the present chapter. Based on the global network-internet system, the network economy has a remarkable growth in our days, reflecting the maximum emergence aspect of knowledge society. In this sense, as the key player in the global economic game, the economic entity needs to change as it goes in order to evolve, but particularly in order to survive.

REFERENCES

Al-Shargabi, B., Al-Jawarneh, S., & Hayajneh, S. M. (2020). A cloudlet based security and trust model for e-government web services. *Journal of Theoretical and Applied Information Technology*, *98*(1), 27–37.

Aljawarneh, S. (Ed.). (2012). *Cloud computing advancements in design, implementation, and technologies*. IGI Global.

Aljawarneh, S., & Malhotra, M. (Eds.). (2017). *Critical Research on Scalability and Security Issues in Virtual Cloud Environments*. IGI Global.

Baars, H., & Kemper, H. G. (2008). Management support with structured and unstructured data—An integrated business intelligence framework. *Information Systems Management*, *25*(2), 132–148. doi:10.1080/10580530801941058

Baars, H., & Kemper, H. G. (2010, July). Business intelligence in the cloud? In PACIS (p. 145). Academic Press.

Berkowitz, J. (2009). *Cloud Computing (Part 1): Advantages, Types and Challenges*. CRM Mastery Weblog. http://crmweblog. crmmastery. com/2009/11/cloud-computing-part1-advantages-types-and-challenges

Birst. (2010). *Why Cloud BI? The 9 Substantial Benefits of Software-as-a Service Business Intelligence*. Birst, Inc.

Cardellini, V., Casalicchio, E., Grassi, V., & Presti, F. L. (2007, July). Flow-based service selection forweb service composition supporting multiple qos classes. In *IEEE International Conference on Web Services (ICWS 2007)* (pp. 743-750). IEEE. 10.1109/ICWS.2007.91

Catteddu, D. (2009, December). Cloud Computing: benefits, risks and recommendations for information security. In *Iberic Web Application Security Conference* (pp. 17-17). Springer.

Chamodrakas, I., Batis, D., & Martakos, D. (2010). Supplier selection in electronic marketplaces using satisficing and fuzzy AHP. *Expert Systems with Applications*, *37*(1), 490–498. doi:10.1016/j.eswa.2009.05.043

Chehbi-Gamoura, S., Derrouiche, R., Malhotra, M., & Koruca, H. I. (2018, June). Adaptive management approach for more availability of big data business analytics. In *Proceedings of the Fourth International Conference on Engineering & MIS 2018* (pp. 1-8). 10.1145/3234698.3234758

Dubey, V. K., & Menascé, D. A. (2010, July). Utility-based optimal service selection for business processes in service oriented architectures. In *2010 IEEE International Conference on Web Services* (pp. 542-550). IEEE. 10.1109/ICWS.2010.33

Esposito, C., Su, X., Aljawarneh, S. A., & Choi, C. (2018). Securing collaborative deep learning in industrial applications within adversarial scenarios. *IEEE Transactions on Industrial Informatics*, *14*(11), 4972–4981. doi:10.1109/TII.2018.2853676

Ghilic-Micu, B., Stoica, M., & Mircea, M. (2008). A framework for measuring the impact of BI solution. *TC, 1*, 3.

Graupner, S., Basu, S., & Singhal, S. (2011, March). Business operating environment for service Clouds. In *2011 Annual SRII Global Conference* (pp. 1-10). IEEE.

Gurjar, Y. S., & Rathore, V. S. (2013). Cloud business intelligence–is what business need today. *International Journal of Recent Technology and Engineering*, *1*(6), 81–86.

ISACA. (2009). *Cloud Computing: Business Benefits With Security, Governance and Assurance Perspectives*. ISACA.

Jaswal, S., & Malhotra, M. (2019, December). A detailed analysis of trust models in cloud environment. In *Proceedings of the Second International Conference on Data Science, E-Learning and Information Systems* (pp. 1-5). 10.1145/3368691.3368740

Kalpana, G., Kumar, P. V., Aljawarneh, S., & Krishnaiah, R. V. (2018). Shifted adaption homomorphism encryption for mobile and cloud learning. *Computers & Electrical Engineering*, *65*, 178–195. doi:10.1016/j.compeleceng.2017.05.022

Knight, D. (2009). *Why Cloud vs. Premise is the Wrong Question*. Cisco Systems Inc.

Korol, T., & Korodi, A. (2010). Predicting bankruptcy with the use of macroeconomic variables. *Economic Computation and Economic Cybernetics Studies and Research*, *44*(1), 201–221.

Li, H., Sedayao, J., Hahn-Steichen, J., Jimison, E., Spence, C., & Chahal, S. (2009). Developing an enterprise cloud computing strategy. *Korea Information Processing Society Review*, *16*(2), 4–16.

Linthicum, D. S. (2009). *Moving to Cloud Computing Step-by-Step*. The Linthicum Group.

Lizcano, D., Lara, J. A., White, B., & Aljawarneh, S. (2020). Blockchain-based approach to create a model of trust in open and ubiquitous higher education. *Journal of Computing in Higher Education*, *32*(1), 109–134.

Malhotra, M., & Singh, A. (2019). Role of Agents to Enhance the Security and Scalability in Cloud Environment. In Cloud Security: Concepts, Methodologies, Tools, and Applications (pp. 552-573). IGI Global. doi:10.4018/978-1-5225-8176-5.ch028

McKnight, W. (2005). Introducing the Data Warehouse Appliance, Part I. *DMReview*.

Menascé, D. A., Casalicchio, E., & Dubey, V. (2010). On optimal service selection in service oriented architectures. *Performance Evaluation*, *67*(8), 659–675. doi:10.1016/j.peva.2009.07.001

Mohammed, T. A., Ghareeb, A., Al-bayaty, H., & Aljawarneh, S. (2019, December). Big data challenges and achievements: applications on smart cities and energy sector. In *Proceedings of the Second International Conference on Data Science, E-Learning and Information Systems* (pp. 1-5). 10.1145/3368691.3368717

Mouchili, M. N., Aljawarneh, S., & Tchouati, W. (2018, October). Smart city data analysis. In *Proceedings of the First International Conference on Data Science, E-learning and Information Systems* (pp. 1-6). Academic Press.

Rehman, Z., Hussain, F. K., & Hussain, O. K. (2011, June). Towards multi-criteria cloud service selection. In *2011 Fifth International Conference on Innovative Mobile and Internet Services in Ubiquitous Computing* (pp. 44-48). IEEE.

Singh, A., Juneja, D., & Malhotra, M. (2017). A novel agent based autonomous and service composition framework for cost optimization of resource provisioning in cloud computing. *Journal of King Saud University-Computer and Information Sciences*, *29*(1), 19–28. doi:10.1016/j.jksuci.2015.09.001

Trummer, I., Leymann, F., Mietzner, R., & Binder, W. (2010, November). Cost-optimal outsourcing of applications into the clouds. In *2010 IEEE Second International Conference on Cloud Computing Technology and Science* (pp. 135-142). IEEE. 10.1109/CloudCom.2010.64

Verizon. (2009). *Start Packing. You're Moving to the Cloud – and We Can Help.* Verizon Business.

Section 2
Cloud Governance and Big Data: A Case Study

Chapter 5

Cloud Governance:
How Cloud ML Is Mobilizing Some Educational Software by Governance and Computation

Anustup Mukherjee
Chandigarh University, India

Harjeet Kaur
Chandigarh University, India

ABSTRACT

Artificial intelligence within the area of computer vision is creating a replacement genre in detection industry. Here, AI is using the power of computer vision in creating advanced educational software LMS that detects student emotions during online classes, interviews, and judges their understanding and concentration level. It also generates automated content in step with their needs. This LMS cannot only judge audio, video, and image of a student; it also judges the voice tone. Through this judgement, the AI model understands how much a student is learning, effectivity, intellect, and drawbacks. In this chapter, the power of deep learning models VGG Net and Alex Net in LMS computer vision are used. This LMS architecture will be able to work like a virtual teacher that will be taking a parental guide to students.

DOI: 10.4018/978-1-7998-5040-3.ch005

I. INTRODUCTION

COVID 19 changed the definition of our contemporary systems. So, we all are into something virtual. Artificial Intelligence is giving a new vision of education system, this AI based LMS by the power of cloud governance judges' students understanding and concentration level as well also generate automated contents according to their needs, a complete virtual teacher by the help of CV models, we are creating facial as well emotion detection systems in an advanced way out. CV systems are well developed enough now to generate facial landmarks out of video or image data and track the objects, it is advancement of object detection API's being started from open CV. Right now deep learning based net models which includes Alex, Res, Mobi or VGG net models to state greater accuracy.

This LMS AI model understand:

- How much a student is learning?
- How much effective the class is?
- How much concentration level a student has?
- What is student intellect?
- How to modify next class based on this classes drawbacks?
- How to generate a best content for a student?

Not only a guide, during this COVID 19 situation when many students are suffering from work, class as well assignment burden, some for stress, frustration, tiredness in online class, as well some for not understanding the online lectures, this all things will be resolved and be taken care of, Hence this AI based computer vision architecture LMS (Giedre Dregvaite & Robertas Damasevicius, 2015) in Figure 1 will be shaping new educational up wave in new normal.

Affective computing is a field of Machine Learning and Computer Science that studies the recognition and the processing of human affects. Multimodal Emotion Recognition is a relatively new discipline that aims to include text inputs, as well as sound and video. This field has been rising with the development of social network that gave researchers access to a vast amount of data (Al-Shargabi et al, 2020; Aljawarneh, 2012; Aljawarneh et al, 2017; Chehbi-Gamoura et al, 2018; Esposito et al, 2018; Jaswal et al, 2019; Kalpana et al, 2018; Lizcano et al, 2020; Malhotra et al, 2019; Mohammed et al, 2019; Mouchili et al, 2018; Singh,2011).

We are exploring state of the art models in multimodal sentiment analysis. We have chosen to explore text, sound and video inputs and develop an ensemble model that gathers the information from all these sources and displays it in a clear and interpretable way.

Figure 1. Overview of services of AI-LMS

Video Classroom

Use the video classroom simulator and get a feedback on how our algorithm interprets your facial emotions compared to other candidates.

You will be provided a feedback on your facial emotions such as :

- Anger
- Happiness
- Fear
- Sadness
- Surprise
- Disgust

Audio Classroom

Use the audio classroom simulator and get a feedback on how our algorithm interprets your vocal emotions compared to other candidates.

You will be provided a feedback on your vocal emotions such as :

- Anger
- Happiness
- Fear
- Sadness
- Surprise
- Disgust

Text

Use the text classroom simulator and get a feedback on how our algorithm interprets your psychological traits through compared to other candidates.

You will be provided a feedback on your Big Five Psychological traits, which include :

- Openness
- Conscientiousness
- Extraversion
- Agreeableness
- Neuroticism

II. TECHSTACK USED

1. Python 3.7
2. Tensorflow
3. Keras
4. Flask – For API building
5. Mongo DB for Data Base set – by using Py-Mongo
6. Html, CSS, Java Script for web app of LMS

III. DATA SOURCE

We have chosen to diversify the data sources we used depending on the type of data considered. All data sets used are free of charge and can be directly downloaded.

1. For the text input, we are using the Stream-of-consciousness dataset that was gathered in a study by Pennebaker and King [1999]. It consists of a total of 2,468 daily writing submissions from 34 psychology students (29 women and 5 men whose ages ranged from 18 to 67 with a mean of 26.4). The writing submissions were in the form of a course unrated assignment. For each assignment, students were expected to write a minimum of 20 minutes per day about a specific topic. The data was collected during a 2-week summer course between 1993 to 1996. Each student completed their daily writing for 10 consecutive days. Students' personality scores were assessed by answering the Big Five Inventory (BFI) [John et al., 1991]. The BFI is a 44-item self-report questionnaire that provides a score for each of the five personality traits. Each item consists of short phrases and is rated using a 5-point scale that ranges from 1 (disagree strongly) to 5 (agree strongly). An instance in the data source consists of an ID, the actual essay, and five classification labels of the Big Five

personality traits. Labels were originally in the form of either yes ('y') or no ('n') to indicate scoring high or low for a given trait.

2. For audio data sets, we are using the Ryerson Audio-Visual Database of Emotional Speech and Song (RAVDESS). This database contains 7356 files (total size: 24.8 GB). The database contains 24 professional actors (12 females, 12 male), vocalizing two lexically- matched statements in a neutral North American accent. Speech includes calm, happy, sad, angry, fearful, surprise, and disgust expressions, and song contains calm, happy, sad, angry, and fearful emotions. Each expression is produced at two levels of emotional intensity (normal, strong), with an additional neutral expression. All conditions are available in three modality formats: Audio-only (16bit, 48kHz .wav), Audio-Video (720p H.264, AAC 48kHz, .mp4), Video-only (no sound)." https://zenodo.org/record/1188976#.XCx-tc9KhQI

3. For the video data sets, we are using the popular FER2013 Kaggle Challenge data set. The data consists of 48x48 pixel grayscale images of faces. The faces have been automatically registered so that the face is more or less centered and occupies about the same amount of space in each image. The data set remains quite challenging to use, since there are empty pictures, or wrongly classified images.

IV. ALGORITHM INBUILT

Our aim is to develop a model able to provide a live sentiment analysis with a visual user interface. Therefore, we have decided to separate two types of inputs:

- Textual input, such as answers to questions that would be asked to a person from the platform
- Video input from a live webcam or stored from an MP4 or WAV file, from which we split the audio and the images

V. TEXT MODEL: PIPELINE

The text-based personality recognition pipeline depicts in Figure 2 has the following structure:

- Text data retrieving
- Custom natural language pre-processing:
  - Tokenization of the document

      ◦   Cleaning and standardization of formulations using regular expressions
      ◦   Deletion of the punctuation
      ◦   Lowercasing the tokens
      ◦   Removal of predefined stop words
      ◦   Application of part-of-speech tags on the remaining tokens

- Lemmatization of tokens using part-of-speech tags for more accuracy.
- Padding the sequences of tokens of each document to constrain the shape of the input vectors.
- 300-dimension in Figure 3 Word2Vec (R. S. Baker, 2006) trainable embedding
- Prediction using our pre-trained model.

Figure 2. Overview of working of the AI based written assignment or test analysis

VI. MODEL

We have chosen a neural network architecture based on both one-dimensional convolutional neural networks and recurrent neural networks. The one-dimensional convolution layer plays a role comparable to feature extraction: it allows finding patterns in text data. The Long-Short Term Memory cell is then used in order to leverage on the sequential nature of natural language

unlike regular neural network where inputs are assumed to be independent of each other, these architectures progressively accumulate and capture information through the sequences. LSTMs have the property of selectively remembering patterns for long durations of time. Our final model first includes 3 consecutive blocks consisting of the following four layers: one-dimensional convolution layer - max pooling - spatial dropout - batch normalization. The numbers of convolution filters are respectively 128, 256 and 512 for each block, kernel size is 8, max pooling size is 2 and dropout rate is 0.3. Following the three blocks, we chose to stack 3 LSTM cells with 180 outputs each. Finally, a fully connected layer of 128 nodes is added before the last classification layer

Figure 3. Text Model Architecture

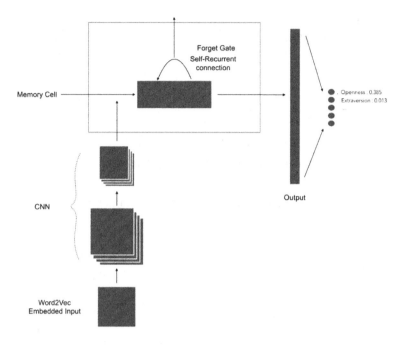

VII. AUDIO: PIPELINE

The speech emotion recognition pipeline in Figure 4 was built the following way:

- Voice recording
- Audio signal discretization
- Log-mel-spectrogram extraction
- Split spectrogram using a rolling window
- Make a prediction using our pre-trained model

The model we have chosen is a Time Distributed Convolutional Neural Network.

The main idea represented in Figure 5 of a Time Distributed Convolutional Neural Network is to apply a rolling window (fixed size and time-step) all along the log-mel-spectrogram. Each of these windows will be the entry of a convolutional neural network, composed by four Local Feature Learning Blocks (LFLBs) and the output of each of these convolutional networks will be fed into a recurrent neural network composed by 2 cells LSTM (Long Short-Term Memory) to learn the long-term contextual dependencies (Adamson et al.,2014). Finally, a fully connected layer with SoftMax activation is used to predict the emotion detected in the voice.

To limit overfitting, we tuned the model with:

- Audio data augmentation
- Early stopping
- And kept the best model

Figure 4. Overview of the Student viva/interview voice analysis

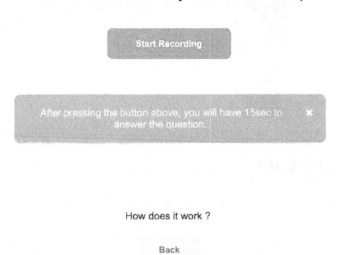

Figure 5. Voice based Natural Language Processing model architecture

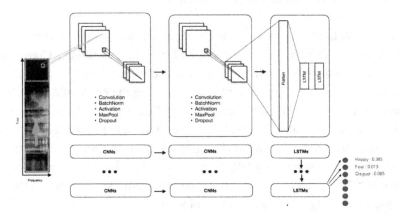

Figure 6. Model Accuracy

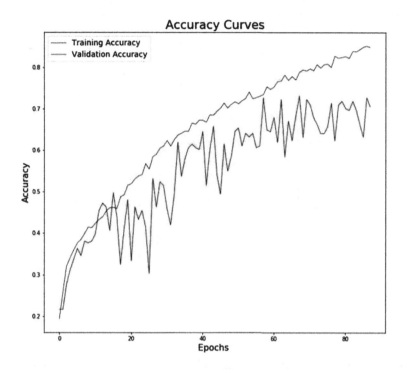

VIII. VIDEO PIPELINE

The video processing pipeline was built the following way:

1. Launch the webcam
2. Identify the face by Histogram of Oriented Gradients
3. Zoom on the face
4. Dimension the face to 48 * 48 pixels
5. Make a prediction on the face using our pre-trained model
6. Also identify the number of blinks on the facial landmarks on each picture

The model we have chosen is an XCeption model in Figure 7 since it outperformed the other approaches we developed so far. We tuned the model with:

*   Data augmentation
*   Early stopping
*   Decreasing learning rate on plateau
*   L2-Regularization

- Class weight balancing
- And kept the best model

Figure 7. Interview Model Accuracy

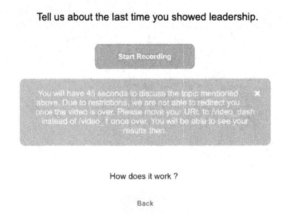

The XCeption architecture is based on Depth Wise Separable convolutions that allow to train much fewer parameters, and therefore reduce training time on Colab's GPUs to less than 90 minutes shown in Figure 8.

When it comes to applying CNNs in real life application, being able to explain the results is a great challenge. Clear ROI in Figure 9. We can indeed plot class activation maps, which display the pixels that have been activated by the last convolution layer. We notice how the pixels are being activated differently depending on the emotion being labelled. The happiness seems to depend on the pixels linked to the eyes and mouth, whereas the sadness or the anger seem for example to be more related to the eyebrow.

IX. RESULT

We tested different combinations of embeddings and classifiers in order to compare results in Figure 10. As explained at the end of the part on Word2Vec embeddings, we tried a hybrid model using averaged vector representations using TF-IDF weights: there is a loss of accuracy compared to the complete Word2Vec embedding, but results are better than the regular TF-IDF embedding. Let's provide the details of the accuracy obtained with each combination that we tested in our pipeline:

Figure 8. Video Model Architecture

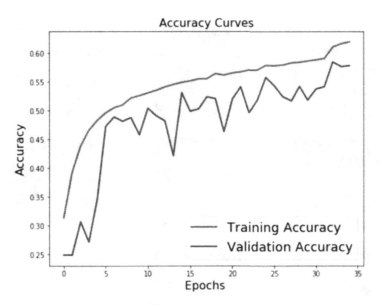

In the Figure 11 we are showing different approached models with their respective accuracy which shows exact model of our us. Output of LMS has shown in Figure 12

Figure 9. ROI Area selection for image recognition

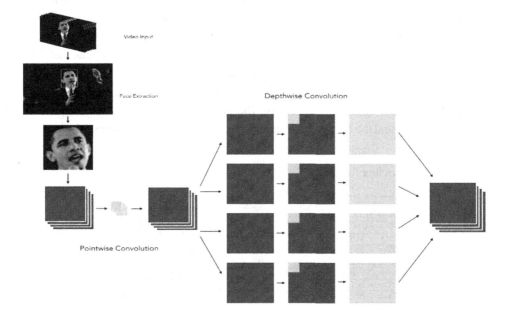

Figure 10. Result

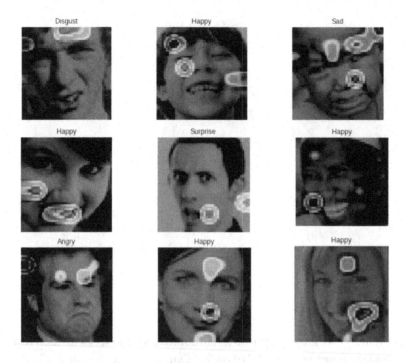

X. CONCLUSION

To conclude, it is possible to construct rather accurate classifiers for both personality traits and emotions recognition for different input types considered separately, each modality requiring its own set of features and hyper-parameters. The following steps for our project will be to design an ensemble model capable of combining the insights gained from both personality traits detection and emotions recognition in order to provide a broader assessment of a user's interview. Our final model would include a type of coherence measure expressing the similarity between a specific user's emotional profile and the average characteristics of people in the same psychological

Figure 11. Approached Models

Model	EXT	NEU	AGR	CON	OPN
TF-IDF + MNB	45.34	45.11	45.24	45.31	45.12
TF-IDF + SVM	45.78	45.91	45.41	45.54	45.56
Word2Vec + MNB	45.02	46.01	46.34	46.38	45.97
Word2Vec + SVM	46.18	48.21	49.65	49.97	50.07
Word2Vec (TF-IDF averaging) + MNB	45.87	44.99	45.38	44.21	44.84
Word2Vec (TF-IDF averaging) + SVM	46.01	46.19	47.56	48.11	48.89
Word2Vec + NN (LSTM)	51.98	50.01	51.57	51.11	50.51
Word2Vec + NN (CONV + LSTM)	**55.07**	**50.17**	**54.57**	**53.23**	**53.84**

Figure 12. Final Results of the LMS

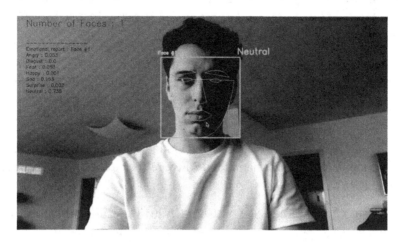

category according to the Big Five model. This would typically imply unsupervised clustering techniques.

REFERENCES

Adamson, D., Dyke, G., Jang, H., & Rosé, C. P. (2014). Towards an agile approach to adapting dynamic collaboration support to student needs. *International Journal of Artificial Intelligence in Education*, *24*(1), 92–124. doi:10.100740593-013-0012-6

Agaoglu, M. (2016). Predicting instructor performance using data mining techniques in higher education. *IEEE Access: Practical Innovations, Open Solutions*, *4*, 2379–2387. doi:10.1109/ACCESS.2016.2568756

Al-Shargabi, B., AlJawarneh, S., & Hayajneh, S. M. (2020). A cloudlet based security and trust model for e-government web services. *Journal of Theoretical and Applied Information Technology*, *98*(1), 27–37.

Aljawarneh, S. (Ed.). (2012). *Cloud computing advancements in design, implementation, and technologies*. IGI Global.

Aljawarneh, S., & Malhotra, M. (Eds.). (2017). *Critical Research on Scalability and Security Issues in Virtual Cloud Environments*. IGI Global.

Babić, I. D. (2017). Machine learning methods in predicting the student academic motivation. *Croatian Operational Research Review*, *8*(2), 443–461. doi:10.17535/crorr.2017.0028

Baker, R. S. (2016). Stupid Tutoring Systems Intelligent Humans. *International Journal of Artificial Intelligence in Education*, *26*(2), 600–614. doi:10.100740593-016-0105-0

Chehbi-Gamoura, S., Derrouiche, R., Malhotra, M., & Koruca, H. I. (2018, June). Adaptive management approach for more availability of big data business analytics. In *Proceedings of the Fourth International Conference on Engineering & MIS 2018* (pp. 1-8). 10.1145/3234698.3234758

Dregvaite, G., & Damasevicius, R. (2015). Integrating Multiple Analytics Techniques in a Custom Moodle Report Information and Software Technologies. 21st International Conference, ICIST 2015 (CVLA), *538*, 115—126.

Esposito, C., Su, X., Aljawarneh, S. A., & Choi, C. (2018). Securing collaborative deep learning in industrial applications within adversarial scenarios. *IEEE Transactions on Industrial Informatics*, *14*(11), 4972–4981. doi:10.1109/TII.2018.2853676

Jain, G. P., Gurupur, V. P., Schroeder, J. L., & Faulkenberry, E. D. (2014). Artificial intelligence-based student learning evaluation: A concept map-based approach for analyzing a student's understanding of a topic. *IEEE Transactions on Learning Technologies*, *7*(3), 267–279.

Jaswal, S., & Malhotra, M. (2019, December). A detailed analysis of trust models in cloud environment. In *Proceedings of the Second International Conference on Data Science, E-Learning and Information Systems* (pp. 1-5). 10.1145/3368691.3368740

Jeschike, M., Jeschke, S., Pfeiffer, O., Reinhard, R., & Richter, T. (2007). Equipping virtual laboratories with intelligent training scenarios. *AACE Journal*, *15*(4), 413–436.

Kalpana, G., Kumar, P. V., Aljawarneh, S., & Krishnaiah, R. V. (2018). Shifted adaption homomorphism encryption for mobile and cloud learning. *Computers & Electrical Engineering*, *65*, 178–195. doi:10.1016/j.compeleceng.2017.05.022

Kalz, M., van Bruggen, J., Giesbers, B., Waterink, W., Eshuis, J., & Koper, R. (2008). A model for new linkages for prior learning assessment. *Campus-Wide Information Systems*, *25*(4), 233–243. doi:10.1108/10650740810900676

Kao, Chen, & Sun. (2010). Using an e-Learning system with integrated concept maps to improve conceptual understanding. *International Journal of Instructional Media*, *37*(2), 151–153.

Lizcano, D., Lara, J. A., White, B., & Aljawarneh, S. (2020). Blockchain-based approach to create a model of trust in open and ubiquitous higher education. *Journal of Computing in Higher Education*, *32*(1), 109–134. doi:10.100712528-019-09209-y

Malhotra, M., & Singh, A. (2019). Role of Agents to Enhance the Security and Scalability in Cloud Environment. In Cloud Security: Concepts, Methodologies, Tools, and Applications (pp. 552-573). IGI Global. doi:10.4018/978-1-5225-8176-5.ch028

Mohammed, T. A., Ghareeb, A., Al-bayaty, H., & Aljawarneh, S. (2019, December). Big data challenges and achievements: applications on smart cities and energy sector. In *Proceedings of the Second International Conference on Data Science, E-Learning and Information Systems* (pp. 1-5). 10.1145/3368691.3368717

Mouchili, M. N., Aljawarneh, S., & Tchouati, W. (2018, October). Smart city data analysis. In *Proceedings of the First International Conference on Data Science, E-learning and Information Systems* (pp. 1-6). Academic Press.

Palocsay, S. W., & Stevens, S. P. (2008). A study of the effectiveness of web-based homework in teaching undergraduate business statistics. *Decision Sciences Journal of Innovative Education*, 6(2), 213–232. doi:10.1111/j.1540-4609.2008.00167.x

Perez, S., Massey-Allard, J., Butler, D., Ives, J., Bonn, D., Yee, N., & Roll, I. (2017). Identifying productive inquiry in virtual labs using sequence mining. In E. André, R. Baker, X. Hu, M. M. T. Rodrigo, & B. du Boulay (Eds.), Artificial intelligence in education. Academic Press.

Singh, A., Juneja, D., & Malhotra, M. (2017). A novel agent based autonomous and service composition framework for cost optimization of resource provisioning in cloud computing. *Journal of King Saud University-Computer and Information Sciences*, 29(1), 19–28. doi:10.1016/j.jksuci.2015.09.001

Chapter 6
Master Data–Supply Chain Management, the Key Lever for Collaborative and Compliant Partnerships in Big Data Era:
Marketing/Sales Case Study

Samia Chehbi Gamoura
https://orcid.org/0000-0002-1239-0873
Strasbourg University, France

Manisha Malhotra
https://orcid.org/0000-0002-9056-9473
Chandigarh University, India

ABSTRACT

With the advent of big data in supply chain information systems (SCIS), data compliance and consistency are becoming vital. Today, SC stakeholders need to pay more attention to data governance, which requires changing traditional management methods. These can be achieved by mastering a single repository through what is usually named master data management (MDM). However, accomplishing this objective is particularly challenging in the complex logistics networks of supply chains (SC). The volatile nature of the logistics flows that increase exponentially because of the facilitation of exchanges' interoperability in the information systems. In this chapter, the authors propose an MDM-based framework for the supply chain information systems as an enabler for strong collaboration and compliance. For proof of concept, a case study of a French hypermarket is examined through

DOI: 10.4018/978-1-7998-5040-3.ch006

benchmarking scenarios. The outcomes of the case validate our approach as a hands-on solution when applied correctly. Finally, the chapter discusses the key findings and the limitations of our framework.

INTRODUCTION

With the inundation of the Data records and the replications in the Big Data era, the distribution of networked Information Systems (IS) in Supply Chain Management (SCM) is facing the challenges of non-compliance and irregularities (Myung, 2016). The different Data lakes and Databases preserve the business objects' depictions in numerous ways with disparate features, even with the same real-world entities (Chehbi Gamoura, 2019). Ideally, managers must align the Data transactions related to these entities for entire business activities across the inter-connected applications (Meriton et al., 2020).

Today, the traditional Enterprise Resource Planning (ERP) systems cannot hold the complexity and heterogeneity in Big Data high-scaled systems (Kamble & Gunasekaran, 2020). In such cases, the Data accumulation without appropriate compliance tends to generate a set of new issues with unpredictable costs of the inconsistency risks in SCM (Chehbi-Gamoura et al., 2020). To address these new growing challenges, the owners of IS strive to invest the required efforts to implement standard repository-based systems such as Master Data Management (MDM) (Al-Shargabi et al, 2020; Aljawarneh, 2012; Aljawarneh et al, 2017; Chehbi-Gamoura et al, 2018; Esposito et al, 2018; Jaswal et al, 2019; Kalpana et al, 2018; Lizcano et al, 2020; Malhotra et al, 2019; Mohammed et al, 2019; Mouchili et al, 2018; Singh,2011).

More than a simple repository, the MDM system may be a real asset to help the network members build a real collaborative, and compliant environment. If it is set up and accomplished appropriately, it can provide reliable reporting, adjusted compliance, and accurate decisions (Han et al., 2017). Despite the awareness of these benefits for academics and industries, the literature in SCM's publications reveals a real research gap in this point (In et al., 2018). Consequently, in this document, the authors propose a new platform to provide a shared bridge for the SC partners to communicate, access, improve, and compliant the information across it. Moreover, this chapter presents a real-world case study as a validation frame to examine our architecture's plausibility and limits. The case study describes the Data compliance issues in the marketing/sales web-based applications of a French hypermarket.

The purposes of this paper are both industrial and academic. From the academic perspective, the objective is to provide a review of MDM research maturity in the interconnected Supply Chain systems and then to depict the landscape and gaps of the current researches in the Big Data era. The paper offers a new architecture to support a collaborative and compliant system for the Supply Chains partners from the industrial view.

The remainder of the paper is organized as follows. Section 2 explores the background and related researches. In section 3, researchers present the fundamental concepts of the proposed architecture. Section 4 describes the case study used to validate the proposed approach. Finally, section 5 discusses the key findings, limits, and open points.

BACKGROUND AND RESEARCH GAPS

Data Compliance in Supply Chain Management

With the maturity and intelligence, an IS can provide adequate collaborative support to application owners only if it allows consistent information sharing with high-quality Data (Bazi et al., 2017). However, with the advent of Big Data, Data consistency has become more imperative and highly challenging (Vilminko-Heikkinen et al., 2017).

According the academic bibliography, the emergence of the massive and heterogeneous Data fallouts in the following points:

- Operational failures in critical business processes (Figl, 2017),
- Strategic decision makings based on the potentially unreliable Data
- Mobilization of the considerable resources to resynchronize the Data across different services (Jeong et al., 2020). The primary reason for the issues mentioned above is the partitioning of the Data within the various existing Data lakes across the chain, which becomes highly challenging to interoperate.

In reality, within a connection of different Big Data environments covering SCM systems, the business Data are not highly valuable because of their duplicity across the several operational silos (Kamble & Gunasekaran, 2020). Indeed, each of the stakeholders operates its own Data lakes and the Databases with its Data items, its labeling system, its taxonomy, and certainly has its business rules base (Wu et al., 2017). In such a context, there are many replicas when the set of IS are networked and operate simultaneously, where the identical Data records are stored redundantly and without hierarchical controls. Even in big organizations, Information Technology (IT) specialists continually develop patchwork and middleware solutions to homogenize the systems' data record (Jung & Lehrer, 2017). It has been reported by (Gartner, 2018) that the global cost spent in developing IT middleware to face the business Data compliance issues (Zhao et al., 2020), grew more than 10% over the last year, and in 2018, it is getting up at 6% growth. That justifies the current increasing need for specialized profiles such as IT business analysts, who closely understand how such systems work together (Fan et al., 2010).

It is challenging to get all the stakeholders of different IS to approve on common definitions of Data items (Xiong et al., 2017) in the context of volatile Big Data where such challenge becomes severe and critical for business (Marodin et al., 2017). Therefore, new tools and techniques need to be set up to address such challenges. The MDM system is one such tool that can be viewed as a consensus-building with the help of IT specialists and business managers (Vilminko-Heikkinen et al., 2017). However, integrating the MDM within disparate IS develops the cross-collaborative IT-enabled business platform from all the participants involved to build the governance process (Xiong et al., 2017).

The research community is aware that there is no governance without an MDM approach (Watson & McGivern, 2016). Still, paradoxically, 25% of IT specialists worked on Data governance issues in almost all the IS that integrate the MDM approach (Xiong et al., 2017). This contradiction highlights the complexity and challenges of da governance in the SC context (Jia et al., 2016). Indeed, building the MDM approach must be a comprehensive integration project, supported by all the stakeholders in a constructive, collaborative manner (Kache & Seuring, 2017).

Mastering Data in Business Information Systems

The reference Data underpins the entire IS of an organization. That is why business data management is a crucial issue in all affiliated organizations in SC networks (Han et al., 2017). For example, several marketing services use the Data from various social network sites to recommend convenient new services to the potential or significant customers in an application. However, they do not overhaul this with compliant Data in customer/prospect applications. In the following example, the authors illustrate the Data inconsistency in customer records.

Example: Customer Data

In an IS, a company deals with its customers, and each customer may be affected by many business processes related to its information lifecycle (In, et al. 2019). For instance, a customer movement may be recorded and handled by the company '*A.*'

But, it will be recorded and processed by the billing service of the other company, *'B.'* The customer may be enrolled in two roles with altered features that are relevant for each business. Therefore, for the same real-world entity (customer), other business activities that reference the same entity may value some features over others in line with the business circumstance.

In both IS of these two companies, each one has recorded its Data attributes in their Data warehouse to be cleaned up, formatted, and then aggregated to be exploited further (Myung, 2016). Unfortunately, these operations may fail because of the recording and data inconsistency duplications, which ultimately represents the same entity for all systems (Figure 1).

Figure 1. Example of compliance challenges in customer Data

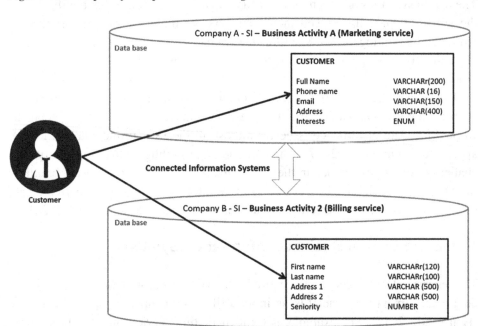

MDM is an approach that appeared in 2002. At this epoch, the concept was attached to security concerns (Sarathy & Muralidhar, 2002) and 'Data Quality Management (DQM)' (Fisher et al. 2003). The first business cases to comply with the dispersed Data were emerged in the Irish Datactics® (Datactics, 2016) and the French public Unidec® (Fauche & Latapie, 2007). Nevertheless, both concepts (MDM and QDM) have turned to the front of the stage to deploy high-distributed systems supporting Big Data since 2010 (Han et al., 2017). In this background, the organizations continue to set-up MDM repositories to the feed middleware for cleansing, compliance, and aggregation of the massive amassed Data. Many industrialized MDM suites already exist and are successfully employed inside or outside the enterprise's boards. As far as the best solution is concerned, it is subject to multiple elements, counting the business requests and the general IT settings (Puzey & Latham, 2016).

There is no industrial solution that integrates MDM for all functionalities of integrated IS (Zhao et al. 2020). That indicates no framework exists, able to achieve MDM maturity at all forms of interconnected IS at all levels. The maturity earns all operations of a Data lifecycle through one common repository. Three main factors may fortify that:

1.   All IS actors are not sufficiently mature, and till today, they still are not aligned to adopt Big Data deployment,
2.   The complexity of the IT infrastructures in implementation of the middleware solutions is usually exorbitant, with additional charges due to maintenance (Chehbi-Gamoura et al. 2020),
3.   The accumulated and dynamic Data are increasingly interdependent, and the business constraints often impose strong dependencies between resulting Data (Vilminko-Heikkinen et al. 2019).

Literature Status

The academic literature related to mastering the Data in the context of SC is not consistent (Gupta et al. 2016), and the majority of research works are closed to specific structures such as manufacturing chains, multi-ERP platforms, etc. (Table 1).

To address this perceived lack of research on the homogenization of efforts, researchers propose architecture as an initiative that aims to transform the accumulated separated Data into one single cross-domain of one unified repository for connected applications. Authors strive and expect to provide a platform for Big Data consistency in NIS-wide governance processes.

RESEARCH APPROACH

MDM Key Concepts: Master Objects, Business Objects, and Business Roles

In a Big Data environment, the business activities usually refer to different roles, with various features, for the same object (Chehbi-Gamoura et al. 2020). The term "Business Role" is commonly used to identify distinct patterns endorsed by the same object in the different IS. That may be either within the same organization

Table 1. Chronological of the most relevant publications in the topic of MDM in SCM context

Chronology	Reference	Goal	Context
2006	(Knolmayer & Röthlin, 2006)	Common Materials Master Data	Multi-ERP instances
2007	(Berson & Dubov, 2007)	Customer Data Integration	Global Enterprise System
2008	(Smith & McKeen, 2008)	Homogenization of Databases	Cross-business services
2010	(Fan et al. 2010)	Data Repairing	Inner-enterprise services
	(Cruz et al. 2010)	Business glossary	Inner-enterprise services
2011	(Silvola et al. 2011)	One Data model	cross-organizations
2012	(Otto, 2012a)	Integrated management	Inner-enterprise services
	(Otto, 2012b)	Master Data quality Model	Global Enterprise System
2015	(Spruit & Pietzka, 2015)	One Master Data Maturity Model	Inner-enterprise services
	(Myung, 2015)	Product Lifecycle Management	Manufacturing chain
2016	(Myung, 2016)	Master and Quality Management	Manufacturing chain

(for example, disparate roles for the same customer between sales and marketing services in the same company) or throughout the network (for example, disparate roles for the same product between the warehouse and the supplier).

In turn, a "Business object" is used to identify all the objects handled in Business Roles: products, resources, customers, retailers, sellers, etc. The business objects usually have different structures, but they all conceptualize one concrete real-world entity.

The core entity that gathers 360° degree views for the same object to cover all the business activities is commonly named "Master Object." It may be considered meta-Data objects that fold attributes (name, address, phone number, etc.), definitions, roles, lifecycle, etc.

Relationships between these essential concepts are illustrated in Figure 2.

Figure 2. Critical concepts in MDM: Business Objects, Business Roles, and Master Objects

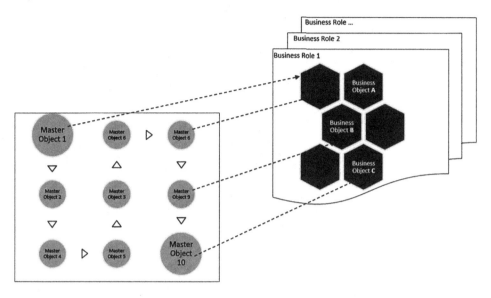

Pull/Push Mechanisms

When connected to IS, MDM can play two different roles: provider or consumer of Data. In most cases, both roles are endorsed by one master repository (Vilminko-Heikkinen et al. 2019). Typically, in such a system, the providers feed the repository with 'authentic' Data and consumers' access to this repository to ingest Data and then update their own attributes (Xiong et al. 2017). In the proposed architecture, authors reuse these two notions in two distinguished pull and push processes (Figure 3).

- **Pull process**: Business owners extract 'authentic' Data from MDM, following a selected mode: real-time interaction (request/reply), regular synchronized batches, or asynchronous mode.
- **Push process:** Repeatedly, updated Data in MDM are sent to business owners (subscribers) by messaging or synchronized batches.

Both flows (Pull and push) are set up in synchronized cadence between the master repository (MDM) and the connected business roles (subscribers). Technically, this can be set up either in batch mode or in real-time exchanges (Rivas et al. 2017). Following particularities are linked to the nature of the collected Data in the Big Data environment; the reference Data in the repository can be associated with unstructured, non-transactional, and non-relational records. Thus, usually, the repositories are

Figure 3. Pull/Push mechanisms in the proposed architecture

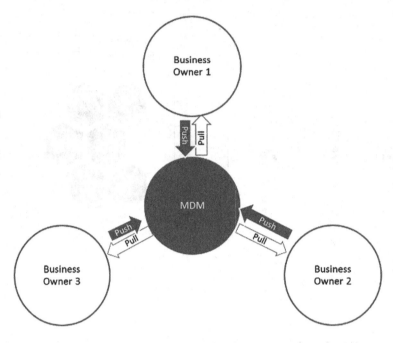

also used to exchange meta-Data. The paradox is that this meta-Data then become Data for the repository.

Governance Rules

Lacking persuasive authority, typically called Data Governance (DG), MDM initiatives unavoidably encounter hurdles due to the da providers (Kucharavy et al. 2020). That may be resolved by placing the rules that control the use/feed of the Data flows. Hence, the authors implicate six categories of the governance rules, as illustrated in the MDM engine in Figure 4:

1. **Consistency Rules (CYR):** A set of rules that serve in Data consistency and accuracy. These rules are used to fix imported errors, manage re-submissions, proactively watch Data changes, and repair corrupted Data rows.
2. **Quality Indicators Rules (QIR):** Procedures that define indicators for measuring the quality of Data. They include measures to qualify Data quality and examine the causes and impacts of quality concerns.
3. **Anomalies Detection Rules (ADR):** Pushing Data to MDM often generates irregularities, uncertainty, and ambiguity (Xiong, Yu, & Zhang, 2017). Therefore, a set of business rules must be implemented to avoid such abnormalities.

4.   **Cleansing Rules (CGR):** Inserted Data in MDM should continuously be kept clean and compliant (Chehbi-Gamoura et al. 2017). Therefore, specific instructions are associated with integration, elimination of duplicates, and consolidation of reference Data.

5.   **Security Rules (SYR):** Security directions in terms of Data protection and accessibility. They are dedicated to checking and managing who uses the Data, which enterprise has read and/or write rights or granted/denied access.

6.   **Maintaining Quality Rules (MQR):** Procedures to sustain Data quality and ensure the availability of services.

Figure 4. Governance rules in the proposed architecture MDM-NIS

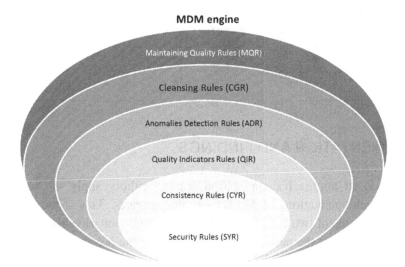

Figure 5 synthesizes an overview of the proposed architecture with a set of selected key concepts, to be generalized and customized in applications: Business Roles (Procurement, product engineering, distribution, sales), Business Objects (Materials, product, customers, factory, wholesaler, suppliers), Master Objects (Materials, Product, Suppliers, customers, end-customers), and Governance Rules (Cleansing, security, integration).

The proposed architecture comprises many other parts and ad-hoc functionalities. Quoting these additional functionalities goes beyond the limits of a single paper. However, the main ad-hoc modules include archiving, event/notification, and analytics.

Figure 5. Example of the proposed MDM-NIS concept in Big Data context

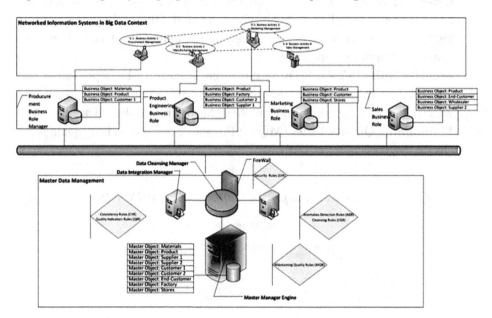

EXPERIMENTATION AND FINDINGS

In the proposed approach's application frame, authors apply the concept to networked web-applications of Marketing/sales services. This section describes the implementation of two use cases with experimental scenarios. But beforehand, they will first present the network of IS, then define the process, and, finally, the authors elaborate on the empirical benchmarking results.

Marketing/Sales Case Study

The French distribution hypermarket, in our case study, owns a vast number of web-applications with a diverse set of flows connected to external IS. The network of these applications is too complicated that it is impossible to model in a comprehensible scheme. Compared to other firms in its business sector, the hypermarket group is ahead in the maturity of using Big Data and MDM. Indeed, the company launched its Big Data project around 2010 and adopted SAS MDM® (SAS, 2016) solution five years later (2015).

In France, the investment management in marketing and sales departments; is one of the crucial problems encountered in the IS that involves the hypermarket and its regional vegetable suppliers (farmers, cultivators, winegrowers, etc.). On one side, hypermarket managers face significant challenges while using their traditional ERP to access and unify both structured and unstructured Data. On the other side, with the multiplication of Data sources in Customer Relationship Management (CRM) applications used by vegetable suppliers, the accumulated Data are housed and distributed to cause tricky problems. A third hurdle is due to vegetable suppliers' volatility depending on seasonality and irregular sales of vegetables. In the dynamic network of these connected web-applications, the main issues are linked to inconsistency, duplication of items, wrong contact information in marketing campaigns, unadjusted schedules in sales, issues in stock management, and so forth.

Key Attributes

1. **Business Roles:** According to the collected Data, two business roles are identified:
    a. **Marketing Business Role:** In the context of Big Data sourcing, producers exploit several channels to send marketing campaigns, such as Facebook® and Twitter® accounts, recovered addresses of new arrivals, relationships of neighbors between inhabitants, etc. Business objects that are handled are:
        i.   Unpackaged-Product Business Object: that represents vegetables without packages (Potatoes, tomatoes, carrots, etc.),
        ii. Potential-Customer Business Object: which denotes all recorded consumers in the region.
    b. **Sales Business Role:** Business objects within this role are:
        i.   Packaged-Product Business Object: representing all packaged vegetables available in the region's stores.
        ii. End-Customer Business Object: which identifies all consumers who have already made at least one purchase.
2. **Master Objects:** Two objects are identified:
    a. **Product Master Object:** represents vegetable products in packaged and unpackaged forms.
    b. **Customer Master Object:** identifies customers and potential customers in the region.

Pull/Push Use Cases

In the pull process, the consumers defined by the business roles send requests to obtain the authentic Data from 'Master Objects' in MDM. For instance, stores request the updated address of the customer in the After-Sales Service (ASS) files (Figure 6).

In the push process, the updated Data defined by 'Business Roles' are sent to business owners. For example, the customer responds to the marketing partner by

Figure 6. Pull use case in marketing/sales case study

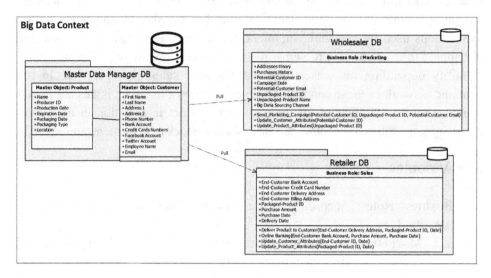

indicating a new address with the specific information he would be interested in using eco-friendly packaging (figure 7).

Figure 7. Push use case in marketing/sales case study

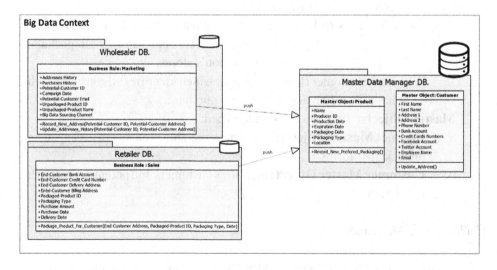

Governance Rules Setting

In the application of this case study, the authors define a set of rules as listed in Table 2.

Table 2. Set of governance rules in the marketing/sales case study

Category	Sub-category	Rule		
		Proposition (P)	**Negation (⌐ P)**	**Type**
Consistency Rules (CYR)	Authenticity	A product must have a certified expiration date	Push flow rejected	Consistency of product data
	Identification	A customer must have one valid email address	Push flow rejected	Consistency of customer data
	Recognition	An email address must have a valid format	Push flow rejected	Consistency of customer data
Quality Indicators Rules (QIR)	Standardization	A product item must have a filled ecological index	Push flow rejected	Quality of product data
	Completion	A customer must have a valid credit card	Push flow not rejected. But notifications should be sent to business roles owners	Quality of customer data
Anomalies Detection Rules (ADR)	Accuracy	A product item may be pulled with two locations	Pull flow not rejected. But notification warnings should be reported by the business role owner	Anomaly in product data
Cleansing Rules (CGR)	Integration	The same product item is under processing by more than one stakeholder	Push flow suspended	Integration of product data
	Elimination of duplicates	Duplicate product items are detected (same id by the same producer)	Push flow rejected	Consolidation of product data
	Deletion of orphans	An orphan product item is detected (without id)	Push flow rejected	The coherence of product data
Security Rules (SYR)	Controlled access	Business roles owners access to pull/push processes of customer master-object	Access denied	Authentication of business owners
Maintaining Quality Rules (MQR)	Sustainability	The it provider must set up maintenance rules. For example, scheduling regular pull batches, every 12 hours for 'product master object,' and every 36 hours for 'customer master object.'	Access denied	Continuity of MDM services

Figure 8. Sequence diagram of scenario 1 in marketing/sales case study (by StarUML 5.0.2®)

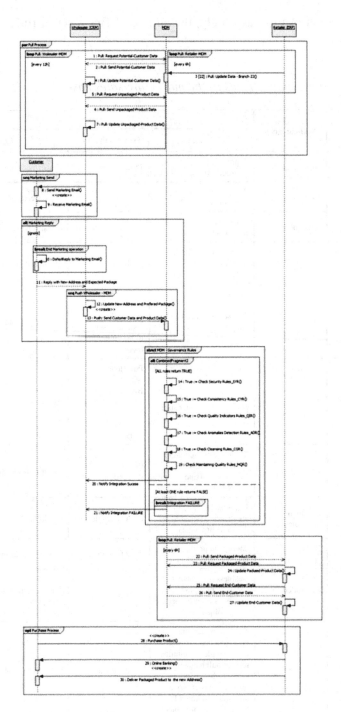

Figure 9. Sequence diagram of scenario 2 in marketing/sales case study (by StarUML 5.0.2®)

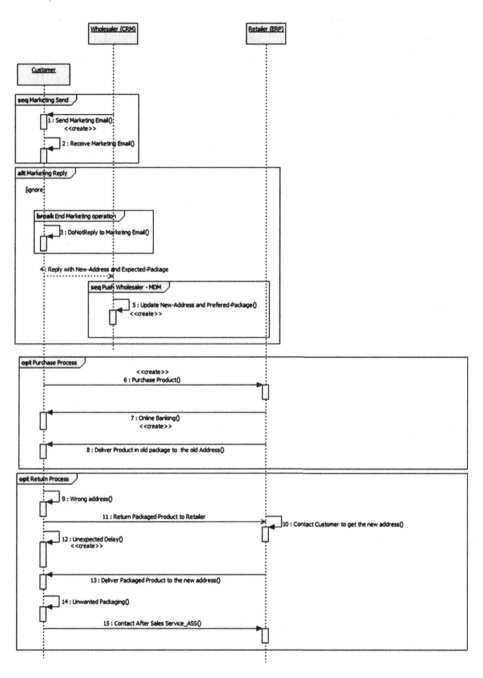

Experimentation Scenarios

The sequence diagrams below summarize the described case study's operations in two different scenarios: with MDM middleware (scenario 1) illustrated in Figure 8, and without MDM middleware (scenario 2) schematized in Figure 9. All experimentation was modeled and simulated by StarUML 5.0.2® from McLab® (MKLab, 2016).

Data Collection

Data collected after running scenarios are recorded in tables 4 and 5, as extracted by StarUML5.0.2® (MKLab, 2016).

Assessment Policy

The benchmarking study of the scenarios described earlier needs a matrix of costs, computed as follows:

Suppose the Boolean variable d_i, which designates if the operation is considered in computation or not, as interpreted by the column 'considered (computed cost)' in tables 4 and 5.

$$\forall i, d_i \in \{0,1\} \tag{1}$$

Suppose, the Boolean variable p_i which indicates if the operation is completed or not, as read in the column 'Performed' in tables 4 and 5.

$$\forall i, p_i \in \{0,1\} \tag{2}$$

Suppose, the variable Ct_i which specifies the cost of the operation's assignment, corresponding to the column 'Transfer cost' in tables 4 and 5.

$$\forall i, \exists Ct_i \geq 0 \tag{3}$$

Suppose, the variable Cr_i which indicates the cost of the operation's transaction, as shown in the column 'Transaction cost' in tables 4 and 5.

$$\forall i, \exists Cr_i \geq 0 \tag{4}$$

Table 3. Generated events in Scenario 1 (with MDM)

Operation Number	Operation Name	Operators *		Process Type **	Considered (Computed cost)[1]	Operation Performed[2]	Transfer Cost[3]	Transaction Cost[4]	Branch Cost[1]	Operation delay Cost[5]	Operation Type
1	pull: request potential-customer data	W* ► MDM	↻	Pull MDM	●	●	●	£	£	●	Loop [12h]
2	pull: send potential-customer data	MDM ►W*	↻	Pull MDM	●	●	●	£	£	●	Loop [12h]
3	pull: update data - branch 22	R*	○	Pull MDM	£	●	£	£	●	£	Loop [12h]
22	pull: request packaged-product data	R* ► MDM	↻	Pull MDM	●	●	●	£	£	●	Loop [6h]
23	pull: send packaged-product data	MDM ► R*	↻	Pull MDM	●	●	●	£	£	●	Loop [6h]
24	pull: update packaged-product data	R*	○	Pull MDM	●	●	£	●	£	£	Loop [6h]
25	pull: request end-customer data	R* ► MDM	↻	Pull MDM	●	●	●	£	£	●	Loop [6h]
26	pull: send end-customer data	MDM -> R*	↻	Pull MDM	●	●	●	£	£	£	Loop [6h]
27	pull: update end-customer data	R*	○	Pull MDM	●	●	£	●	£	£	Loop [6h]
4	pull: update potential-customer data	W*	○	Pull MDM	●	●	£	●	£	£	Loop [12h]
5	pull: request unpackaged-product data	W* ► MDM	↻	Pull MDM	●	●	●	£	£	●	Loop [12h]
6	pull: send unpackaged-product data	MDM ► W*	↻	Pull MDM	●	●	●	£	£	●	Loop [12h]
7	pull: update unpackaged-product data	W*	○	Pull MDM	●	●	£	●	£	£	Loop [12h]
8	send marketing email	W* ► C*	↻	MS**	●	●	●	£	£	●	Sequential
9	receive marketing email	C*	○	MS**	£	●	£	£	£	£	Sequential
10	reply to marketing email	C*	○	MS**	£	£	£	£	£	£	Alt° [Break]
11	reply with new-address and package	C* ► W*	○	MS**	●	●	●	£	£	●	Alt°
12	update new-address and package	W*	0	Push MDM	●	●	£	●	£	£	Sequential
13	push: send customer and product data	W* ► MDM	↻	Push MDM	●	●	●	£	£	●	Sequential
14	true:= check security RULES_SYR	MDM	○	MDM	●	●	£	●	£	£	Alt°
15	true:= check consistency RULES_SYR	MDM	○	MDM	●	●	£	●	£	£	Alt°
16	true:= check quality RULES_QIR	MDM	○	MDM	●	●	£	●	£	£	Alt°
17	true:= check anomalies RULES_ADR	MDM	○	MDM	●	●	£	●	£	£	Alt°
18	true:= check cleansing RULES_CGR	MDM	○	MDM	●	●	£	●	£	£	Alt°
19	check maintaining quality RULES_MGR	MDM	○	MDM	●	●	£	●	£	£	Alt°
20	notify integration success	MDM ► W*	↻	Push MDM	●	●	●	£	£	●	Alt°
21	notify integration failure	MDM ► W*	↻	Push MDM	●	£	●	£	£	●	Alt°[Break]

continued on following page

Table 3. Continued

Operation Number	Operation Name	Operators *		Process Type **	Considered (Computed cost)[1]	Operation Performed[2]	Transfer Cost[3]	Transaction Cost[4]	Branch Cost[1]	Operation delay Cost[5]	Operation Type
22	pull: request packaged-product data	R* ► MDM	↻	Pull MDM	●	●	●	£	£	●	Loop [6h]
23	pull: send packaged-product data	MDM ► R*	↻	Pull MDM	●	●	●	£	£	●	Loop [6h]
24	pull: update packaged-product data	R*	O	Pull MDM	●	●	£	●	£	£	Loop [6h]
25	pull: request end-customer data	R* ► MDM	↻	Pull MDM	●	●	●	£	£	●	Loop [6h]
26	pull: send end-customer data	MDM ► R*	↻	Pull MDM	●	●	●	£	£	●	Loop [6h]
27	pull: update end-customer data	R*	O	Pull MDM	●	●	£	●	£	£	Loop [6h]
28	purchase product	C* ► R*	↻	SS**	●	●	●	●	£	●	Optional
29	online banking	R* ► C*	↻	SS**	●	●	●	●	£	●	Optional
30	deliver product to the new address	R* ► C*	↻	SS**	£	●	£	£	£	●	Optional

(by StarUML5.0.2® (MKLab 2016))

Note: R*: Retailer, C*: Customer, W*: Wholesaler. MS**: Marketing Service, SS**: Sales Service, Alt°: Alternative. ●: Yes, £: No

Suppose, the variable Cb_i which interprets the cost of operation roaming, conforming to the column 'branch' in tables 4 and 5.

$$\forall i \ , \ \exists Cb_i \geq 0 \tag{5}$$

Suppose, the variable Cd_i which indicates the cost of the operation's duration corresponding to the column' Operation delay cost' in tables 4 and 5.

$$\forall i, \exists Cd_i \geq 0 \tag{6}$$

Suppose, the matrix of costs M_{CT} from formula (1), (2), (3), (4), (5), and (6):

$$M_{CT} = \begin{bmatrix} d_1 & p_1 & Ct_1 & Cr_1 & Cb_1 & Cd_1 \\ \dots & \dots & \dots & \dots & \dots & \dots \\ d_i & p_i & Ct_i & Cr_i & Cb_i & Cd_i \end{bmatrix}_{i=Number\ of\ operations} \tag{7}$$

Accordingly, the global cost CT can be computed in the following formula:

$$CT = \sum_i \left(d_i \times p_i \right) \times \left(Ct_i + Cr_i + Cb_i + Cd_i \right) \tag{8}$$

Table 4. Generated events in Scenario 2 (without MDM)

Operation Number	Operation Name	Operators*		Process Type**	Considered (Computed Cost)	Operation Performed	Transfer Cost	Transaction Cost	Branch Cost	Operation Delay Cost	Operation Type
1	Send Marketing Email	W* ► C*	3	MS**	●	●	●	£	£	●	Sequential
2	Receive Marketing Email	C*	0	MS**	£	●	£	£	£	£	Sequential
3	Do0tReply to Marketing Email	C*	0	MS**	£	£	£	●	£	£	Alt° [Break]
4	Reply with New-Address and Package	C* ► W*	3	MS**	●	●	●	£	£	●	Alternative
5	Update New-Address and Package	W*	0	MS**	●	●	£	●	£	£	Sequential
6	Purchase Product	C* ► R*	3	SS*	●	●	●	●	£	●	Optional
7	Online Banking	R* ► C*	3	SS*	●	●	●	●	£	●	Optional
8	Deliver Product to the old Address	R* ► C*	3	SS*	£	●	£	£	£	●	Optional
9	Wrong address	C*	0	RS*	£	●	£	●	£	●	Optional
10	Return Packaged Product to Retailer	C* ► R*	3	RS*	●	●	●	£	£	●	Optional
11	Contact Customer to get the new address	R* ► C*	3	RS*	●	●	●	£	£	●	Optional
12	Unexpected Delay	C*	0	RS*	●	●	£	£	£	●	Optional
13	Deliver Product to the new address	R* ► C*	3	RS*	£	●	£	£	£	●	Optional
14	Contact After Sales SERVICE_SS	C* ► R*	3	RS*	●	●	£	●	£	●	Optional

(by StarUML5.0.2®)

Note: C*: Customer, R*: Retailer, W*: Wholesaler. MS**: Marketing Sales, SS*: Sales Service, RS*: Return Service. Alt°: Alternative. ●: Yes, £: No

Empirical Benchmarking (Scenario 1 vs. Scenario 2)

Based on the assessment policy's costs, the primary outcomes are discussed in the empirical graphics below.

Overview of Costs Distribution

Figure 10 shows two different overall tendencies: With MDM, all the cost types evolve according to stable trends (transaction cost at 30%, transfer cost at 20%, delay cost at 40%) except the branch cost (only 10% beginning). However, despite relatively low costs in the front (40%) without MDM, delay costs burst from period 9 to more than 250% at period 14. That is due to the unexpected delays because of the customer's returned items and the wrong customer Data.

Overview of Costs Distribution Distributed by Type

Summarizing, the results of the bar graphs in Figure 11 indicate the following observations:

Figure 10. Overview of normalized costs in scenarios 1 and 2 (by StarUML5.0.2®)
(unit costs: UCt1= 20%, UCr1= 30%, UCb1= 10%, UCd1= 40%)

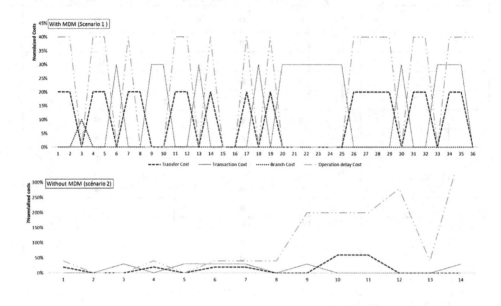

- Transfer cost exceeds in both scenarios at an approximatively equal rate (60%). The use of MDM places a high speed in the MDM-pull procedure, while in the traditional case (without MDM), the same rate is moved to the return processing operation. That may be interpreted by the hefty charges related to unsatisfied customers.

- The distribution of transaction cost tends towards the consumption of MDM in case of its use, with 40% for the MDM engine's internal operations and 40% in Pull activity. However, this cost is zero at the last step of return as there is no need for a return investment.

- Pull activities from MDM exclusively bear branch cost. It is important to note that this cost is directly related to this case study. In practice, it is usually aggregated into other types of expenses (for example, transaction cost).

- Cost due to delay explodes in the classic case (without MDM) in the processing of customer returns (87%) but remains moderate at 58% in MDM operations (scenario 1, with MDM). That is coherent as returns processing delays increase in a very high trend. That is why it is recommended to invest upstream to avoid such a high spending rate and customers' dissatisfaction who may flee to join the competitors.

Figure 11. Overview of total normalized costs distributed by type in scenarios 1 and 2 (unit costs: UCt1= 20%, UCr1= 30%, UCb1= 10%, UCd1= 40%)

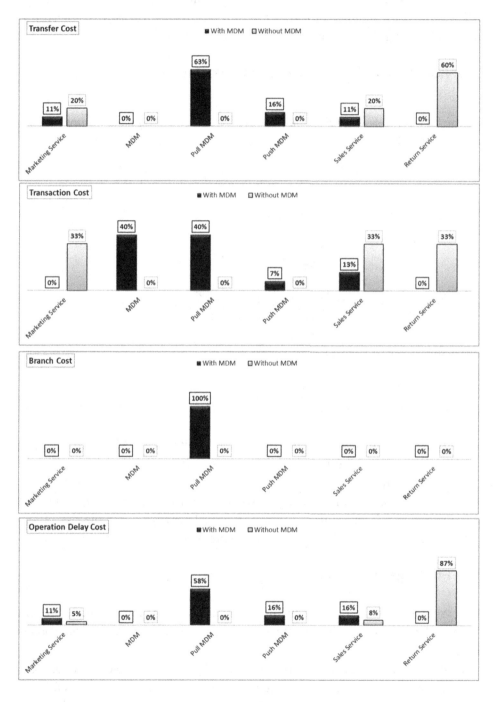

The details of these first results led us to go further in the analysis by aggregating the costs into business operations (sales, marketing), pre-investment operations (MDM expenses), and post-investment (return processing expenses), as illustrated in the following graph of figure 12.

Overview of Total Cost vs. Pre/Post Investments

Figure 12. Overview of total normalized costs aggregated in phases of investments (unit costs: UCt1= 20%, UCr1= 30%, UCb1= 10%, UCd1= 40%)

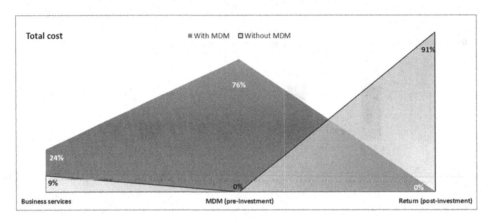

In Figure 12, the aggregated view of areas graph offers a synopsis of the option to take:

- **Option 1:** Financing in pre-investment capital with MDM deployment (76%) to gain in returns later (~0%) with the assurance of sustainability and customer loyalty,
- **Option 2:** Instead of financing in MDM (pre-investment) (~0%), supporting exorbitant post-investment capital of returns later (91%) with the risk of loss of customer satisfaction and a potential break of market share.

Key Findings and Limits

The case study reveals that introducing a standard of MDM architecture to govern the overall information connected flows is a tricky task. To summarize, three points are highlighted:

Firstly, one standard centralized model for NIS would mean a continuous roam of Data from the involved IS to the federal system and vice versa. That is feasible in the majority of cases but engenders high maintenance costs and organizational constraints. Thus, stakeholders should be aware that this kind of solution is not a panacea and have to choose between submitting to MDM service or living with the heterogeneity and not following the group policy's strategies.

Secondly, the IS stakeholder can choose between investing in MDM solution for the homologation and pooling of Data traffic (the costs will be very high in Data exchanges), but saved on the customer satisfaction gain and reduced return costs after-sales service. Or not to invest in MDM and stay on heterogeneous Data in an isolated system, but the cost of return and customer dissatisfaction will increase significantly in the long-term.

Lastly, the existing middleware solutions of MDM are designed to fit big companies in general, but the effort to implement elaborate MDM would be exaggerated for small enterprises. This prejudice is the source of the low Data quality in NIS and maybe the origin of the significant issues, which prevent the governing Data overall the network.

This case study was deliberately conducted in a systematic stepwise presentation. A researcher would apply the proposed solution to another NIS case and is expected to achieve the same outcomes. Likewise, the afore-presented results can be used as input for further case studies since this is the first study in the particular field of Big Data NIS-MDM context.

CONCLUSION AND OPEN VIEWS

In contemporary Big Data-driven management, information consistency has become a significant competitive factor, and information obtained by connected systems has become valuable and highly coveted. Therefore, such a network of Information Systems has to integrate and pool all efforts efficiently. Indeed, a synergy may arise from good the Data management if the several distinct and disparate Information Systems are benefitted from one repository of the accumulated Data. This repository may be implemented through the Master Data Management (MDM) system for all the networks.

To address this growing challenge, the authors propose an architecture founded on MDM. The approach provides a platform for the Big Data consistency to efficiently govern the Networked Information Systems' information flow. The solution is based on three key concepts (Business Roles, Business Objects, and Master Objects), organized in pull/push flows and federated by a set of governance rules.

A benchmarking study was depicted in the case of marketing/sales applications of a French hypermarket to validate the proposed approach's feasibility. Even though the outcomes achieved look positive, substantial work is still required in the short term. Stressing a POC (Proof of Concept) prototype in the real IT production environment may defend the more massive credibility of the proposed approach. Likewise, implementing other large-scaled networked connected Information Systems may reveal other capabilities and challenges that may open further research concerns and discussions.

This paper's key finding is that the Master Data Management approach may the best way today to govern the Big Data down-flooding, but it must not be considered the solution to all Data problems. It remains a conceptual approach with a significant contribution imparted to oversee and control the transverse Data flows.

REFERENCES

Al-Shargabi, B., AlJawarneh, S., & Hayajneh, S. M. (2020). A cloudlet based security and trust model for e-government web services. *Journal of Theoretical and Applied Information Technology, 98*(1), 27–37.

Aljawarneh, S. (Ed.). (2012). *Cloud computing advancements in design, implementation, and technologies*. IGI Global.

Aljawarneh, S., & Malhotra, M. (Eds.). (2017). *Critical Research on Scalability and Security Issues in Virtual Cloud Environments*. IGI Global.

Bazi, G., El Khoury, J., & Srour, F. J. (2017). Integrating Data Collection Optimization into Pavement Management Systems. *Business & Information Systems Engineering, 59*(3), 135–146. doi:10.100712599-017-0466-4

Berson, A., & Dubov, L. (2007). *Master data management and customer data integration for a global enterprise*. McGraw-Hill, Inc.

Chehbi Gamoura, S. (2019). A Cloud-Based Approach for Cross-Management of Disaster Plans: Managing Risk in Networked Enterprises. In Emergency and Disaster Management: Concepts, Methodologies, Tools, and Applications (pp. 857-881). IGI Global.

Chehbi-Gamoura, S., & Derrouiche, R. (2017). Big valuable data in supply chain: Deep analysis of current trends and coming potential. In *Collaboration in a Data-Rich World* (pp. 230–241). Springer. doi:10.1007/978-3-319-65151-4_22

Chehbi-Gamoura, S., Derrouiche, R., Damand, D., & Barth, M. (2020). Insights from big Data Analytics in supply chain management: An all-inclusive literature review using the SCOR model. *Production Planning and Control, 31*(5), 355–382. doi:10.1080/09537287.2019.1639839

Chehbi-Gamoura, S., Derrouiche, R., Damand, D., Kucharavy, D., & Barth, M. (2020). Cross-management of risks in big data-driven industries by the use of fuzzy cognitive maps. *Logistique & Management, 28*(2), 155–166. doi:10.1080/125079 70.2019.1686437

Chehbi-Gamoura, S., Derrouiche, R., Malhotra, M., & Koruca, H. I. (2018, June). Adaptive management approach for more availability of big data business analytics. In *Proceedings of the Fourth International Conference on Engineering & MIS 2018* (pp. 1-8). 10.1145/3234698.3234758

Cruz, N. D., Schiefelbein, P., Anderson, K., Hallock, P., & Barden, D. (2010). ORM and MDM/MMS: integration in an enterprise level conceptual data model. In R. Meersman, T. Dillon, & P. Herrero, In *Proceeding of OTM Confederated International Conferences On the Move to Meaningful Internet Systems* (pp. 457-463). Rhodes, Greece: Springer International Publishing.

Datactics. (2016). Retrieved 05 22, 2017, from https://www.datactics.com/

Esposito, C., Su, X., Aljawarneh, S. A., & Choi, C. (2018). Securing collaborative deep learning in industrial applications within adversarial scenarios. *IEEE Transactions on Industrial Informatics, 14*(11), 4972–4981. doi:10.1109/TII.2018.2853676

Fan, W., Li, J., Ma, S., Tang, N., & Yu, W. (2010). Towards certain fixes with editing rules and master data. *Proceedings of the VLDB Endowment International Conference on Very Large Data Bases, 3*(1-2), 173–184. doi:10.14778/1920841.1920867

Fauche, H., & Latapie, P. (2007). *Un exemple de décisionnel de très grande volumétrie: le SID de l'UNEDIC*. UNIDEC.

Figl, K. (2017). Comprehension of procedural visual business process models. *Business & Information Systems Engineering, 59*(1), 41–67. doi:10.100712599-016-0460-2

Fisher, C. W., Chengalur-Smith, I., & Ballou, D. P. (2003). The impact of experience and time on the use of data quality information in decision making. *Information Systems Research, 14*(2), 170–188. doi:10.1287/isre.14.2.170.16017

Gartner. (2018). *IT Spending Forecast, 3Q18 Update: Ride the Innovation Wave*. Orlando, FL: Gartner.

Gupta, A., Xu, W., Ruiz-Juri, N., & Perrine, K. (2016). A workload aware model of computational resource selection for big data applications In *Big Data (Big Data), IEEE International Conference on* (pp. 2243-2250). IEEE.

Han, W., Borges, J., Neumayer, P., Ding, Y., Riedel, T., & Beigl, M. (2017). Interestingness Classification of Association Rules for Master Data. In *Industrial Conference on Data Mining* (pp. 237-245). Springer. 10.1007/978-3-319-62701-4_18

In, J., Bradley, R., Bichescu, B. C., & Autry, C. W. (2018). Supply chain information governance: Toward a conceptual framework. *International Journal of Logistics Management*.

In, J., Bradley, R., Bichescu, B. C., & Autry, C. W. (2019). Supply chain information governance: Toward a conceptual framework. *International Journal of Logistics Management, 30*(2), 506–526. doi:10.1108/IJLM-05-2017-0132

Jaswal, S., & Malhotra, M. (2019, December). A detailed analysis of trust models in cloud environment. In *Proceedings of the Second International Conference on Data Science, E-Learning and Information Systems* (pp. 1-5). 10.1145/3368691.3368740

Jeong, J. H., Woo, J. H., & Park, J. (2020). Machine Learning Methodology for Management of Shipbuilding Master Data. *International Journal of Naval Architecture and Ocean Engineering, 12*, 428–439. doi:10.1016/j.ijnaoe.2020.03.005

Jia, F., Gao, R., Lamming, R., & Wilding, R. (2016). Adaptation of supply management towards a hybrid culture: the case of a Japanese automaker. *Supply Chain Management: An International Journal, 1*(45-62), 21.

Jung, R., & Lehrer, C. (2017). Guidelines for Education in Business and Information Systems Engineering at Tertiary Institutions. *Business & Information Systems Engineering, 59*(3), 189–203. doi:10.100712599-017-0473-5

Kache, F., & Seuring, S. (2017). Challenges and opportunities of digital information at the intersection of Big Data Analytics and supply chain management. *International Journal of Operations & Production Management, 37*(1), 10–36. doi:10.1108/IJOPM-02-2015-0078

Kalpana, G., Kumar, P. V., Aljawarneh, S., & Krishnaiah, R. V. (2018). Shifted adaption homomorphism encryption for mobile and cloud learning. *Computers & Electrical Engineering, 65*, 178–195. doi:10.1016/j.compeleceng.2017.05.022

Kamble, S. S., & Gunasekaran, A. (2020). Big data-driven supply chain performance measurement system: A review and framework for implementation. *International Journal of Production Research, 58*(1), 65–86. doi:10.1080/00207543.2019.1630770

Knolmayer, G. F., & Röthlin, M. (2006). Quality of material master data and its effect on the usefulness of distributed ERP systems. *International Conference on Conceptual Modeling,* 362-371. 10.1007/11908883_43

Kucharavy, D., Damand, D., Chehbi-Gamoura, S., Barth, M., & Mornay, S. (2020). Warehouse of the future: The concept of contradiction mapping. *Logistique & Management*, *28*(1), 48–56. doi:10.1080/12507970.2019.1686436

Lizcano, D., Lara, J. A., White, B., & Aljawarneh, S. (2020). Blockchain-based approach to create a model of trust in open and ubiquitous higher education. *Journal of Computing in Higher Education*, *32*(1), 109–134. doi:10.100712528-019-09209-y

Malhotra, M., & Singh, A. (2019). Role of Agents to Enhance the Security and Scalability in Cloud Environment. In Cloud Security: Concepts, Methodologies, Tools, and Applications (pp. 552-573). IGI Global. doi:10.4018/978-1-5225-8176-5.ch028

Marodin, G. A., Tortorella, G. L., Frank, A. G., & Godinho Filho, M. (2017). The moderating effect of Lean supply chain management on the impact of Lean shop floor practices on quality and inventory. *Supply Chain Management: An International Journal*, *6*(473-485), 22.

Meriton, R., Bhandal, R., Graham, G., & Brown, A. (2020). An examination of the generative mechanisms of value in big data-enabled supply chain management research. *International Journal of Production Research*, 1–28. doi:10.1080/00207 543.2020.1832273

MKLab. (2016). https://staruml.io/

Mohammed, T. A., Ghareeb, A., Al-bayaty, H., & Aljawarneh, S. (2019, December). Big data challenges and achievements: applications on smart cities and energy sector. In *Proceedings of the Second International Conference on Data Science, E-Learning and Information Systems* (pp. 1-5). 10.1145/3368691.3368717

Mouchili, M. N., Aljawarneh, S., & Tchouati, W. (2018, October). Smart city data analysis. In *Proceedings of the First International Conference on Data Science, E-learning and Information Systems* (pp. 1-6). Academic Press.

Myung, S. (2015). Master Data Management in PLM for the Enterprise Scope. In *Proceeding of IFIP International Conference on Product Lifecycle Management* (pp. 771-779). Doha, Qatar: Springer International Publishing.

Myung, S. (2016). Innovation Strategy for Engineering Plant Product Lifecycle Management based on Master Data Management, Project Management and Quality Management. *Korean Journal of Computational Design and Engineering*, *21*(2), 170–176. doi:10.7315/CADCAM.2016.170

Otto, B. (2012). How to design the master data architecture: Findings from a case study at Bosch. *International Journal of Information Management, 32*(4), 337–346. doi:10.1016/j.ijinfomgt.2011.11.018

Otto, B., Hüner, K. M., & Österle, H. (2012). Toward a functional reference model for master data quality management. *Journal of Information Systems and e-Business Management*, 395-425.

Puzey, M., & Latham, S. (2016). Enabling operational excellence through the effective management of master data. *APPEA Journal, 56*(2), 575–575. doi:10.1071/AJ15081

Rivas, B., Merino, J., Caballero, I., Serrano, M., & Piattini, M. (2017). Towards a service architecture for master data exchange based on ISO 8000 with support to process large datasets. *Computer Standards & Interfaces, 54*, 94–104. doi:10.1016/j.csi.2016.10.004

Sarathy, R., & Muralidhar, K. (2002). The security of confidential numerical data in databases. *Information Systems Research, 13*(4), 389-403.

SAS. (2016). *SAS MDM*. Retrieved 05 22, 2017, from https://www.sas.com/fr_fr/software/data-management/master-data-management.html

Silvola, R., Jaaskelainen, O., Kropsu-Vehkapera, H., & Haapasalo, H. (2011). Managing one master data–challenges and preconditions. *Industrial Management & Data Systems, 111*(1), 146–162. doi:10.1108/02635571111099776

Singh, A., Juneja, D., & Malhotra, M. (2017). A novel agent based autonomous and service composition framework for cost optimization of resource provisioning in cloud computing. *Journal of King Saud University-Computer and Information Sciences, 29*(1), 19–28. doi:10.1016/j.jksuci.2015.09.001

Smith, H. A., & McKeen, J. D. (2008). Developments in practice XXX: master data management: salvation or snake oil? *Communications of the Association for Information Systems, 23*(1), 4. doi:10.17705/1CAIS.02304

Spruit, M., & Pietzka, K. (2015). MD3M: The master data management maturity model. *Computers in Human Behavior, 51*, 1068–1076. doi:10.1016/j.chb.2014.09.030

Vilminko-Heikkinen, R., & Pekkola, S. (2019). Changes in roles, responsibilities and ownership in organizing master data management. *International Journal of Information Management, 47*, 76–87. doi:10.1016/j.ijinfomgt.2018.12.017

Vilminko-Heikkinen, R., & Pekkola, S. (2019). Changes in roles, responsibilities and ownership in organizing master data management. *International Journal of Information Management, 47*, 76–87. doi:10.1016/j.ijinfomgt.2018.12.017

Vilminko-Heikkinen, R., Vilminko-Heikkinen, R., Pekkola, S., & Pekkola, S. (2017). Master data management and its organizational implementation: An ethnographical study within the public sector. *Journal of Enterprise Information Management, 30*(3), 454–475. doi:10.1108/JEIM-07-2015-0070

Watson, H. J., & McGivern, M. (2016). Getting started with business-driven data governance. *Business Intelligence Journal, 21*(1), 4–7.

Wu, K. J., Liao, C. J., Tseng, M. L., Lim, M. K., Hu, J., & Tan, K. (2017). Toward sustainability: Using big data to explore the decisive attributes of supply chain risks and uncertainties. *Journal of Cleaner Production, 142*, 663–676. doi:10.1016/j.jclepro.2016.04.040

Xiong, J., Yu, G., & Zhang, X. (2017). Research on Governance Structure of Big Data of Civil Aviation. *Journal of Computer and Communications, 5*(05), 112–118. doi:10.4236/jcc.2017.55009

Zhao, C., Ren, L., Zhang, Z., & Meng, Z. (2020). Master data management for manufacturing big data: A method of evaluation for data network. *Journal of the World Wide Web: Internet and Web Information Systems, 23*(2), 1407–1421. doi:10.100711280-019-00707-8

Chapter 7
Web Usage Mining
Issues in Big Data:
Challenges and Opportunities

Sunny Sharma
Chandigarh University, India

Manisha Malhotra
ⓘ https://orcid.org/0000-0002-9056-9473
Chandigarh University, India

ABSTRACT

Web usage mining is the use of data mining techniques to analyze user behavior in order to better serve the needs of the user. This process of personalization uses a set of techniques and methods for discovering the linking structure of information on the web. The goal of web personalization is to improve the user experience by mining the meaningful information and presented the retrieved information in a way the user intends. The arrival of big data instigated novel issues to the personalization community. This chapter provides an overview of personalization, big data, and identifies challenges related to web personalization with respect to big data. It also presents some approaches and models to fill the gap between big data and web personalization. Further, this research brings additional opportunities to web personalization from the perspective of big data.

DOI: 10.4018/978-1-7998-5040-3.ch007

INTRODUCTION

World Wide Web is an internet server which hosts the abundant amount of information in the form of web pages. Search Engines like Google, Yahoo, Bing, DuckDuckGo use data mining techniques to extract the web pages from the web and the whole process is known as web mining (WM) (Furukawa et al., 2015). According to analysis targets, Web Mining is organized into three main areas: web content mining (WCM), web structure mining (WSM) and web usage mining (WUM). Content Mining is process of analyzing the contents of web pages. WSM is the process of mining the knowledge about the web pages like the ranking of web pages, how these web pages are interlinked with one another (Kumar & Singh, 2017). In WUM, web log data related to a user is analyzed while the user surfs the web (Neelima & Rodda, 2015). This usage information is further used in order to predict the future needs of the user and for the neighboring users. Nevertheless, the abundant amount of information available on the web creates a challenge to both the customers and the companies. The customer is presented with multiple choices of products for a specific need which leads to product overload. Consequently, the need for computing based advertising strategies like one to one marketing and client Relationship Management (CRM) has been stressed upon by both researchers and companies. An effective strategy to overcome this product overload is by providing personalized web recommendations in which the user is interested in. Malik and Fyfe (2012) describe web personalization in three different phases: Learning, Matching and Recommendation. The Learning phase is further subdivided into two types: Implicit Learning and Explicit Learning. The second phase is matching. Matching phase includes filtration processes which are Collaborative Filtering (CF), Content Based Filtering (CBF), and Hybrid Filtering. The last phase that is recommendation phase is responsible for providing the set of personalized results to the users (Al-Shargabi et al, 2020; Aljawarneh, 2012; Aljawarneh et al, 2017; Chehbi-Gamoura et al, 2018; Esposito et al, 2018; Jaswal et al, 2019; Kalpana et al, 2018; Lizcano et al, 2020; Malhotra et al, 2019; Mohammed et al, 2019; Mouchili et al, 2018; Singh,2011).

The speed and ease with which electronic transactions can be carried out on the web have been the key force behind the instant growth of electronic business. Eirinaki and Vazirgiannis (2003) describe the need for combining the e-commerce and semantic web and evaluated the benefit of this grouping. Their work further insists on the importance of semantic web technique and emphasized that the modern web technology has the ability to extremely encourage the prospect improvement on the internet. The beginning of big data and data technologies instigated novel research issues to the personalization community. Big data is a novel field that deals with large collection of data- both structured and unstructured- which is increasing exponentially with time. The development of big data has occurred only recently.

The act of collecting and storing enormous amount of data started in the early 1950s when mainframe computers were came to the market. In the period from 1950s to 1990s, the data generated slowly because of high cost of computers, storage devices, network; hence expensive access to computers. The data during this period was exceptionally structured, essentially to support operationally information systems. The advent of World Wide Web in the 1990s generated enormous amount of data hence development of big data analytics. The hugeness, robustness, and versatility of huge data shift Web personalization into a new research situation.

TERMINOLOGY

Web Mining

Web Mining is exploitation of data mining techniques to retrieve information from the web. It is categorized into three main areas, shown in the figure 1:

1. **Web Content Mining:** WCM is process of analyzing the contents of the web pages, images, videos etc. The techniques of web content mining are comparable to the text mining and data mining. The major difference is that in Web content mining, the data over the web is available in semi- structured form.
2. **Web Structure Mining:** WSM is the process of mining the knowledge about the web pages such as ranking of web pages, how these web pages are interlinked with one another on the web (Sharma et al., 2019). The most prominent tools used to find the ranking of a web page are Page Rank Algorithm, HITS, and Alexa Ranking etc.
3. **Web usage Mining:** WUM is an approach of using data mining techniques to collect and understand the usage information from the web log data in order to personalize the contents of a website. The phases of WUM are further divided into three phases: data collection, pattern discovery and pattern analysis. The log data file contains usage patterns of users which can be stored either at server side or client side. A log file contains information about a user like clicked documents, referrer pages, access time for a website etc. By analyzing such data, a webmaster can conclude the life time value of customers. In WUM, all information about a user is analyzed while the user surfs the web (Gerrikagoitia et al., 2015). This usage information is further used in order to predict the future needs of the user and for the neighboring users. Nevertheless, the abundant amount of information available on the web creates a challenge to both the customers and the companies. The customer is presented with multiple choices

of products for a specific need which leads to product overload. An effective strategy to overcome this product overload is by recommending personalized web recommendations in which the user is mostly interested in.

Figure 1. Taxonomy of Web Mining

Web Personalization

It is the process of personalizing a website according to the need of specific users or to provide certain recommendations based on their past history. The process of web personalization is based on two categorizes: web search personalization and recommendation based web personalization. In search personalization, the intuition is done by the user; whereas in recommendation based personalization, the action is itself taken by the system. The both categorization can be understood in figure 2. As shown in the figure 2.a, the user is retrieving the information from the web through the use of search engine. And in figure 2.b, the user is presented with the personalized interface by the recommender system based on past experience of the user. Web Recommender Systems inherit filtering process to predict the need of users in which the users might have a tendency to express (Forsati et al., 2009). For an instance, think of Netflix model where the users are recommended the contents based on their past behaviors, or the way in which products are shown on Amazon.

Web Personalization research exploits many other research areas like Artificial Intelligence, Machine Learning, Natural Language Processing, and Web Mining. (Malik & Fyfe, 2012) describe web personalization in three different phases: Learning, Matching and Recommendation. The Learning phase is further subdivided into two types: Implicit Learning and Explicit Learning. The second phase is matching. Matching phase includes filtration processes which are Collaborative Filtering (CF), Content Based Filtering (CBF), Rule Based and Hybrid Filtering. The last phase that is recommendation phase is responsible for providing the set of personalized results to the users. Many merchants store the data about the customers related to the buying of the products. Different products are bought by different customers. Moreover, more than one costumer can buy the same product. So in order to know, which customer would like to purchase what product, it is important to know what other customers with the same background purchase. This is the main idea behind the collaborative filtering. Collaborative Filtering based recommended systems have been used in wide areas (Isinkaye et al, 2015, Elkahky et al, 2015, Li & Karahanna, 2015). GroupLens (Miller, 2003) is a news based system which exploits Collaborative Filtering Technique in order to provide news recommendations from massive news database to its users. Ringo (Shardanand & Maes, 1995) is an online social application which uses Collaborative Filtering in order to build users profile using the ratings of the users given to the music albums. The Ecommerce platform, Amazon employs topic diversification algorithms for generating the recommendation list (Smith & Linden, 2017). To overcome the scalability issue, Amazon uses collaborative filtering methods by producing a table of similar products offline by using the item-to-item matrix.

Content Based Filtering is based on the contents the user has previously browsed or liked. There are so many techniques for content based filtering. Content based is feasible only if there is data that defines what an individual user likes that represents the user's needs. For instance, it is easy to recommend shoes out of many clothing items stored in database on the basis of user's previous history (or user's interest), but it is impossible to find out the best shoes or a perfect item out of all the shoes. For that, one has to exploit Collaborative Filtering. Moreover, in order to perform content based filtering, it is required to structure the data as most of data available is in unstructured form. But for both structured and unstructured, it is valuable to incorporate preprocessing phase. Some systems that use Content Based Filtering to assist users to locate the information online include Letizia, MyBestBets etc; (Pazzani & Billsus, 2007). Letizia makes use of user interface to provide personalized information and to collect user's profile (Lieberman, 1995).

Big Data

Big data is a novel field that deals with large collection of data- both structured and unstructured- which is increasing exponentially with time. The development of big data is accepted as one of the most prominent areas of prospect information technology which is evolving at a quick speed, driven in part by blogging, web development, social media and the Internet of Things (IoT) fact (Oussous et al., 2018).

EVOLUTION OF BIG DATA

The development of big data has occurred only recently. The act of collecting

Figure 2a. Web Search Personalization

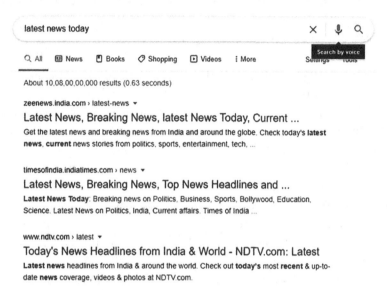

Figure 2b. Web Recommendation

and storing enormous amount of data started in the early 1950s when mainframe computers were came to the market. In the period from 1950s to 1990s, the data generated slowly because of high cost of computers, storage devices, network; hence expensive access to computers. The data during this period was exceptionally structured, essentially to support operationally information systems. The advent of World Wide Web in the 1990s generated enormous amount of data hence development of big data analytics. Since the approach of the World Wide Web, big data and data analytics have advanced through three significant stages.

1. **Big Data 1.0 (1994—2004):** The advent of e-commerce was the main contributor to the big data 1.0 at which the major sources were online businesses. Owing to the technological limitations of web applications, user generated content was only a limited part of the web content. Web mining techniques were developed in this period (1994—2004) to examine users' online activities. Web mining can be divided into three different types: web usage mining, web structure mining, and web content mining.
2. **Big Data 2.0 (2005—2014):** In web 1.0, internet users were not allowed to contact with the content provider as well as another users on the web. Big Data 2.0 is evolved by Web 2.0 and the social phenomenon where users were allowed to interact with websites and contribute their data to the website.
3. **Big Data 3.0 (2015 - Present):** Big Data 3.0 incorporates data from Big Data 1.0 and Big Data 2.0 data. The IoT applications that produce data in the form of images, audio, and video are the key contributors to Big Data 3.0. The IoT refers to environment in which computers and sensors have specific signatures capable of exchanging information and communicating even without human involvement over the internet (Lieberman, 1995). With the exponential growth of IoT, the key sources of big data are smart devices and sensors that will overtake social media and e-commerce websites.

WEB PERSONALIZATION CHALLENGES IN BIG DATA

1. **Huge Data:** It is cleared from the big data 3.0, that data on web is increasing exponentially with time. The huge amount of data needs to be explored to extract knowledge for effective web personalization.
2. **Cold Start Problem:** It is difficult to deal with cold start problem in personalization process on big data. Cold start problem arises when the recommendation system doesn't hold the knowledge related to the user whom to provide the personalized results.
3. **Unstructured Data:** It is cleared that most of data on the web is in unstructured form. For effective personalization, data analysis and machine learning

techniques is required to employ on the web to make the information machine understandable.

4. **Data Quality:** There are many definitions related to data quality, but data is generally considered high quality if it fits for the intended use. As most of data on the web is in unstructured form and collected from a number of sources, the data quality tends to reduce. It is always recommended to preprocess the data prior to actual use for effective results.

CONCLUSION

The omnipresence of data will most likely move research towards the creation of techniques and methods that will provide more generic, open-corpus and functional applications which will face the big data challenges. To close the gap between big data and the Semantic Web, community needs to create systems that will integrate both in a single framework. The purpose of this article was to present a brief introduction to personalization of the Web along with the present state of the art, from the perspective of both big data and the Semantic Web, and to outline the associated problems.

REFERENCES

Al-Shargabi, B., AlJawarneh, S., & Hayajneh, S. M. (2020). A cloudlet based security and trust model for e-government web services. *Journal of Theoretical and Applied Information Technology*, *98*(1), 27–37.

Aljawarneh, S. (Ed.). (2012). *Cloud computing advancements in design, implementation, and technologies*. IGI Global.

Aljawarneh, S., & Malhotra, M. (Eds.). (2017). *Critical Research on Scalability and Security Issues in Virtual Cloud Environments*. IGI Global.

Chehbi-Gamoura, S., Derrouiche, R., Malhotra, M., & Koruca, H. I. (2018, June). Adaptive management approach for more availability of big data business analytics. In *Proceedings of the Fourth International Conference on Engineering & MIS 2018* (pp. 1-8). 10.1145/3234698.3234758

Eirinaki, M., & Vazirgiannis, M. (2003). Web mining for web personalization. *ACM Transactions on Internet Technology*, *3*(1), 1–27. doi:10.1145/643477.643478

Elkahky, A. M., Song, Y., & He, X. (2015, May). A multi-view deep learning approach for cross domain user modeling in recommendation systems. In *Proceedings of the 24th International Conference on World Wide Web* (pp. 278-288). International World Wide Web Conferences Steering Committee. 10.1145/2736277.2741667

Esposito, C., Su, X., Aljawarneh, S. A., & Choi, C. (2018). Securing collaborative deep learning in industrial applications within adversarial scenarios. *IEEE Transactions on Industrial Informatics, 14*(11), 4972–4981. doi:10.1109/TII.2018.2853676

Forsati, R., Meybodi, M. R., & Rahbar, A. (2009, May). An efficient algorithm for web recommendation systems. In *2009 IEEE/ACS International Conference on Computer Systems and Applications* (pp. 579-586). IEEE. 10.1109/AICCSA.2009.5069385

Furukawa, T., Mori, K., Arino, K., Hayashi, K., & Shirakawa, N. (2015). Identifying the evolutionary process of emerging technologies: A chronological network analysis of World Wide Web conference sessions. *Technological Forecasting and Social Change, 91*, 280–294. doi:10.1016/j.techfore.2014.03.013

Gerrikagoitia, J. K., Castander, I., Rebón, F., & Alzua-Sorzabal, A. (2015). New trends of Intelligent E-Marketing based on Web Mining for e-shops. *Procedia: Social and Behavioral Sciences, 175*(1), 75–83. doi:10.1016/j.sbspro.2015.01.1176

Isinkaye, F. O., Folajimi, Y. O., & Ojokoh, B. A. (2015). Recommendation systems: Principles, methods and evaluation. *Egyptian Informatics Journal, 16*(3), 261–273. doi:10.1016/j.eij.2015.06.005

Jaswal, S., & Malhotra, M. (2019, December). A detailed analysis of trust models in cloud environment. *In Proceedings of the Second International Conference on Data Science, E-Learning and Information Systems* (pp. 1-5). 10.1145/3368691.3368740

Kalpana, G., Kumar, P. V., Aljawarneh, S., & Krishnaiah, R. V. (2018). Shifted adaption homomorphism encryption for mobile and cloud learning. *Computers & Electrical Engineering, 65*, 178–195. doi:10.1016/j.compeleceng.2017.05.022

Khan, M. A., & Salah, K. (2018). IoT security: Review, blockchain solutions, and open challenges. *Future Generation Computer Systems, 82*, 395–411. doi:10.1016/j.future.2017.11.022

Kumar, A., & Singh, R. K. (2017). A study on web structure mining. *International Research Journal of Engineering and Technology, 4*(1), 715–720.

Li, S. S., & Karahanna, E. (2015). Online recommendation systems in a B2C E-commerce context: A review and future directions. *Journal of the Association for Information Systems, 16*(2), 72–107. doi:10.17705/1jais.00389

Lieberman, H. (1995). Letizia: An agent that assists web browsing. *IJCAI (United States)*, *1995*(1), 924–929.

Lizcano, D., Lara, J. A., White, B., & Aljawarneh, S. (2020). Blockchain-based approach to create a model of trust in open and ubiquitous higher education. *Journal of Computing in Higher Education*, *32*(1), 109–134. doi:10.100712528-019-09209-y

Malhotra, M., & Singh, A. (2019). Role of Agents to Enhance the Security and Scalability in Cloud Environment. In Cloud Security: Concepts, Methodologies, Tools, and Applications (pp. 552-573). IGI Global. doi:10.4018/978-1-5225-8176-5.ch028

Malik, Z. K., & Fyfe, C. (2012). Review of web personalization. *Journal of Emerging Technologies in Web Intelligence*, *4*(3), 285–296. doi:10.4304/jetwi.4.3.285-296

Miller, B. N., Ried, J. T., & Konstan, J. A. (2003). GroupLens for Usenet: Experiences in applying collaborative filtering to a social information system. In *From Usenet to CoWebs* (pp. 206–231). Springer. doi:10.1007/978-1-4471-0057-7_10

Mohammed, T. A., Ghareeb, A., Al-bayaty, H., & Aljawarneh, S. (2019, December). Big data challenges and achievements: applications on smart cities and energy sector. In *Proceedings of the Second International Conference on Data Science, E-Learning and Information Systems* (pp. 1-5). 10.1145/3368691.3368717

Mouchili, M. N., Aljawarneh, S., & Tchouati, W. (2018, October). Smart city data analysis. In *Proceedings of the First International Conference on Data Science, E-learning and Information Systems* (pp. 1-6). Academic Press.

Neelima, G., & Rodda, S. (2015). An overview on web usage mining. In *Emerging ICT for Bridging the Future-Proceedings of the 49th Annual Convention of the Computer Society of India CSI* Volume 2 (pp. 647-655). Springer.

Oussous, A., Benjelloun, F. Z., Lahcen, A. A., & Belfkih, S. (2018). Big Data technologies: A survey. *Journal of King Saud University-Computer and Information Sciences*, *30*(4), 431–448. doi:10.1016/j.jksuci.2017.06.001

Pazzani, M. J., & Billsus, D. (2007). Content-based recommendation systems. In *The adaptive web* (pp. 325–341). Springer. doi:10.1007/978-3-540-72079-9_10

Shardanand, U., & Maes, P. (1995, May). Social information filtering: algorithms for automating" word of mouth". In Chi (Vol. 95, pp. 210-217). ACM.

Sharma, S., Mahajan, S., & Rana, V. (2019). A semantic framework for ecommerce search engine optimization. *International Journal of Information Technology*, *11*(1), 31–36. doi:10.100741870-018-0232-y

Singh, A., Juneja, D., & Malhotra, M. (2017). A novel agent based autonomous and service composition framework for cost optimization of resource provisioning in cloud computing. *Journal of King Saud University-Computer and Information Sciences, 29*(1), 19–28. doi:10.1016/j.jksuci.2015.09.001

Smith, B., & Linden, G. (2017). Two decades of recommender systems at Amazon.com. *IEEE Internet Computing, 21*(3), 12–18. doi:10.1109/MIC.2017.72

Chapter 8

A Novel Resource Allocation and Scheduling Based on Priority Using Metaheuristic for Cloud Computing Environment

Meenakshi Garg
Government Bikram College of Commerce, India

Amandeep Kaur
Sri Guru Granth Sahib World University, India

Gaurav Dhiman
Government Bikram College of Commerce, India

ABSTRACT

In cloud computing systems, current works do not challenge the database failure rates and recovery techniques. In this chapter, priority-based resource allocation and scheduling technique is proposed by using the metaheuristic optimization approach spotted hyena optimizer (SHO). Initially, the emperor penguins predict the workload of user server and resource requirements. The expected completion time of each server is estimated with this predicted workload. Then the resources activities are classified based on the criteria of the deadline and the asset. Further, the employed servers are classified based on the workload and the estimated completed time. The proposed approach is compared with existing resource utilization techniques in terms of percentage of resource allocation, missed deadlines, and average server workload.

DOI: 10.4018/978-1-7998-5040-3.ch008

INTRODUCTION

Cloud Computing

Cloud computing is different from traditional computing, which relies mainly on personal devices. This enables mobile sharing of computing resources. It offers, at minimum time, versatile and limited access to resources. Hardware or software can be the shared tools. Cloud offers various products such as Service Software (SaaS), Service Platform Service (PaaS), Service Infrastructure (IaaS) (Sheetal & Ravindranath, 2019).

The advantages of Cloud Computing are:

1. Applications can be accessed as utilities throughout the web.
2. No specific software installation needed for accessing cloud applications.
3. The PaaS service provides various deployment tools and runtime environments
4. It provides platform independent access to all clients.
5. Supports load balancing (Bhavani & Guruprasad, 2014).

The advantages of Cloud Computing's are:

1. Applications can be accessed throughout the web as utilities.
2. No installation of specific software required to access cloud applications.
3. PaaS provides different implementation methods and runtime environments
4. Provides separate application access for all customers.
5. Supports balance of load (Bhavani & Guruprasad, 2014).

RESOURCE ALLOCATION AND SCHEDULING IN CLOUD

The allocation of resources can be static or dynamic. The cloud client proactively asks for a fixed amount of resources in static allocation. Nonetheless, static allocation results in poor or over-use of resources (Sareen et. al,2015; Al-Shargabi et al, 2020; Aljawarneh, 2012; Aljawarneh et al, 2017; Chehbi-Gamoura et al, 2018; Esposito et al, 2018; Jaswal et al, 2019; Kalpana et al, 2018; Lizcano et al, 2020; Malhotra et al, 2019; Mohammed et al, 2019; Mouchili et al, 2018; Singh,2011).

In dynamic allocation, on-demand users request resources depending on application requirements. If the requested resources are unavailable, other cloud data centers are allocated by the cloud service provider (CSP) (Asha & Rao, 2013), (Patel & Patel, 2013).

PROBLEM IDENTIFICATION

The resource usage and energy consumption parameters were mainly considered for the allocation of VM in the multi-agent-based VM allocation approach (Wang et. al, 2016). But the work load forecast or future asset needs are not addressed. In fact, there was no understanding of the deadline for each mission (Dhiman, 2020), (Dhiman & Kaur, 2019), (Dhiman & Kumar, 2019).

In (Student, 2015), when a job with high priority (with a low deadline) arrives, the job with low priority (with a high deadline) has been preempted, allowing the job with high priority to be carried out in its capacity. But it does not control the workload of the PMs, nor does it check the size of the resources requested. In (Xiao et. al, 2012), (Choi & Lim, 2016), (Kumar et. al, 2017), the workload is predicted based on the need for future resources. It then migrates the VM from a hot spot to a resource-based cold spot. But the energy cost for the services used was not included in this method. In fact, there was no understanding of the deadline for each mission (Dhiman & Kaur, 2018), (Singh & Dhiman, 2017), (Kaur & Dhiman, 2019).

Some works on cloud-based task scheduling based on ABC are available (Kruekaew & Kimpan, 2014), (Kimpan & Kruekaew, 2016). In the fitness function, they consider the VM load to select the VMs (Hesabian et. al, 2015) considers making pan time and load balancing (these metrics have not been defined) for fitness function (Sheetal & Ravindranath, 2019), (Garg & Malhotra, 2017) also considers completion time and loading as a fitness function for selecting VMs (Garg et. al,2018), (Garg et. al,2019), (Garg et. al,2019).

But the main advantages of the solution over these works are:

1. Using EWMA from past values, predicted the loading and completion time. The fitness function is built only from these expected values (Garg et. al, 2019).
2. Algorithm does not select a single VM but selects a server instead (Dhiman, 2019).
3. Listed databases on the basis of client query preferences (Dhiman, 2019).

RELATED WORKS

(Song et. Al, 2011) proposed a two-tiered on-demand resource allocation mechanism, including the local and global resource allocation. A local on demand resource allocation algorithm is applied by the VM with a threshold value. In global resource allocation, the threshold value of local allocation can be adjusted adaptively.

(Maguluri et. al, 2014) have discussed about traffic optimal resource allocation algorithms.

(Di & Wang, 2012) have designed a deadline-based resource allocation algorithm and an error free technique for job completion time.

(Wang et. al, 2016) have introduced a decentralized multiagent (MA) based VM allocation approach. A local negotiation-based VM consolidation mechanism is developed to exchange the assigned VMs of agents for energy cost saving.

(Upadhye & Dange, 2014) have proposed Utility Accrual (UA) approach to associate each task with a Time Utility Function (TUF). The TUF denotes the utility attained by a system at the time when a task is completed to improve the performance.

(Weng & Wang, 2012) have designed adaptive neural fuzzy inference system (ANFIS) algorithm for predicting the load and deciding the resource allocation policy for VMS.

(Veeramallu, 2014) have presented the many dynamic resource allocation techniques. Resource provisioning was done by parallel processing using different types of scheduling heuristics.

PROPOSED SOLUTION

Overview

A Priority based Resource Allocation and Scheduling Technique using Spotted Hyena Optimizer (SHO) (Singh & Dhiman, 2017), (Kaur & Dhiman 2019), (Dhiman, 2019), (Dhiman, 2019),),(Dhiman, 2020),(Dhiman & Kaur, 2019), Dhiman et. al, 2019) (PRA-SHO) for cloud environment. Initially, the work load of server and resource requirements of users are predicted by the scout bees by monitoring the past resource utilizations and size of the allocated VM. With this predicted workload, the expected completion time of each server is estimated. Then the tasks requesting the resources are categorized based on the deadline and resource requirements. Then based on the work load and expected completed time, the servers are categorized. Then each category of task will be allocated to the respective category of servers. The proposed approach is implemented in CloudSim environment of Java and compared with existing techniques in terms of resource utilization, percentage of resources successfully allocated, percentage of missed deadlines, average work load of server etc.

Figure 1. System architecture

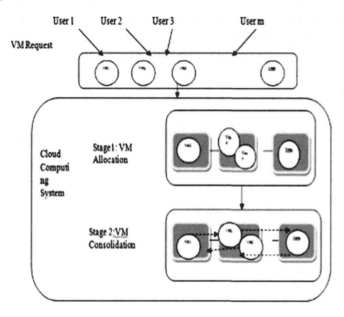

SPOTTED HYENA OPTIMIZER (SHO)

SHO algorithm has four key phases that are encouraged by spotted hyena's usual activities. These activities are scanning, encircling, stalking and fighting for prey as follows, which are mathematically modelled.

Encircling Prey

The finest solution for encircling the prey is called the target prey and the other search agents or spotted hyenas will change their positions according to this optimal solution defined as

$$\vec{D}_m = \left| \vec{B} \times \vec{P}_p(y) - \vec{P}(y) \right| \tag{1}$$

$$\vec{P}(y+1) = \vec{P}_p(y) - \vec{E} \times \vec{D}_m \tag{2}$$

Where Dm is the distance vector among the prey and the spotted hyena, y is the present iteration, Pp represents the prey position vector, P signifies the spotted hyena position vector, B and E are the coefficient vector.

The B and E vectors are computed as following:

$$\vec{B} = 2 \times r\vec{d}_1 \tag{3}$$

$$\vec{E} = 2 \times \vec{m} \times r\vec{d}_2 - \vec{m} \tag{4}$$

$$\vec{m} = 5 - \left(Iteration \times \left(5 \, / \, Max_{Iteration}\right)\right), where \, Iteration = 0,1,2,...,Max_{Iteration} \tag{5}$$

Hunting

SHO's next step is the hunting approach that makes a cluster of optimal solutions against the finest search agent and updates other search agents ' positions.

$$\vec{D}_m = \left| \vec{B} \times \vec{P}_m - \vec{P}_k \right| \tag{6}$$

$$\vec{P}_k = \vec{P}_m - \vec{E} \times \vec{D}_m \tag{7}$$

$$\vec{C}_m = \vec{P}_k + \vec{P}_{k+1} + ... + \vec{P}_{k+N} \tag{8}$$

Where Pm determines the first best spotted hyena location, Pk is the position of other spotted hyenas and N is the number of spotted hyenas determined as follows:

$$N = count_{ns} \left(\vec{P}_m, \vec{P}_{m+1}, \vec{P}_{m+2}, ..., \left(\vec{P}_m + \vec{M}\right)\right) \tag{9}$$

Where M is a random variable in range [0.5, 1], ns is the number of solutions, and cm is the number of optimal solutions in group N.

Attacking Prey (Exploitation)

There's a need to decrease the value of vector m for exploitation. The variation in E is also decreased, however, due to a change in the value in m which can decrease from 5 to 0 during iterations. The mathematical formulation for the proposed SHO to attack behavior is defined as follows:

$$\vec{P}(y+1) = \frac{\vec{C}_m}{N}$$

(10)

where P(y+1) saves the best solution, and updates other search agent positions.

Search for Prey (Exploration)

The search mechanism defines an algorithm's explorative capacity. Therefore, the proposed SHO algorithm ensures ability to use E with random values greater than or less than 1. Often responsible for demonstrating SHO's more unpredictable behavior is vector B, and preventing local optimum.

Assumptions

Let X = (M, N) be the cloud system

M = {m1, m2, …, m_i} be the set of servers interconnected by the communication network

$$\forall \left(m_i, m_j \right) \in N$$

(11)

This indicates that m_i and m_j communicate with each other through only ones which
Let c (p_i, p_j) be the communication distance between server's m_i and m_j.
This is computed as the number of switches along the shortest path between m_i and m_j
Let $\delta = \left\{ \alpha_1, \alpha_2, ...\alpha_n \right\}$ be the set of VM resource request required by users.
Let w_i be the amount of resources required by VM $\alpha \in \delta$.
Each server owns number of resources that are capable of running multiple VMs.
Let c the amount of resources at the server m_i

VM Allocation

VM allocation $\left[\delta_{(m1)}, \delta_{(m2)}, \ldots, \delta_{(mi)}\right]$ is defined as mapping of server to set a set of VMs that should satisfy the following two conditions:

1.   1. Each VM should be allocated to at least one server and no VM is allocation to more than one server.

$$\bigcup_{mi \in m} \Theta(m_i) = \Theta \tag{12}$$

$$\Theta(m_i) \cap \Theta(m_j) = \Phi, \forall 1 \le i, j \le y, i \ne j \tag{13}$$

2.   2. For each server, the total resource requirements of its hosted VM does not exceed its available resources.

$$\sum_{\theta_j \in \Theta(m_i)} c_j \le w_i, \forall 1 \le i \le y \tag{14}$$

Prediction of Work Load

Each server maintains a resource utilization history (RUT) per VM which contains the total resources utilized and total time taken to complete each services of users.

The workloads of each VM can be predicted using exponentially weighted moving average (EWMA) of past workloads of all VMs.

$$EL(t) = \alpha \cdot EL(t-1) + (1-\alpha) \cdot OL(t) \tag{15}$$

where EL and OL are the estimated and observed loads at time t and α is a constant.

Similarly, expected completion time of each server can be determined by estimating EWMA of past completion times of all VMs.

$$ECT(t) = \beta \cdot ECT(t-1) + (1-\beta) \cdot OCT(t) \tag{16}$$

Where ECT and OCT are the expected and observed completion time of VMs at time t and β is a constant.

Classification of Users Tasks

When the users submit their service requirements, then the cloud server broker will classify the services and allocates priorities as shown in Table 1.

Table 1. Classification of User Tasks

Deal Line	Resources Size	Priority
Short	High	1
Short	Medium	2
High	High	3
High	Low	4

Priority Based Resource Allocation and Scheduling Technique

The technique of priority-based resource allocation is as follows:

1. Let Q be the solutions
2. Let C is the number of optimization parameters
3. Let T be the maximum number of cycles that the algorithm would run.
   a. Initially scout bees are deployed in the network which collects the past resource utilizations and size of the allocated VM.
   b. Based on the collected information, work load of server and resource requirements of users are predicted.
   c. 3. c. A fitness function is formed for each server Si, i=1,2…n using EL and ECT as

$$g_i = \left(\lambda_1 * EL\right) + \left(\lambda_2 * ECT\right), where\ \lambda_1\ and\ \lambda_2\ are\ the\ weight\ values \qquad (17)$$

   d. Then, roulette wheel selection method (of ABC) will be applied to find the best solution. In this method,
      i. The initial positions of food sources are randomly generated.
      ii. During each iteration, the employed and onlooker bees seek for better solutions by performing neighbor search.
      iii. 3. d. iii. For each solution qi, determine a neighbor b_i.

$$q_{ij} = b_{ij} + \sigma_{ij}\left(b_{ij} - b_{kj}\right), where$$
$$k \in \{1,2,3,...,Q\} \, and \, k \neq i,$$
$$\sigma = random \, number \, in \, the \, range \, [-1,1], \tag{18}$$
$$j = 1,2,3,...,V$$

k and j are randomly selected

iv.   A better solution is then selected between bi and qi.
v.   The onlooker bees are deployed near the food sources using the roulette wheel selection method.
vi. It selects a food source at position bi with a probability Zi calculated as follows:

$$\frac{fit_i}{\sum_{n=1}^{S} fit_n} \tag{19}$$
$$fit_i = \begin{cases} \dfrac{1}{1+g_i}, & if \, g_i \geq 0 \\ 1 + abs(g_i), & if \, g_i < 0 \end{cases}$$

Where gi =fitness of the solution

vii.   A solution is rejected by an employed bee if it could not be enhanced for a fixed number of trials.
viii. The employed bee is then changed into a scout bee to generate a new solution randomly.
ix.   The value of limit is chosen as $Q \times C$.
x.   The best solutions are recorded till now.
xi.   Steps c and h are repeated until T cycles are completed.
xii.   Determine the global best solution among the best local solutions recorded at each processor. The scout bees then visit each server and determine the fitness function. Based on the best solution observed, the servers are categorized as follows:

Then each category of task will be allocated to the respective category of servers. The low priority tasks (3) and (4) are preempted when high priority task (1) or (2) arrives.

Table 2. Category of Servers

Server	Work Load	Expected Completion Time
1	Least	Less
2	Medium	Less
3	Less	High
4	High	High

EXPERIMENTAL RESULTS

The NASA workload (Arlitt & Williamson, 1997) was used as the emulator for access point (AP) requests from Web users. This workload reflects practical variations in load over a time period. This consists of 100960 user requests submitted during a day to the Web servers. Abnormal deviations will activate the load balancing mechanism in this workload. Research shows that the pattern of delivery of user requests to websites is very close to the pattern of that workload. The experimental parameters assigned to this work are shown in Table 3.

Performance Metrics

The experimental results of the proposed PRAS-ABC scheme in CloudSim Simulator (Calheiros et. al,2011) is explained here. The performance metrics considered for evaluation are as follows: Response delay: The response time R(t) represents the latency. It is calculated (in minutes) according to Eq. (20).

$$R(t) = \frac{\sum_{j=1}^{Re\,q_{ans}} W_j}{Re\,q_{ans}} \qquad (20)$$

Where Req_{ans} is the number of answers

Whereas W_j is the waiting time of answered requests

$$W_j = [F_j(t) - A_j(t)].Ser_j(t) \qquad (21)$$

Where the finishing time, arrival time and service time are F(t), A(t) and Ser(t). Arrival time and end time are the times the user receives the request, and the time the user receives the response from their VM, respectively. Service time is the estimated time which the incoming user request requires.

Table 3. Experimental Parameters

Parameter	Value
Work load	NADA traces
Resource Utilization Thresholds	$U^{low-thr} = 20\%$ and $U^{high\_thr} = 80\%$
Response Time Thresholds	$RT^{low-thr} = 200ms$ and $RT^{high\_thr} = 1000ms$
Scaling Intervals	$\Delta t = 10min$
Desired Response Time	DRT = 1000ms=1s
Load Balancing Policy	Round-Robin
Configuration of VMs	t2.medium and t2.Large
Maximum On-demand VM Limitation	MaxVM=10VM
Task and Resources Scheduling Policy	Time-Shared

- **Throughput:** It represents the ratio of answered requests (Req_{ans}) to the total number of received requests (Req_{rec}) in percentage.
- **Resource utilization**: It represents the mean % of the CPU utilization by calculating the average of all VMs utilization.

$$R_u = \frac{\sum_{j=1}^{RVM} U\left(VM_j\right)}{RVM} \tag{22}$$

Here RVM is the number of rented VMs and U(VMj) represent the utilization of VMj.

- **Missed deadlines (Md):** Requests experiencing the response delay of greater than the requested deadline (Rd) are considered as missed deadline.

$$M_d = \sum_{j=1}^{Tot\,Req} W_j - R_d \tag{23}$$

Results

Performance of PRAS-ABC is as following:-

Figure 2. Time vs Response Delay

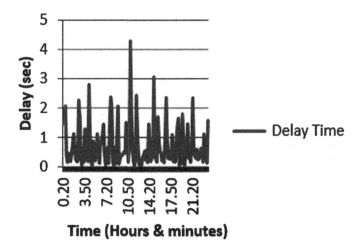

As time taken as x-axis and corresponding delay is calculated. The performance can be evaluated through the graph.

Figure 3. Time vs VMs Allocation

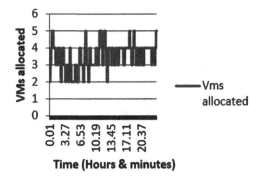

As time taken as x-axis and the VMs allocation is calculated. The performance can be evaluated through the graph.

Figure 4. Time vs Allocation Decision

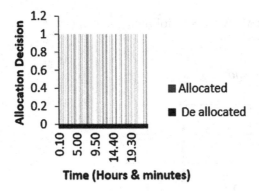

In this experiment time taken as x-axis and the corresponding allocation decision is calculated. The performance can be evaluated through the graph.

Performance of PRAS-ABC With Suprex

PRASABC is compared with the super professional executor (Suprex) (Mingprasert & Masuchun, 2017), (Gupta & Ghrera, 2016), (Aslanpour et. al,2017). In Suprex, if the resources are under provisioned, the executor adds a new VM. In contrast, if the resources are over-provisioned, the executor releases a VM on-demand by selecting a VM.

Figure 5 shows the CPU Utilization measured for PRASABC and Suprex when number of VMs are varied. The VMs are increased from 2 to 5, as we can see from

Figure 5. No. of VMs CPU Utilization

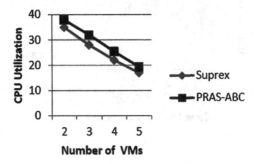

the figure, the CPU Utilization of PRAS-ABC decreases from 38 to 19.4, the CPU Utilization of Suprex decreases from 35 to 17. Hence the CPU Utilization of PRAS-ABC is 13% of higher when compared to Suprex.

Figure 6. No. of VMs vs Throughput

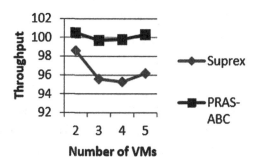

Figure 6 shows the Throughput measured for PRAS-ABC and Suprex when number of VMs are varied. The VMs are increased from 2 to 5, as we can see from the figure, the Throughput of PRAS-ABC decreases from 100.5 to 100.3, the Throughput of Suprex decreases from 98.6 to 96.2. Hence the Throughput of PRAS-ABC is 4% of higher when compared to Suprex.

Figure 7 shows the CPU Load measured for PRAS-ABC and Suprex when number of VMs are varied. The VMs are increased from 2 to 5, as we can see from the figure, the CPU Load of PRAS-ABC decreases from 160 to 21, the CPU Load of Suprex decreases from 172 to 39. Hence the CPU Load of PRAS-ABC is 42% of higher when compared to Suprex.

Figure 7. No. of VMs vs CPU Load

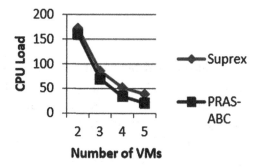

Figure 8. No. of VMs vs Percentage of missed deadlines

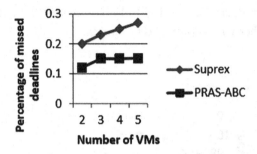

Figure 8 shows the percentage of missed deadlines for the requested services when the number of VMs is varied. The figure shows that PRAS-ABC attains 66% lesser missed deadlines than Suprex scheme. The average values of each metrics for both the schemes are shown in Table 4.

Table 4. Average Values for both the Schemes

Scheme	Time (Hrs & Mins)	CPU Utili-zation	Throughput	Delay (sec)	% of Missed deadline	CPU Load
PRAS-ABC	0.01-23.01	26.52	100.97	0.7218	0.1695	59.404
Suprex	0.01-23.01	23.52	96.2	0.788	0.2095	71.404

CONCLUSION

A Priority based Resource Allocation & Scheduling Technique using Artificial Bee Colony Optimization (ABC) (PRA-ABC) for cloud environment. Initially, the work load of server and resource requirements of users are predicted by the scout bees by monitoring the past resource utilizations and size of the allocated VM. With this predicted workload, the expected completion time of each server is estimated. Then the tasks requesting the resources are categorized based on the deadline and resource requirements. Then based on the work load and expected completed time, the servers are categorized. Then each category of task will be allocated to the respective category of servers. The proposed approach have been implemented in CloudSim environment of Java and compared with existing techniques in terms of resource utilization, percentage of resources successfully allocated, percentage of missed deadlines, average work load of server etc.

REFERENCES

Al-Shargabi, B., AlJawarneh, S., & Hayajneh, S. M. (2020). A cloudlet based security and trust model for e-government web services. *Journal of Theoretical and Applied Information Technology*, *98*(1), 27–37.

Aljawarneh, S. (Ed.). (2012). *Cloud computing advancements in design, implementation, and technologies*. IGI Global.

Aljawarneh, S., & Malhotra, M. (Eds.). (2017). *Critical Research on Scalability and Security Issues in Virtual Cloud Environments*. IGI Global.

Arlitt, M. F., & Williamson, C. L. (1997). Internet web servers: Workload characterization and performance implications. *IEEE/ACM Transactions on Networking*, *5*(5), 631–645. doi:10.1109/90.649565

Asha, N., & Rao, G. R. (2013). A Review on Various Resource Allocation Strategies in Cloud Computing. *International Journal of Emerging Technology and Advanced Engineering*, *3*(7).

Aslanpour, M. S., Ghobaei-Arani, M., & Toosi, A. N. (2017). Auto-scaling web applications in clouds: A cost-aware approach. *Journal of Network and Computer Applications*, *95*, 26–41. doi:10.1016/j.jnca.2017.07.012

Bhavani, B. H., & Guruprasad, H. S. (2014). Resource provisioning techniques in cloud computing environment: A survey. *International Journal of Research in Computer and Communication Technology*, *3*(3), 395–401.

Calheiros, R. N., Ranjan, R., Beloglazov, A., De Rose, C. A., & Buyya, R. (2011). CloudSim: A toolkit for modeling and simulation of cloud computing environments and evaluation of resource provisioning algorithms. *Software, Practice & Experience*, *41*(1), 23–50. doi:10.1002pe.995

Chehbi-Gamoura, S., Derrouiche, R., Malhotra, M., & Koruca, H. I. (2018, June). Adaptive management approach for more availability of big data business analytics. In *Proceedings of the Fourth International Conference on Engineering & MIS 2018* (pp. 1-8). 10.1145/3234698.3234758

Choi, Y., & Lim, Y. (2016). Optimization approach for resource allocation on cloud computing for iot. *International Journal of Distributed Sensor Networks*, *12*(3), 3479247. doi:10.1155/2016/3479247

Dhiman, G. (2019). ESA: A hybrid bio-inspired metaheuristic optimization approach for engineering problems. *Engineering with Computers*, 1–31. doi:10.100700366-019-00826-w

Dhiman, G. (2019). *Multi-objective Metaheuristic Approaches for Data Clustering in Engineering Application (s)* (Doctoral dissertation).

Dhiman, G. (2020). MOSHEPO: A hybrid multi-objective approach to solve economic load dispatch and micro grid problems. *Applied Intelligence*, *50*(1), 119–137. doi:10.100710489-019-01522-4

Dhiman, G., & Kaur, A. (2017, December). Spotted hyena optimizer for solving engineering design problems. In *2017 international conference on machine learning and data science (MLDS)* (pp. 114-119). IEEE.

Dhiman, G., & Kaur, A. (2018). Optimizing the design of airfoil and optical buffer problems using spotted hyena optimizer. *Designs*, *2*(3), 28. doi:10.3390/designs2030028

Dhiman, G., & Kaur, A. (2019). STOA: A bio-inspired based optimization algorithm for industrial engineering problems. *Engineering Applications of Artificial Intelligence*, *82*, 148–174. doi:10.1016/j.engappai.2019.03.021

Dhiman, G., & Kumar, V. (2017). Spotted hyena optimizer: A novel bio-inspired based metaheuristic technique for engineering applications. *Advances in Engineering Software*, *114*, 48–70. doi:10.1016/j.advengsoft.2017.05.014

Dhiman, G., & Kumar, V. (2018). Emperor penguin optimizer: A bio-inspired algorithm for engineering problems. *Knowledge-Based Systems*, *159*, 20–50. doi:10.1016/j.knosys.2018.06.001

Dhiman, G., & Kumar, V. (2018). Multi-objective spotted hyena optimizer: A multi-objective optimization algorithm for engineering problems. *Knowledge-Based Systems*, *150*, 175–197. doi:10.1016/j.knosys.2018.03.011

Dhiman, G., & Kumar, V. (2019). KnRVEA: A hybrid evolutionary algorithm based on knee points and reference vector adaptation strategies for many-objective optimization. *Applied Intelligence*, *49*(7), 2434–2460. doi:10.100710489-018-1365-1

Dhiman, G., & Kumar, V. (2019). Seagull optimization algorithm: Theory and its applications for large-scale industrial engineering problems. *Knowledge-Based Systems*, *165*, 169–196. doi:10.1016/j.knosys.2018.11.024

Dhiman, G., & Kumar, V. (2019). Spotted hyena optimizer for solving complex and non-linear constrained engineering problems. In *Harmony search and nature inspired optimization algorithms* (pp. 857–867). Springer. doi:10.1007/978-981-13-0761-4_81

Di, S., & Wang, C. L. (2012). Error-tolerant resource allocation and payment minimization for cloud system. *IEEE Transactions on Parallel and Distributed Systems*, *24*(6), 1097–1106. doi:10.1109/TPDS.2012.309

Esposito, C., Su, X., Aljawarneh, S. A., & Choi, C. (2018). Securing collaborative deep learning in industrial applications within adversarial scenarios. *IEEE Transactions on Industrial Informatics*, *14*(11), 4972–4981. doi:10.1109/TII.2018.2853676

Garg, M., & Malhotra, M. (2017). Retrieval of Images on the Basis of Content: A Survey. *International Journal of Engineering Development and Research*, *5*, 757–760.

Garg, M., Malhotra, M., & Singh, H. (2018). Statistical Feature Based Image Classification and Retrieval Using Trained Neural Classifiers. *International Journal of Applied Engineering Research: IJAER*, *13*(8), 5766–5771.

Garg, M., Malhotra, M., & Singh, H. (2019). A Novel CBIR-Based System using Texture Fused LBP Variants and GLCM Features. *International Journal of Innovative Technology and Exploring Engineering*, *9*(2), 1247–1257.

Garg, M., Malhotra, M., & Singh, H. (2019). Comparison of deep learning techniques on content-based image retrieval. *Modern Physics Letters A*, *34*, 1950285. doi:10.1142/S0217732319502857

Garg, M., Singh, H., & Malhotra, M. (2019). Fuzzy-NN approach with statistical features for description and classification of efficient image retrieval. *Modern Physics Letters A*, *34*(3), 1950022. doi:10.1142/S0217732319500226

Gupta, P., & Ghrera, S. P. (2016). Power and fault aware reliable resource allocation for cloud infrastructure. *Procedia Computer Science*, *78*, 457–463. doi:10.1016/j.procs.2016.02.088

Hesabian, N., Haj, H., & Javadi, S. (2015). Optimal scheduling in cloud computing environment using the bee algorithm. *Int J Comput Netw Commun Secur*, *3*, 253–258.

Jaswal, S., & Malhotra, M. (2019, December). A detailed analysis of trust models in cloud environment. In *Proceedings of the Second International Conference on Data Science, E-Learning and Information Systems* (pp. 1-5). 10.1145/3368691.3368740

Kalpana, G., Kumar, P. V., Aljawarneh, S., & Krishnaiah, R. V. (2018). Shifted adaption homomorphism encryption for mobile and cloud learning. *Computers & Electrical Engineering*, *65*, 178–195. doi:10.1016/j.compeleceng.2017.05.022

Kaur, A., & Dhiman, G. (2019). A review on search-based tools and techniques to identify bad code smells in object-oriented systems. In *Harmony search and nature inspired optimization algorithms* (pp. 909–921). Springer. doi:10.1007/978-981-13-0761-4_86

Kimpan, W., & Kruekaew, B. (2016, August). Heuristic task scheduling with artificial bee colony algorithm for virtual machines. In *2016 Joint 8th International Conference on Soft Computing and Intelligent Systems (SCIS) and 17th International Symposium on Advanced Intelligent Systems (ISIS)* (pp. 281-286). IEEE. 10.1109/SCIS-ISIS.2016.0067

Kruekaew, B., & Kimpan, W. (2014, March). Virtual machine scheduling management on cloud computing using artificial bee colony. In *Proceedings of the International MultiConference of engineers and computer scientists* (*Vol. 1*, pp. 12-14). Academic Press.

Kumar, A., Kumar, D., & Jarial, S. K. (2017). A review on artificial bee colony algorithms and their applications to data clustering. *Cybernetics and Information Technologies*, *17*(3), 3–28. doi:10.1515/cait-2017-0027

Lizcano, D., Lara, J. A., White, B., & Aljawarneh, S. (2020). Blockchain-based approach to create a model of trust in open and ubiquitous higher education. *Journal of Computing in Higher Education*, *32*(1), 109–134. doi:10.100712528-019-09209-y

Maguluri, S. T., Srikant, R., & Ying, L. (2014). Heavy traffic optimal resource allocation algorithms for cloud computing clusters. *Performance Evaluation*, *81*, 20–39. doi:10.1016/j.peva.2014.08.002

Malhotra, M., & Singh, A. (2019). Role of Agents to Enhance the Security and Scalability in Cloud Environment. In Cloud Security: Concepts, Methodologies, Tools, and Applications (pp. 552-573). IGI Global. doi:10.4018/978-1-5225-8176-5.ch028

Mingprasert, S., & Masuchun, R. (2017, February). Adaptive artificial bee colony algorithm for solving the capacitated vehicle routing problem. In *2017 9th International Conference on Knowledge and Smart Technology (KST)* (pp. 23-27). IEEE. 10.1109/KST.2017.7886072

Mohammed, T. A., Ghareeb, A., Al-bayaty, H., & Aljawarneh, S. (2019, December). Big data challenges and achievements: applications on smart cities and energy sector. In *Proceedings of the Second International Conference on Data Science, E-Learning and Information Systems* (pp. 1-5). 10.1145/3368691.3368717

Mouchili, M. N., Aljawarneh, S., & Tchouati, W. (2018, October). Smart city data analysis. In *Proceedings of the First International Conference on Data Science, E-learning and Information Systems* (pp. 1-6). Academic Press.

Patel, R., & Patel, S. (2013). Survey on resource allocation strategies in cloud computing. *International Journal of Engineering Research & Technology (Ahmedabad)*, *2*(2), 1–5.

Sareen, P., Kumar, P., & Singh, T. D. (2015). Resource Allocation Strategies in Cloud Computing. *International Journal of Computer Science & Communication Networks*, *5*(6), 358–365.

Sheetal, A. P., & Ravindranath, K. (2019). Priority based resource allocation and scheduling using artificial bee colony (ABC) optimization for cloud computing systems. *International Journal of Innovative Technology and Exploring Engineering*, *8*(6), 39–44.

Sheetal, A. P., & Ravindranath, K. (2019). Priority based resource allocation and scheduling using artificial bee colony (ABC) optimization for cloud computing systems. *International Journal of Innovative Technology and Exploring Engineering*, *8*(6), 39–44.

Singh, A., Juneja, D., & Malhotra, M. (2017). A novel agent based autonomous and service composition framework for cost optimization of resource provisioning in cloud computing. *Journal of King Saud University-Computer and Information Sciences*, *29*(1), 19–28. doi:10.1016/j.jksuci.2015.09.001

Singh, P., & Dhiman, G. (2017, December). A fuzzy-LP approach in time series forecasting. In *International Conference on Pattern Recognition and Machine Intelligence* (pp. 243-253). Springer. 10.1007/978-3-319-69900-4_31

Song, Y., Sun, Y., & Shi, W. (2011). A two-tiered on-demand resource allocation mechanism for VM-based data centers. *IEEE Transactions on Services Computing*, *6*(1), 116–129. doi:10.1109/TSC.2011.41

Student, U. G. (2015). Dynamic resource allocation scheme in cloud computing. *Procedia Computer Science*, *47*, 30–36. doi:10.1016/j.procs.2015.03.180

Upadhye, G., & Dange, T. (2014, July). Cloud resource allocation as non-preemptive approach. In *Second International Conference on Current Trends In Engineering and Technology-ICCTET 2014* (pp. 352-356). IEEE. 10.1109/ICCTET.2014.6966314

Veeramallu, G. (2014). Dynamically Allocating the Resources Using Virtual Machines. *International Journal of Computer Science and Information Technologies*, *5*(3), 4646-4648.

Verma, S., Kaur, S., Dhiman, G., & Kaur, A. (2018, December). Design of a novel energy efficient routing framework for wireless nanosensor networks. In *2018 First International Conference on Secure Cyber Computing and Communication (ICSCCC)* (pp. 532-536). IEEE. 10.1109/ICSCCC.2018.8703308

Wang, W., Jiang, Y., & Wu, W. (2016). Multiagent-based resource allocation for energy minimization in cloud computing systems. *IEEE Transactions on Systems, Man, and Cybernetics. Systems*, *47*(2), 205–220. doi:10.1109/TSMC.2016.2523910

Weng, C. F., & Wang, K. (2012, August). Dynamic resource allocation for MMOGs in cloud computing environments. In *2012 8th International Wireless Communications and Mobile Computing Conference (IWCMC)* (pp. 142-146). IEEE. 10.1109/IWCMC.2012.6314192

Xiao, Z., Song, W., & Chen, Q. (2012). Dynamic resource allocation using virtual machines for cloud computing environment. *IEEE Transactions on Parallel and Distributed Systems*, *24*(6), 1107–1117. doi:10.1109/TPDS.2012.283

Section 3
Metaheuristic Approach and Cloud Security

Chapter 9

Task Scheduling in Cloud Computing Using Spotted Hyena Optimizer

Amandeep Kaur
Sri Guru Granth Sahib World University, India

Gaurav Dhiman
Government Bikram College of Commerce, India

Meenakshi Garg
Government Bikram College of Commerce, India

ABSTRACT

Cloud computing provides internet users with quick and efficient tools to access and share the data. One of the most important research problems that need to be addressed is the effective performance of cloud-based task scheduling. Different cloud-based task scheduling algorithms based on metaheuristic optimization techniques like genetic algorithm (GA) and particle swarm optimization (PSO) scheduling algorithms are demonstrated and analyzed. In this chapter, cloud computing based on the spotted hyena optimizer (SHO) is proposed with a novel task scheduling technique. SHO algorithm is population-based and inspired by nature's spotted hyenas to achieve global optimization over a given search space. The findings show that the suggested solution performs better than other competitor algorithms.

DOI: 10.4018/978-1-7998-5040-3.ch009

INTRODUCTION

Cloud-computing is a decentralized network. It provides the facilities to the users of internet by several service providers like Microsoft, Apple, Google, and Amazon etc. It used the internet technology to provide the scalable infrastructure leading to inconstant loads and versatile access to resources of computer. Most cloud computing work has centred on the efficacy of the task scheduling. Item phases on the effective routing of activities to suitable resources. In cloud computing, NP-complete problem is the best solution. Scheduling algorithm is based upon various strategies. The most important widely used techniques are time, price, strength, fault tolerance and quality of service (QoS) (Chandrashekar, 2015), (Almezeini & Hafez, 2017). For cloud systems, numerous scheduling algorithms like heuristic, Min-Min, Heterogeneous Earliest Finish Time (HEFT) (Masdari et. al, 2016), (Madni et. al, 2017), and Max-Minare used. Also, various metaheuristic algorithms for scheduling tasks have been developed to produce optimum schedules, like Particle Swarm Optimization (PSO) and Genetic Algorithm (GA) (Masdari et. al, 2016). The newly developed spotted hyena optimizer (SHO) (Dhiman & Kumar, 2017) is used in cloud environment for task scheduling in this chapter. SHO is an algorithm inspired by the sported hyena's natural behaviours. Using metaheuristics (Dhiman & Kumar, 2018), (Dhiman & Kumar, 2018), (Singh & Dhiman, 2018), (Dhiman & Kaur (2017), (Chandrawat et. al, 2017), (Singh & Dhiman, 2018), (Dhiman & Kumar, 2019), (Dhiman & Kumar, 2019), (Dhiman & Kaur (2019), (Dhiman & Kumar, 2019) researchers are attempted to develop the complex techniques in real life (Garg & Malhotra, 2017), (Garg et. al, 2018), (Garg et. al, 2019), (Garg et. al, 2019), (Garg et. al, 2019). A reasonable analysis is performed among the available algorithms, task scheduling using the PSO algorithm and GA is used to assess the efficiency of the algorithm being proposed. The main objective is the usage of a scheduling strategy for the cloud computing activities by using the SHO to reduce the overall resources of cloud and the implementation time of task (Al-Shargabi et al, 2020; Aljawarneh, 2012; Aljawarneh et al, 2017; Chehbi-Gamoura et al, 2018; Esposito et al, 2018; Jaswal et al, 2019; Kalpana et al, 2018; Lizcano et al, 2020; Malhotra et al, 2019; Mohammed et al, 2019; Mouchili et al, 2018; Singh,2011).

SPOTTED HYENA OPTIMIZER (SHO) BASED TASK SCHEDULING

In SHO algorithm, there are four important steps, that are stimulated by natural behaviours of the spotted hyena. The behaviours like hunting prey, searching prey, encircling prey, and attacking prey are as following. i

Encircling Prey

Encircling the prey is also called a target prey. In this the search agents will change their locations or positions according to the optimal solution. It is represented as follows:

$$\vec{D}_m = \left| \vec{B} \times \vec{P}_p(y) - \vec{P}(y) \right| \tag{1}$$

$$\vec{P}(y+1) = \vec{P}_p(y) - \vec{E} \times \vec{D}_m \tag{2}$$

where Dm is the distance vector in between the prey and the spotted hyena, y is the present iteration, Pp signifies the prey position vector, whereas P signifies the spotted hyena position vector, and B and E are the coefficient vector.

$$\vec{B} = 2 \times r\vec{d}_1 \tag{3}$$

$$\vec{E} = 2 \times \vec{m} \times r\vec{d}_2 - \vec{m} \tag{4}$$

$$\vec{m} = 5 - \left(Iteration \times \left(5 \, / \, Max_{Iteration} \right) \right), where\ Iteration = 0,1,2,...,Max_{Iteration} \tag{5}$$

Hunting

SHO's next move is hunting the prey strategy. For this, it make a cluster of optimal solutions in contrast to the finest search agent and updates other search agents i' positions. In this process the following equations will be described:

$$\vec{D}_m = \left| \vec{B} \times \vec{P}_m - \vec{P}_k \right| \tag{6}$$

$$\vec{P}_k = \vec{P}_m - \vec{E} \times \vec{D}_m \tag{7}$$

$$\vec{C}_m = \vec{P}_k + \vec{P}_{k+1} + ... + \vec{P}_{k+N} \qquad (8)$$

where Pm determines the first best spotted hyena location, P_k is the position of other spotted Ihyenas and N is the number of spotted hyenas are as following:

$$N = count_{ns}\left(\vec{P}_m, \vec{P}_{m+1}, \vec{P}_{m+2}, ..., \left(\vec{P}_m + \vec{M}\right)\right) \qquad (9)$$

where M is a random variable in the range i[i0.5, i1], ins is the number of solutions, and cm is the number of optimal solutions in category N.

Attacking Prey (Exploitation)

Now, there is a need to reduce the value of vector m for exploitation. The variance in E is decreased because of the change in the value of m, that can be decreased from 5 to 0 during the different iterations. The representation of the proposed SHO to attack action is as follows:

$$\vec{P}(y+1) = \frac{\vec{C}_m}{N} \qquad (10)$$

where P(y+1) saves the finest solution, and changes other search agent positions.

Search for Prey (Exploration)

The searching policy shows the algorithm's explorative ability. Therefore, the proposed SHO algorithm ensures the ability with E at random values i.e. more than 1 or less than 1. It is also the duty of vector B to demonstrate the SHO's with more unpredictable behaviour and prevent maximum local behaviour as shown in Fig. 1.

EXPERIMENTAL METHODOLOGY

In this, the proposed algorithm is implemented by the CloudSim and uses cloud network simulation, modeling, and observation tool (Buyya et. al, 2009). ClouSim's key nodes are data centres, servers, VMs, cloudlets, and brokers (Goyal et. al, 2012). The Datacenter is answerable for the creation of infrastructure resources. This serves as cloud service providers and composed of similar or dissimilar configuration server.

Figure 1. Searching and Attacking behaviours of spotted hyenas

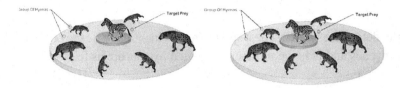

Host of datacenter describes the features of the physical resources like storage server or computing server and defined by the host, RAM, storage, bandwidth, processing power i.e. MIPS, and no. of processing elements etc. Host is responsible for the creation and handling of VM supply, VM migration and destruction of VMs. The VM is created on the host are VM I d, image size, RAM, bandwidth, MIPS and PE etc.

CloudSim are the functions of the Cloudlets that must be submitted in the cloud for processing. Cloudlet consumes a predefined length, input file size, and size of output file. Broker is an intermediator for user-to-cloud service provider. It maps client demands to the respective provider to ensure that the requirements for quality Within CloudSim, the CPU scheduling resources like PE is modelled onto the 2 levels: Host and VM. Each PE are shared between host-level VMs that run ion the server, called a VmScheduler, and is a variable for the host builder. Each VM splits the received resources at VM level and shared with every cloudlet that is running on the VM and called a Cloudlet-Scheduler.

There are 2 default strategies in both levels: one is space-shared and other is time-shared. Means, Vm-Scheduler and Cloudlet-Scheduler are present at any of these combinations. Vm-Scheduler: Time Shared and Cloudlet-Scheduler: you can use Space Shared, or vice versa. The same strategy may be extended to both schedulers as well. In Space Shared scheme, only one VM per cloudlet can be implemented at a time. It allows multiple VMs per cloudlets in Time Shared scheduling policy to multi-task and also run concurrently within a host per VM (Sidhu, 2014).

The cloud is modelled in CloudSim with one datacenter. Two hosts are created in the datacenter, out of which each host has the following configuration: RAM= i2048 MB, storage= i1 GB, and bandwidth= i10 Gbps. That VM contains the following characteristics: RAM= i512 MB with processing power ranges from i100-1000 MIPS, bandwidth= i1 Gbps, and having the image size= i10 GB. Cloudlet features include: file size= i300 MB, output file= i300 MB, and length varies from 1000 to i2000 MI. For our analysis both Vm Scheduler and Cloudlet-Scheduler used the Time-Shared law.

An analytical database will be generated at random. Cloudlets are generated having various lengths randomly from 1000 to 2000 million instructions i(MI). VMs are generated randomly with the capacity ranging from 100 million to 900 million instructions per second (MIPS). The value of services depending on the configuration of VM is as follows: $0.12, $0.13, $0.17, $0.48, $0.52, and $0.96 per hour. Table 1 (Madni et. al, 2017) shows the list of CloudSim parameters.

Table 1. Parameters of Cloudsim

Entity	Parameter	Values
Cloudlet	No. iof icloudlets	50-500
	Length	1000-2000
Virtual iMachine	No. iof iVMs	15
	RAM	512 iMB
	MIPS	100-1000
	Size	10000
	bandwidth	1000
	Policy itype	Time iShared
	VMM	Xen
	Operating iSystem	Linux
	No iof iCPUs	1
Host	No iof iHosts	2
	RAM	2048MB
	Storage	1000000
	Bandwidth	10000
	Policy itype	Time iShared
Data iCenter	No iof iData iCenter	2

EXPERIMENTAL METRICS

The performance is based on makespan, expense, average use, and imbalance degree. The quality metrics listed below are (Madni et. al, 2017), (Almezeini & Hafez, 2017):

Makespan

It measures the overall time to complete by calculating the completion time of the last mission. To Minimize the Makespan is the most common optimisation criterion for the task scheduling and determined with the following formula:

Makepan i= $\max_{taski} i(Fn_{time})$

Where, Fn_{Time} is the ioncluding time of task i.

Cost

It is the total payment amount of the resource utilization to the cloud provider. Cloud provider's main purpose is to increase income and cloud user's purpose is to decrease costs with effective use. The formula to calculate the cost is as follows:

Cost i= $\sum_{resource\ ii} (c_i * t_i)$

Where, Ci shows the cost of VM_i/time unit and T_i represents the time for VM_i utilization.

Average Utilization

To maximize the resource usage is one more significant criterion for cloud providers by keeping the resources as busy as possible to make more profit. The formula to measure average utilization is as follows:

Average Utilization i= $\sum_{i=1}^{n}$ Execution time of resource i/Makespan * n

where, n represents the total number of resources.

Degree of Imbalance

It refers to the distribution of the amount of load between VMs with respect to the capacity for execution. DI's small value shows the system's load is more balanced. It is calculated by:

DI = T_{max} i-T_{min}/T_{avg}

Where, T_{max}, T_{min}, and T_{avg} are the max, min, and avg. time of execution of all VMs.

RESULTS AND EVALUATION

Comparison with planning algorithms, based on two common metaheuristic algorithms: PSO and GA (Ibrahim et. al, 2016), (Ibrahim et. al, 2017). In all instances the size of the population is 100 and there are 100 variants. Such algorithms are compared by size, cost, average resource utilization and degree of imbalance. Fig. 2 shows comparison of SHO, PSO and GA makepan. The x-axis is the number of cloudlets, and the y-axis is the makepan. If the number of clouds is smaller, the mapping of the three algorithms converges.

However, SHO produces even better time of makepan when the number of cloudlets increases. In the fig. 3, cost differences are shown between SHO, PSO and GA. The x-axis represents the number of tasks and the y-axis indicates the magnitude of the tasks per hour. The results show that between PSO and GA is the cost of SHO, although the difference does not matter.

Figure 2. Comparison results of Makespan

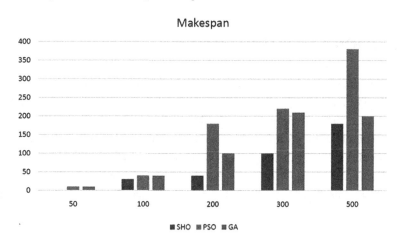

Fig. 4 displays a comparison between SHO, PSO and GA for the average use of resources and when compared to PSO and GA, SHO provides a very high resource utilization. Fig. 5 explains the comparison between SHO, PSO and GA of the degree of imbalance. The x-axis refers to the number of clouds and the y-axis to the point of disequilibrium. The results of the analysis show that the SHO is significantly higher than PSO and GA. It is obvious that the SHO-based task planning algorithm is highly efficient and results much better than the other two algorithms. Through high-performance task planning, it can tackle optimization issues, because the solution finds the optimum solution using different approaches. They have their own strategies to find the optimal solution, as previously explained, and each solution has a particular gender and is classified as resident or nomads.

Figure 3. Comparison results of Cost

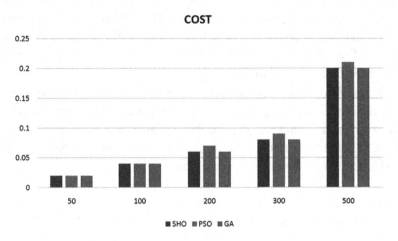

CONCLUSION AND FUTURE WORKS

The development of cloud computing for task scheduling techniques involves different structured metaheuristic algorithms. A new cloud task scheduling algorithm based on the SHO concept, which is a newly built lion life style based algorithm, has been proposed. The efficiency of the proposed algorithm has been compared with that of the PSO and GA metaheuristic algorithms. The consequence in the reduction of maquilas and the degree of mismatch has been exceptional. The organization has also used capital exceptionally. In future work we are aimed at increasing the proposed algorithm by using cloud pricing models to reduce tasks on cloud resources

Figure 4. Results of average resource utilization

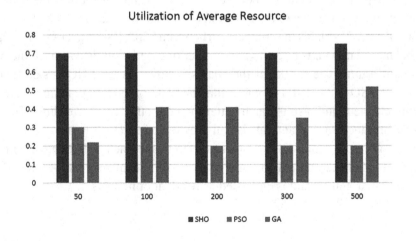

Figure 5. Results of degree of Imbalance

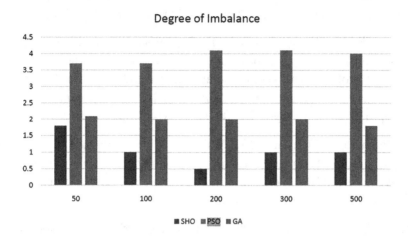

and various complex real-life engineering issues (Singh & Dhiman, 2017), (Kaur & Dhiman 2019), (Dhiman, 2019),),(Dhiman, 2019),),(Dhiman, 2020),(Dhiman & Kaur, 2019), Dhiman et. al, 2019), (Garg & Malhotra, 2017), (Garg et. al, 2018), (Garg et. al, 2019), (Garg et. al, 2019), (Garg et. al, 2019).

REFERENCES

Al-Shargabi, B., AlJawarneh, S., & Hayajneh, S. M. (2020). A cloudlet based security and trust model for e-government web services. *Journal of Theoretical and Applied Information Technology, 98*(1), 27–37.

Aljawarneh, S. (Ed.). (2012). *Cloud computing advancements in design, implementation, and technologies.* IGI Global.

Aljawarneh, S., & Malhotra, M. (Eds.). (2017). *Critical Research on Scalability and Security Issues in Virtual Cloud Environments.* IGI Global.

Almezeini, N., & Hafez, A. (2017). Task scheduling in cloud computing using lion optimization algorithm. *Algorithms, 5,* 7.

Buyya, R., Ranjan, R., & Calheiros, R. N. (2009, June). Modeling and simulation of scalable Cloud computing environments and the CloudSim toolkit: Challenges and opportunities. In *2009 international conference on high performance computing & simulation* (pp. 1-11). IEEE.

Chandrashekar, D. P. (2015). *Robust and fault-tolerant scheduling for scientific workflows in cloud computing environments* (Doctoral dissertation).

Chandrawat, R. K., Kumar, R., Garg, B. P., Dhiman, G., & Kumar, S. (2017). An analysis of modeling and optimization production cost through fuzzy linear programming problem with symmetric and right angle triangular fuzzy number. In *Proceedings of Sixth International Conference on Soft Computing for Problem Solving* (pp. 197-211). Springer. 10.1007/978-981-10-3322-3_18

Chehbi-Gamoura, S., Derrouiche, R., Malhotra, M., & Koruca, H. I. (2018, June). Adaptive management approach for more availability of big data business analytics. In *Proceedings of the Fourth International Conference on Engineering & MIS 2018* (pp. 1-8). 10.1145/3234698.3234758

Dhiman, G. (2019a). ESA: A hybrid bio-inspired metaheuristic optimization approach for engineering problems. *Engineering with Computers*, 1–31. doi:10.100700366-019-00826-w

Dhiman, G. (2019b). *Multi-objective Metaheuristic Approaches for Data Clustering in Engineering Application (s)* (Doctoral dissertation).

Dhiman, G. (2020). MOSHEPO: A hybrid multi-objective approach to solve economic load dispatch and micro grid problems. *Applied Intelligence*, *50*(1), 119–137. doi:10.100710489-019-01522-4

Dhiman, G., & Kaur, A. (2017, December). Spotted hyena optimizer for solving engineering design problems. In *2017 international conference on machine learning and data science (MLDS)* (pp. 114-119). IEEE.

Dhiman, G., & Kaur, A. (2018). Optimizing the design of airfoil and optical buffer problems using spotted hyena optimizer. *Designs*, *2*(3), 28.

Dhiman, G., & Kaur, A. (2019). A hybrid algorithm based on particle swarm and spotted hyena optimizer for global optimization. In *Soft Computing for Problem Solving* (pp. 599–615). Springer. doi:10.1007/978-981-13-1592-3_47

Dhiman, G., & Kaur, A. (2019). STOA: A bio-inspired based optimization algorithm for industrial engineering problems. *Engineering Applications of Artificial Intelligence*, *82*, 148–174. doi:10.1016/j.engappai.2019.03.021

Dhiman, G., & Kumar, V. (2017). Spotted hyena optimizer: A novel bio-inspired based metaheuristic technique for engineering applications. *Advances in Engineering Software*, *114*, 48–70. doi:10.1016/j.advengsoft.2017.05.014

Dhiman, G., & Kumar, V. (2018). Emperor penguin optimizer: A bio-inspired algorithm for engineering problems. *Knowledge-Based Systems, 159*, 20–50. doi:10.1016/j.knosys.2018.06.001

Dhiman, G., & Kumar, V. (2018). Multi-objective spotted hyena optimizer: A multi-objective optimization algorithm for engineering problems. *Knowledge-Based Systems, 150*, 175–197. doi:10.1016/j.knosys.2018.03.011

Dhiman, G., & Kumar, V. (2019). KnRVEA: A hybrid evolutionary algorithm based on knee points and reference vector adaptation strategies for many-objective optimization. *Applied Intelligence, 49*(7), 2434–2460. doi:10.100710489-018-1365-1

Dhiman, G., & Kumar, V. (2019). Seagull optimization algorithm: Theory and its applications for large-scale industrial engineering problems. *Knowledge-Based Systems, 165*, 169–196. doi:10.1016/j.knosys.2018.11.024

Dhiman, G., & Kumar, V. (2019). Spotted hyena optimizer for solving complex and non-linear constrained engineering problems. In *Harmony search and nature inspired optimization algorithms* (pp. 857–867). Springer. doi:10.1007/978-981-13-0761-4_81

Esposito, C., Su, X., Aljawarneh, S. A., & Choi, C. (2018). Securing collaborative deep learning in industrial applications within adversarial scenarios. *IEEE Transactions on Industrial Informatics, 14*(11), 4972–4981. doi:10.1109/TII.2018.2853676

Garg, M., & Malhotra, M. (2017). Retrieval of Images on the Basis of Content: A Survey. *International Journal of Engineering Development and Research, 5*, 757–760.

Garg, M., Malhotra, M., & Singh, H. (2018). Statistical Feature Based Image Classification and Retrieval Using Trained Neural Classifiers. *International Journal of Applied Engineering Research: IJAER, 13*(8), 5766–5771.

Garg, M., Malhotra, M., & Singh, H. (2019). A Novel CBIR-Based System using Texture Fused LBP Variants and GLCM Features. *International Journal of Innovative Technology and Exploring Engineering, 9*(2), 1247–1257.

Garg, M., Malhotra, M., & Singh, H. (2019). Comparison of deep learning techniques on content-based image retrieval. *Modern Physics Letters A, 34*, 1950285. doi:10.1142/S0217732319502857

Garg, M., Singh, H., & Malhotra, M. (2019). Fuzzy-NN approach with statistical features for description and classification of efficient image retrieval. *Modern Physics Letters A, 34*(3), 1950022. doi:10.1142/S0217732319500226

Goyal, T., Singh, A., & Agrawal, A. (2012). Cloudsim: Simulator for cloud computing infrastructure and modeling. *Procedia Engineering, 38*, 3566–3572.

Ibrahim, E., El-Bahnasawy, N. A., & Omara, F. A. (2016, March). Task scheduling algorithm in cloud computing environment based on cloud pricing models. In *2016 World Symposium on Computer Applications & Research (WSCAR)* (pp. 65-71). IEEE. 10.1109/WSCAR.2016.20

Ibrahim, E., El-Bahnasawy, N. A., & Omara, F. A. (2017). Load Balancing Scheduling Algorithm in Cloud Computing System with Cloud Pricing Comparative Study. *Menoufia Journal of Electronic Engineering Research, 26*(1), 129–152.

Jaswal, S., & Malhotra, M. (2019, December). A detailed analysis of trust models in cloud environment. In *Proceedings of the Second International Conference on Data Science, E-Learning and Information Systems* (pp. 1-5). 10.1145/3368691.3368740

Kalpana, G., Kumar, P. V., Aljawarneh, S., & Krishnaiah, R. V. (2018). Shifted adaption homomorphism encryption for mobile and cloud learning. *Computers & Electrical Engineering, 65*, 178–195. doi:10.1016/j.compeleceng.2017.05.022

Kalra, M., & Singh, S. (2015). A review of metaheuristic scheduling techniques in cloud computing. *Egyptian Informatics Journal, 16*(3), 275-295.

Kaur, A., & Dhiman, G. (2019). A review on search-based tools and techniques to identify bad code smells in object-oriented systems. In *Harmony search and nature inspired optimization algorithms* (pp. 909–921). Springer. doi:10.1007/978-981-13-0761-4_86

Lizcano, D., Lara, J. A., White, B., & Aljawarneh, S. (2020). Blockchain-based approach to create a model of trust in open and ubiquitous higher education. *Journal of Computing in Higher Education, 32*(1), 109–134. doi:10.100712528-019-09209-y

Madni, S. H. H., Abd Latiff, M. S., Abdullahi, M., Abdulhamid, S. I. M., & Usman, M. J. (2017). Performance comparison of heuristic algorithms for task scheduling in IaaS cloud computing environment. *PLoS One, 12*(5), e0176321. doi:10.1371/journal.pone.0176321 PMID:28467505

Madni, S. H. H., Abd Latiff, M. S., Abdullahi, M., Abdulhamid, S. I. M., & Usman, M. J. (2017). Performance comparison of heuristic algorithms for task scheduling in IaaS cloud computing environment. *PLoS One, 12*(5), e0176321. doi:10.1371/journal.pone.0176321 PMID:28467505

Malhotra, M., & Singh, A. (2019). Role of Agents to Enhance the Security and Scalability in Cloud Environment. In Cloud Security: Concepts, Methodologies, Tools, and Applications (pp. 552-573). IGI Global. doi:10.4018/978-1-5225-8176-5.ch028

Masdari, M., ValiKardan, S., Shahi, Z., & Azar, S. I. (2016). Towards workflow scheduling in cloud computing: A comprehensive analysis. *Journal of Network and Computer Applications*, *66*, 64–82. doi:10.1016/j.jnca.2016.01.018

Mehmi, Verma, & Sangal. (2017). Simulation modeling of cloud computing for smart grid using CloudSim. *J. Electr. Syst. Inf. Technol.*, *4*(1), 159–172.

Mohammed, T. A., Ghareeb, A., Al-bayaty, H., & Aljawarneh, S. (2019, December). Big data challenges and achievements: applications on smart cities and energy sector. In *Proceedings of the Second International Conference on Data Science, E-Learning and Information Systems* (pp. 1-5). 10.1145/3368691.3368717

Mouchili, M. N., Aljawarneh, S., & Tchouati, W. (2018, October). Smart city data analysis. In *Proceedings of the First International Conference on Data Science, E-learning and Information Systems* (pp. 1-6). Academic Press.

Sidhu, H. S. (2014). Comparative analysis of scheduling algorithms of Cloudsim in cloud computing. *International Journal of Computers and Applications*, *975*, 8887.

Singh, A., Juneja, D., & Malhotra, M. (2017). A novel agent based autonomous and service composition framework for cost optimization of resource provisioning in cloud computing. *Journal of King Saud University-Computer and Information Sciences*, *29*(1), 19–28. doi:10.1016/j.jksuci.2015.09.001

Singh, P., & Dhiman, G. (2017, December). A fuzzy-LP approach in time series forecasting. In *International Conference on Pattern Recognition and Machine Intelligence* (pp. 243-253). Springer. 10.1007/978-3-319-69900-4_31

Singh, P., & Dhiman, G. (2018). A hybrid fuzzy time series forecasting model based on granular computing and bio-inspired optimization approaches. *Journal of Computational Science*, *27*, 370–385. doi:10.1016/j.jocs.2018.05.008

Singh, P., & Dhiman, G. (2018). Uncertainty representation using fuzzy-entropy approach: Special application in remotely sensed high-resolution satellite images (RSHRSIs). *Applied Soft Computing*, *72*, 121–139. doi:10.1016/j.asoc.2018.07.038

Chapter 10
Impacts and Challenges of Cost–Effective Approaches Using Hybrid Cloud Infrastructure Model in Business Analytics

Yogesh Madhukar Ghorpade
Bharathiar University, India

R. Kamatchi Iyer
ISME School of Management and Entrepreneurship, India

ABSTRACT

The cost-effective methodology and its implementation are the primary approaches towards cost computing to bring effectiveness with the proper requirements and provide the proper solution. This chapter focuses on the discussion about the cost-effective method using cloud infrastructure model for building and management of on-premise with the off-premise cloud service provider in business analytics. This chapter also elaborates the methodology undertaken and design considerations for implementation of cloud infrastructure with non-virtualized and on-premise infrastructure environment. The experiment using YGCIS (YG-cloud infrastructure solution) methodology is built for business analytics platform where infrastructure and its resources play a vital role. The cost-effective approach for total cost ownership (TCO) is implemented using YGCCS (YG-cost computing solution) framework. Thus, the solution obtained after implementing the above frameworks increases ROI % and reduces the TCO, impacting the business analytics needs.

DOI: 10.4018/978-1-7998-5040-3.ch010

INTRODUCTION

The cost-effective methodology and its implementation are primary approach towards cost computing to bring effectiveness with the proper requirements and provides proper solution. The productive learning with different approach is the vital requirement for today's Cloud infrastructure building from student's perspective needs to be understood (Yogesh et al., 2012-15). The technology that is used for the experiments are open-source and Proprietary.

This chapter focuses on the cost-effective approach using cloud infrastructure model for building and management of on-premises with off-premises cloud service providers for educational infrastructure. The chapter also elaborates about methodology undertaken and design considerations for implementation of cloud infrastructure with non-virtualized, and on-premises infrastructure environment.

BACKGROUND

Need for Cloud Infrastructure

As per IDC the Cloud computing spending grew at 4.5 times the rate of IT spending since 2009. It is expected to grow more than six times in 2015 through 2020 (CS YEO et al., 2006). The requirement and building of advance lab in Academic for Cloud infrastructure building is a major challenge and it impacts student's productive learning. There are some courses in computer science stream such as cloud computing, advance cloud computing, cloud solution (Al-Shargabi et al, 2020; Aljawarneh, 2012; Aljawarneh et al, 2017; Chehbi-Gamoura et al, 2018; Esposito et al, 2018; Jaswal et al, 2019; Kalpana et al, 2018; Lizcano et al, 2020; Malhotra et al, 2019; Mohammed et al, 2019; Mouchili et al, 2018; Singh,2011).

This cloud courses consists the topics such as TCO, ROI, computing methodology, where hands-on approach is unavailable (Y. Lee and A. Zomaya, 2009; R. Moreno-Vozmediano et al., 2012).

Due to this disadvantage there is lack in labs building and creating advance lab for best productive learning (Amy Apon et al., 2004; AVANADE, 2009; Barham P et al., 2003). If this learning is developed by students, and then they must face major challenges in industries on pro-duction operations. As per the expanding digital transformation in IT infrastructure is observed, it is lacking in Indian academic organization. Further this challenge should not lose the carrier opportunities and proper direction toward the domain work as per academic concern (Do More for Less, 2008; Mark Peters, 2012; "IT Value Transformation Road Map Vision, Value, and Virtualization", 2000; Ana-Ramona Bologa and Razvan Bologa., 2011).

MAIN FOCUS OF THE CHAPTER

Cloud Infrastructure Deployment Model

The Cloud deployment model plays a vital role in Cloud Infrastructure building (Barham P, et al., 2003; Behrend Tara S and Wiebe Eric N, 2011; Cs Yeo and R Buyya, 2006). The On-premise private cloud is built in the premises of the enterprise as shown in Figure 1. The important components in On-premise private cloud infrastructure are enterprise resources such as hardware, hypervisor which creates virtual machines for deployment of operating system, applications; network with proper high computing servers as shown in Figure 1.

Figure 1. Cloud Infrastructure Architecture

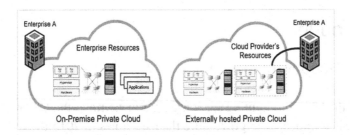

Cloud Infrastructure Building: Implementing 'YGCIS' Methodology

In, private cloud infrastructure the resource availability is the major challenge, if not meet than it becomes critical for the enterprise to provide better solution. The challenge can be mitigated using the public cloud infrastructure, where the availability is not the concern but well planning for the resource utilization is important. For, implementation of the experiment in academic environment the 'YGCIS' [YG-Cloud Infrastructure Solution] methodology is built as shown in Figure 2. Each student has a cluster access with available VM with the host machine that is connected through network. The experiment using 'YGCIS' methodology is built for advance lab where infrastructure and its resources play a vital role (Beloglazov Anton et.al., 2010).

TCO: Using 'YGCCS' Methodology for Cost Effective Approach

The cost-effective approach for Total Cost Ownership [TCO] is implemented using 'YGCCS' [YG-Cost Computing Solution] framework as shown in Figure

3. The framework consists of three stages. The first stage is for building of TCO computing framework using parameters such as core requirement, compute, storage, network, and IT labor by collecting required information from different enterprise and different vendors.

The second stage is for infrastructure testing for different vendor's i.e. collecting all the cost details and making different categories as per the stage 1 and computing the cost. The last stage is predicting analysis obtained through stage 2 for cost effectiveness by different computing methods as shown in Figure 3. Thus, the result obtained by implementing 'YGCCS' methodology is cost effective or not needs to be well observed and computed.

Implementation section covers cloud infrastructure implementation on On-premises, public cloud with proper configuration, checklist, and testing of lab requirement.

Following are the components present and used in the 'YGCCS' Methodology:

- Compute Resources
- Host Machine
- VM Cluster
- Hypervisor Type I or Type II
- Network Devices
- Cloud Service Provider
- Datacenter and Software Defined Datacenter (SDDC)
- Storage internal and external

Figure 2. VM Cluster and VM Host

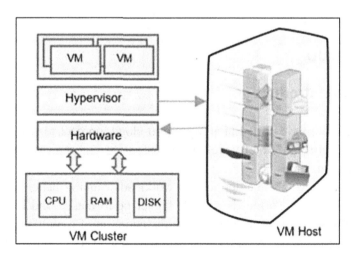

The On-premise infrastructure resources is seen in above figure 2. Where the host machine is connected with VM cluster.

Figure 3. 'YGCIS' Methodology: Cloud Infrastructure Building

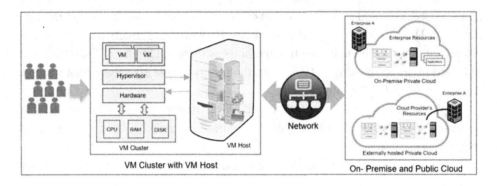

Figure 4. 'YGCCS' Methodology Framework for cost Effective Approach in TCO.

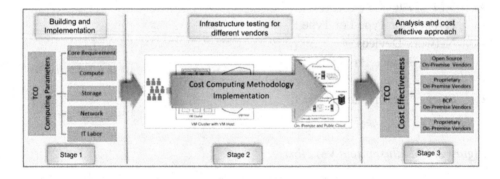

MULTI-CLOUD

Multi-Cloud Introduction

Many organization have started adopting a multi-cloud approach to meet the business demands since no single cloud model can suit the varied requirements and workloads across the organizations.

This section covers some application workloads running better on one cloud platform while other workloads achieve higher performance and lower cost on another platform. The chapter also covers the adoption of a multi-cloud strategy, organizations can choose services from different cloud service providers to create the best possible solution for their business. This chapter also covers how the infrastructure implementation is carried out for academic environment for cost-effectiveness implementation of multi-cloud strategy. The comparison between on premise data-center with public cloud providers are measured and calculated.

Multi-Cloud Architecture

A single heterogeneous architecture is the key feature of multi-cloud. As multi-cloud environments use a broad spectrum of various deployment models, it is difficult to pinpoint a single reference architecture that can serve as a blueprint for all conceivable multi-cloud implementations. Multi-cloud architecture should be able to quickly evolve in order to support new digital initiatives, such as Big Data analytics, IoT platforms, and AI that will impose new service requirements.

While requirements for multi-cloud architecture are determined by the application portfolio that is unique for every company, some common patterns can be identified.

1. Multi-Cloud Adoption Strategy

Organic cloud adoption by different groups within the same organization commonly creates a shadow IT and results in using various cloud providers in a multi-cloud environment. Hence, the organization has become a multi-cloud user, but it happened without any IT governance.

Figure 5. Multi-Cloud Architecture

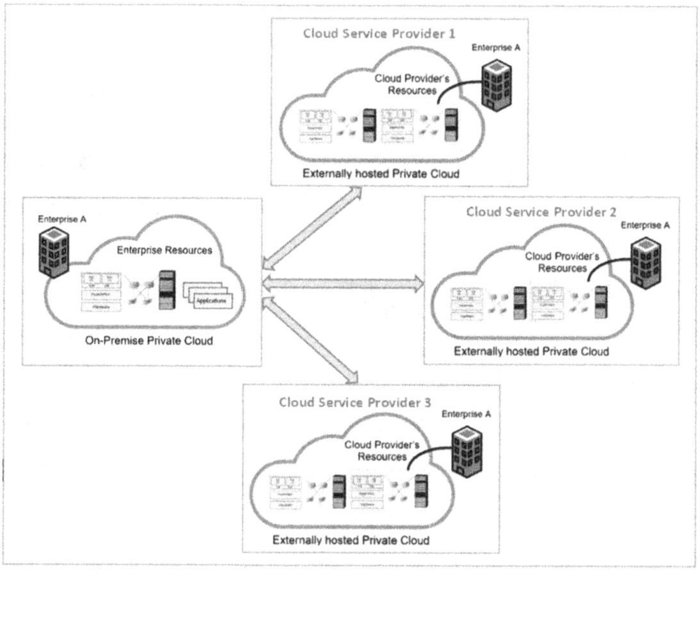

Figure 6. Multi-Cloud Adoption Strategy

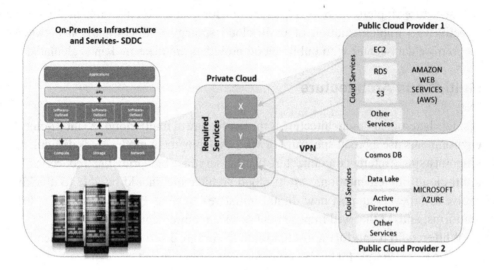

2. Disaster Recovery in Multi-Cloud

It is observed that disaster plays a vital role in Multi-cloud due to adoption strategy to adopt the available resources at the failure time. This adoption strategy for failure or disaster recovery can be utilized using multi region and multi zone using cloud service provider. The snapshots, replicas, RAID are the functionalities carried out in these CSP's for disaster recovery as shown in the below figure.

Figure 7. Fail Over: Private Cloud

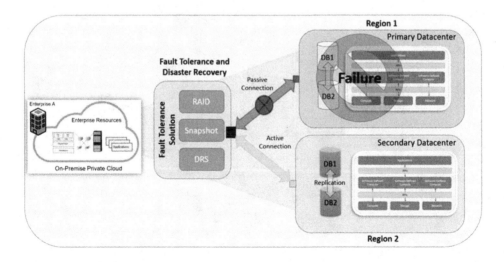

Figure 8. Fail Over: Multi-Cloud

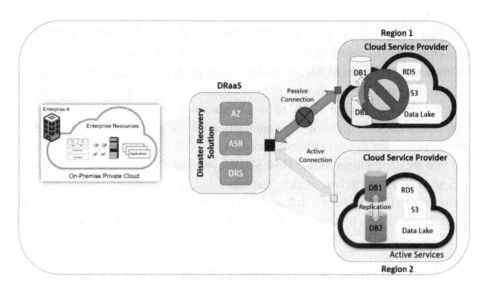

3. VMware Cloud on AWS

VMware Cloud on AWS allows you to create vSphere data centers on Amazon Web Services. These vSphere data centers include vCenter Server for managing your data center, vSAN for storage, and VMware NSX for networking.

Figure 9. VMware Cloud on AWS

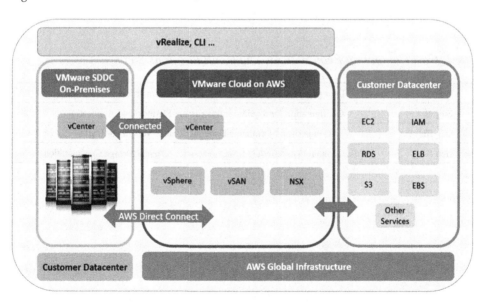

Using Hybrid Linked Mode, you can connect an on-premises data center to your cloud SDDC, and managed both from a single vSphere Client interface. Using your connected AWS account, you can access AWS services such as EC2 and S3 from virtual machines in your SDDC.

When you deploy an SDDC on VMware Cloud on AWS, it is created within an AWS account and VPC dedicated to your organization and managed by VMware. You must also connect the SDDC to an AWS account belonging to you, referred to as the customer AWS account. This connection allows your SDDC to access AWS services belonging to your customer account.

If you are deploying a Single Host SDDC, you can delay linking your customer AWS account for up to two weeks. You cannot scale up a Single Host SDDC to a multiple host SDDC until you link an AWS account. If you are deploying a multiple host SDDC, you must link your customer AWS account when you deploy the SDDC.

COST COMPUTING REQUIREMENTS AND CONFIGURATIONS

Introduction

This topic focuses on the cost computing requirements and configurations. These requirements and configuration are represented in the form of tables for the implemented models of virtualization, cloud infrastructure, non-virtualized, and on-premise infrastructure for the provided academic environment.

Various design consideration in cost computing and configuration are identified. Box 1 shows the steps which are used for computing cost requirements and configurations for the provided infrastructure environment.

Box 1. Cost Computing Requirements and Configurations Steps

Step I	Data requirement gathering from different Infrastructure Resources
Step II	Configuration for required Infrastructure Platform and Application
Step III	Comparison of available Data of Different Vendors or CSP's
Step IV	Cost Computing and finding Effectiveness for different Design Consideration

SDDC Configuration

See Table 1.

Table 1. Total Cost of Ownership for Software Defined Data-Center (SDDC)

	On-Premises	Vendor 1		Vendor 2	
	YGPSDDI $	VMware (INR)	VMware $	Microsoft (INR)	Microsoft $
Capital Expenses					
Servers (12 VM)	27692	2,541,500	39,100	5,083,000	78,200
Storage	5662	195,000	3,000	650,000	10,000
Networking	4432	422,500	6,500	422,500	6,500
Virtualization Platform software	15,543	1,532,375	23,575	1,406,730	21,642
Total HW and Virt SW	**53,329**	**4,691,375**	**72,175**	**7,562,230**	**116,342**
Host Windows Server &SQL Server licenses, other open source	10586	1,800,630	27,702	3,601,260	55,404
Third-party software licenses	0	0	0	421,590	6,486
Total CapEx cost	**63,915**	**6,492,005**	**99,877**	**11,585,080**	**178,232**
		6,492,005	99,877	**0**	
Operating Expenses (3 years)					
Power and cooling	3078	326,625	5,025	653,315	10,051
Data center space	5313	1,526,850	23,490	1,526,850	23,490
Virtualization software support	2324	1,011,595	15,563	1,420,120	21,848
Windows Server &SQL Server Host software support	8000	1,350,505	20,777	2,700,945	41,553
Third-party software support	0	0	0	234,000	3,600
IT administrative time cost	11223	446,875	6,875	4,002,245	61,573
Third-party SW integration	0	0	0	139,165	2,141
Total OpEx cost	**29,938**	**4,662,450**	**71,730**	**10,676,640**	**164,256**
Totals	93,853	**11,154,455**	171,607	**22,261,720**	342,488
Cost per workload VM	7821.11	929,565	14301	1,855,165	28541
% VMware savings over Microsoft solution		**50.11**			

TCO for SDDC: YGPSDDI

See Table 2.

Table 2. Cost effective TCO for SDDC: Experiment Hands ON

Overall Effectiveness			
	YGPSDDI	**VMware**	**Microsoft**
Required Time [T]	66.67	33.33	26.67
Resource Utilization [R]	90.00	60.00	30.00
Space Utilization [S]	50.00	30.00	25.00
Eff. Avg of TRS	68.89	41.11	27.22
Exp. Hands ON [H]	73.06	50.00	73.44
Productive Learning [P]	75.00	73.33	61.67
Average of Learning Effective	74.03	61.67	67.56
Avg of Total Cost Effective	71.38	52.49	10.43
Average of All Effectiveness	71.43	51.76	35.07

Cloud Configuration

Batch Lab Configuration Requirement

See Table 3.

Table 3. Batch lab configuration for 'YGCIS' Methodology

Batch Lab Configuration Requirement				
Sr.	**LAB Configuration**	**Group**	**Each Student**	**Each VM**
1	Students	30	1	0
2	VM	100	3	1
3	CPU	180	6	2
4	RAM [GB]	300	10	3.5
5	Storage [GB]	5000	150	50
6	NW [Bandwidth MB]- OP	5000	167	50
7	NW [Bandwidth MB]- CV	1000	30	10
8	Backup for BCP [GB]	1000	33	11
9	Archive for Data Protection	500	16.5	5.5

TCO Primary Requirement Details for On-Premises and Cloud Vendors

See Table 4.

Table 4. TCO Primary requirement details for On-Premises and Cloud Vendors

TCO Primary Requirement Details for On-Premises and Cloud Vendors			
Layer	**Components**	**Type I**	**Type II**
Core Requirement	TCO- Basic / Advance	Advance	Advance
	Currency- INR	INR	INR
	Environment Type- On-Premises / Colocation	On-Premises	Colocation
	Region- Datacenter / Service Provider	Asia Pacific	Asia Pacific
	Workload Type- General / Other	General	General
	Manual Input	Yes	Yes
	Servers [Physical Servers / Virtual Machines]	VM	VM
Compute	Compute- Service Category [DB / Non-DB]	DB	DB
	Environment- Physical / VM	One Region	Multi Region
	Operating System [Guest OS]	Open Source OS	Window OS and Open Source OS
	VM's	100	100
	Virtualization- Hypervisor	VMware / Xen KVM	VMware, Hyper-V
	Virtualization- Host	Host- CPU, Core & RAM	Host- CPU, Core & RAM
	Cores	2 to 5	2 to 5
	RAM [GB]	3.5	3.5
	Optimization [CPU/RAM]	RAM	CPU & RAM
Storage	Storage Type FSAN, NAS, Local Disk, Object, BLOB]	SAN	SAN
	Disk Type [HDD, SDD]	HDD	HDD
	Capacity [Raw Storage]	50-65	65
	Backup %	30-50%	100% [Business Continuity] 10 TB
	Archive	10-20%	40-60%
	GRS Geo Redundant Storage [Enable or Not]	No	Yes
NW	Networking Bandwidth [On Premise]	1 Gbps	1 Gbps
	Bandwidth [Datacenter Bandwidth]	5 Gbps	5 Gbps
IT Labor	Burdened Annual Salary [Administrator and Datacenter Staff]	Average	Average
	Number of VMs per Admin	200	200

Open Source Use: On-Premise Vs. Cloud Vendors

See Tables 5 and 6.

Table 5. Type I- Open Source use: On-Premises vs. Cloud vendors

		On-Premises Vendors		Cloud Vendors	
Sr	**TCO Comp Parameters**	**Vendor 1 Cost [₹]**	**Vendor 2 Cost [₹]**	**Vendor 1 Cost [₹]**	**Vendor 2 Cost [₹]**
1	Compute	92,275,509	52,552,478	29,912,200	22,743,849
2	Data center	4,532,385	4,234,485	0	0
3	Networking	16,420,735	3,265,370	0	0
4	Storage	9,454,058	14,749,083	3,551,054	6,466,046
5	IT labor	7,433,194	6,722,334	3,795,591	3,765,761
	Total cost	130,115,881	81,523,750	37,258,845	32,975,656

Table 6. Type II- Proprietary use and BCP: On-Premises vs. Cloud vendors

		On-Premises Vendors		Cloud Vendor	
Sr	**TCO Comp Parameters**	**Vendor 1 Cost [₹]**	**Vendor 2 Cost [₹]**	**Vendor 1 Cost [₹]**	**Vendor 2 Cost [₹]**
1	Compute	32,708,866	29,619,561	27,701,598	0
2	Data center	5,476,405	4,234,485	0	0
3	Networking	938,010	505,200	0	12,180,764
4	Storage	29,279,740	26,070,306	6,961,494	16,965,971
5	IT labor	159,233	130,008	58,865	600,000
	Total cost	68,562,254	60,559,560	34,721,957	29,746,735

COST COMPUTING ANALYSIS

Introduction

This topic focuses on the methodologies undertaken for equations building, and obtaining final equations for implemented models for virtualization, cloud infrastructure, non-virtualized, and on-premise infrastructure environment. This chapter also provides the final equation which are used for cost effective calculation of TCO and ROI.

Private Datacenter Infrastructure: YGPDI Model

Implementation section 'on premises' covers 'YGPDI' type 1 methodology, which is used for implementing basic operation in infrastructure building of virtualization and to develop fundamental skills in students with higher cost-effective approach utilizing old resources. The 'on premises' also covers 'YGPDI' Type 2 methodology which is used for implementing advance operation in infrastructure building of private datacenter and to develop operational skills in students with cost effective approach utilizing new and old resources.

Analysis section covers computing of TCO of 'on premises' with 'off premises' methodology for building of datacenter infrastructure using infrastructure or cloud service providers (CSP) like VMware and Microsoft. The result section in analysis covers cost effective and best methodology approach for different requirement and operational needs.

Total cost of ownership (TCO) is the sum of all cost items separated into capital expenditures (CapEx) and operating expenditures (OpEx) over a selected period, and cost per virtual machine (VM) as that amount divided by the number of virtual machines in the environment [6]. Appendix 3 is the checklist for variable value for all equations, required for computing.

Capital Expenses Equation (CapEx)

For private datacenter infrastructure the capital expenses with respect to new and available old infrastructure are as follows:

$$CapEx_{(NEW)} = \sum\left(\sum H_{HW} + \sum H_{NW} + \sum H_{St} + \sum V_{SW(lic)} + \sum H_{OS(lic)} + \sum TP_{(lic)}\right)_{i=1,n} \qquad (1)$$

$$CapEx_{(OLD)} = \sum\left(\sum H_{HW} + \sum H_{NW} + \sum H_{St} + \sum V_{SW(lic)} + \sum H_{OS(lic)} + \sum TP_{(lic)}\right)_{i=1,n} \qquad (2)$$

$$CapEx_{(EFF)} = [CapEx_{(OLD)} - CapEx_{(NEW)}] + OT_{(REQ)} \qquad (3)$$

Where H_{HW} is Host hardware server cost; H_{NW} is Host networking hardware costs; H_{St} is Host storage costs; $V_{SW(lic)}$ is Virtualization software license costs; $H_{OS(lic)}$ is Host operating system license costs; $TP_{(lic)}$ is Applicable third-party license costs; $CapEx_{(NEW)}$ is Capital Expenditure for new infrastructure, OLD is old infrastructure,

EFF is cost effective infrastructure; $OT_{(REQ)}$ is other cost required while building physical datacenter.

Operating Expenses Equation (OpEx)

$$OpEx_{(NEW)} = \sum(\sum PC + \sum DC_{SP} + \sum Sc(\sum V_{SW} + \sum H_{OS} + \sum(n * \sum G_{OS}) +$$

$$\sum TP_{SW}) + \sum TP_{SW} + \sum IT_{AD} + \sum V_{MG})_{i=1,n} \qquad (4)$$

$$OpEx_{(OLD)} = \sum(\sum PC + \sum DC_{SP} + \sum Sc(\sum V_{SW} + \sum H_{OS} + \sum(n * \sum G_{OS}) +$$

$$\sum TP_{SW}) + \sum TP_{SW} + \sum IT_{AD} + \sum V_{MG})_{i=1,n} \qquad (5)$$

$$OpEx_{(EFF)} = [OpEx_{(OLD)} - OpEx_{(NEW)}] + OT_{(REQ)} \qquad (6)$$

Note: Above equation OpEx cost is of one year.
So, three years total cost for OpEx will be

$$T(Opex) = 3 * (OpEx - VarCost) \qquad (7)$$

Where PC is Power and cooling costs; DC_{SP} is Data center space costs; $Sc(V_{SW})$ is Virtualization software support costs; $Sc(H_{OS})$, $Sc(G_{OS})$ is Host and guest operating system support costs; $Sc(TP_{SW})$ is Third-party software support costs; $\int TP_{SW}$ is Third-party software integration costs; IT_{AD} is IT administrative time costs; V_{MG} is VM migration costs (if applicable); VarCost is Profit Variable Cost in OpEx with respect to contract made in years.

Total Cost of Ownership (TCO)

$$TCO_{k} = T(CapEx_{k}) + T(OpEx_{k}) \qquad (8)$$

Total Cost per Virtual Machine Equation (TCPVM)

$$TCPVMk = [(TCOk) / n(VMk)] \qquad (9)$$

Note: Condition of variable should be same across the equation.

Where 'k' is the infrastructure variable for new, old and cost-effective infrastructure; T(CapEx) is Total CapEx costs; T(OpEx) is Total OpEx costs (over selected period); n(VM) is Number of virtual machines; TCPVM is Total Cost of Ownership per virtual machine.

CLOUD INFRASTRUCTURE SOLUTION: HYBRID CLOUD

TCO Cost Computing: Cost Effective Model

The following equations are required for analysis of cost computing and to find the cost-effective model for best solution for different enterprises.

Total Compute Resources Required

$$\sum_{V1}^{N} COMPUTE = \sum_{V1}^{N} HW\left(1..N\right) + \sum_{V1}^{N} SW\left(1..N\right) + \sum_{V1}^{N} PW\left(1..N\right) + \sum_{V1}^{N} VIRT\left(1..N\right)$$
(1)

Where V is vendor, HW is Hardware, SW is Software, PW is Power and VIRT is Virtualization.

Total Datacenter Resources Required

$$\sum_{V1}^{N} DC = \sum_{V1}^{N} DCR1\left(1..N\right) + \sum_{V1}^{N} DCR2\left(1..N\right) + \sum_{V1}^{N} DCR3\left(1..N\right) + \sum_{V1}^{N} DCR..N\left(1..N\right)$$
(2)

Where DC is Datacenter, DCR1 is Datacenter Resource 1 and so on.

Total Network Resources Required

$$\sum_{V1}^{N} NW = \sum_{V1}^{N} NWR1\left(1..N\right) + \sum_{V1}^{N} NWR2\left(1..N\right) + \sum_{V1}^{N} NWR3\left(1..N\right) + \sum_{V1}^{N} NWR..N\left(1..N\right)$$
(3)

Where NW is Network, NWR1 is Network Resource 1 and so on.

Total Storage Resources Required

$$\sum\nolimits_{V1}^{N} ST = \sum\nolimits_{V1}^{N} STR1\left(1..N\right) + \sum\nolimits_{V1}^{N} STR2\left(1..N\right) + \sum\nolimits_{V1}^{N} STR3\left(1..N\right) + \sum\nolimits_{V1}^{N} STR..N\left(1..N\right)$$

(4)

Where ST is Storage, STR1 is Storage Resource 1 and so on.

Total IT Labor Resources Required

$$\sum\nolimits_{V1}^{N} ITL = \sum\nolimits_{V1}^{N} ITLR1\left(1..N\right) + \sum\nolimits_{V1}^{N} ITLR2\left(1..N\right) + \sum\nolimits_{V1}^{N} ITLR3\left(1..N\right) + \sum\nolimits_{V1}^{N} ITLR..N\left(1..N\right)$$

(5)

Where ITL is IT Labor, ITLR1 is IT Labor Resource 1 and so on.

Total Cost of Ownership [TCO]

$$\mathrm{Min}\left(\sum\nolimits_{V1}^{N} TCO\left(1..N\right)\right) = \mathrm{Min}\left(\sum\nolimits_{V1}^{N} COMPUTE\left(1..N\right)\right) + \mathrm{Min}\left(\sum\nolimits_{V1}^{N} DC\left(1..N\right)\right)$$
$$+\mathrm{Min}\left(\sum\nolimits_{V1}^{N} NW\left(1..N\right)\right) + \mathrm{Min}\left(\sum\nolimits_{V1}^{N} ST\left(1..N\right)\right) + \mathrm{Min}\left(\sum\nolimits_{V1}^{N} ITL\left(1..N\right)\right)$$

(6)

Where TCO is Total Cost of ownership.

TCO for Opensource

$$\mathrm{Cost\ Eff}\left(\sum\nolimits_{V1}^{N} TCOopensource\left(1..N\right)\right) = \mathrm{Min}\left(\sum\nolimits_{V1}^{N} TCOop\left(1..N\right)\right), \mathrm{Min}\left(\sum\nolimits_{V1}^{N} TCOcv\left(1..N\right)\right)$$

(7)

Where TCOopensource is Total Cost of ownership for Open Source, TCOop is TCO On-Premise, TCOcv is TCO Cloud Vendor.

TCO for Proprietor and BCP

$$\text{Cost Eff}\left(\sum_{V1}^{N}TCOpropbcp\left(1..N\right)\right) = \text{Min}\left(\sum_{V1}^{N}TCOprop\left(1..N\right)\right), \text{Min}\left(\sum_{V1}^{N}TCObcp\left(1..N\right)\right)$$

(8)

Where TCOpropbcp is Total Cost of ownership for Proprietor and BCP (Business Continuity Plan).

TCO for Cost Effective Model

$$\text{Cost Eff}\left(\sum_{V1}^{N}TCOcosteffm\left(1..N\right)\right) = \text{Cost Eff}\left(\sum_{V1}^{N}TCOopensource\left(1..N\right)\right),$$
$$\text{Cost Eff}\left(\sum_{V1}^{N}TCOpropbcp\left(1..N\right)\right)$$

(9)

Where TCOcosteffm is Total Cost of ownership for Cost Effective Model.

RESULTS

Introduction

This chapter focuses on the results of cost-effective approach using different virtualization and cloud infrastructure models for building and management of educational infrastructure. This chapter also provides the percentile results for cost effective measurement of TCO and ROI.

Private Datacenter Infrastructure: YGPDI Model Results and Solutions

TCO: Total Capital and Operating Expenses

The TCO result in expenses with two major categories of capital and operational, shows that the type I and type II (with 1-30%) are more cost effective methodology compared to VMware (with 31-55%) and Microsoft (with above 85%) technology as shown in Figure 10.

Figure 10. Total Expenses [CapEx and OpEx]

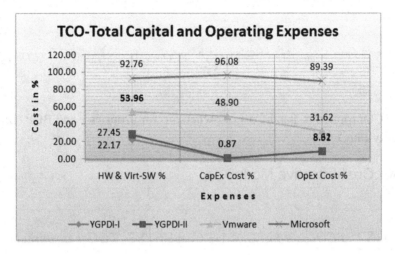

TCO: Overall Comparison

The overall result of TCO comparison between methodology implemented i.e. 'YGPDI' I and II is below 10% and datacenter service providers as Vmware between 39% to 46% and Microsoft above 90% as shown in Figure 11.

Figure 11. TCO including all parameters

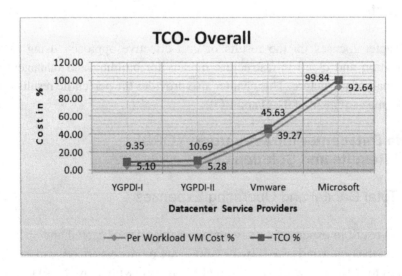

TCO: Cost Effective Result

In the result of TCO cost effective the average 'YGPDI' I and II methodology implemented is highly cost effective and is above 90% and datacenter service providers as Vmware between 40-60% and Microsoft less cost effective above 0 to 10% as shown in Figure 12.

Figure 12. TCO- Cost Effective Comparison

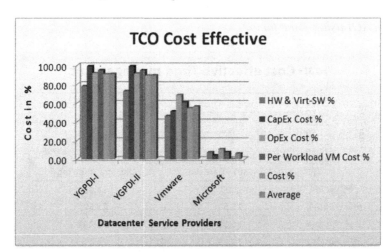

TCO Result Table

The result TCO Table 7 is obtained by computing various TCO parameters with a period of three years for different implementing methodology and different datacenter service providers using all equations from 1 to 9. The cost values are converted to percantage value for analysis and making it easier to understand.

Table 7. TCO Final Result Table

COST Parameters	Datacenter Service Provider [DSP]			
	YGPDI-I	*YGPDI-II*	*VMware*	*Microsoft*
HW & Virt-SW %	22.17	27.45	53.96	92.76
CapEx Cost %	0.87	0.87	48.90	96.08
OpEx Cost %	8.31	8.62	31.62	89.39
Per Workload VM Cost %	5.10	5.28	39.27	92.64
Cost %	9.35	10.69	45.63	99.84

ROI: Cost Effective With Time Management

In Time effective factor, the result obtained is more effective in datacenter service provider i.e. Vmware and Microsoft cosmpared to time required for 'YGPDI' I methodology implemented which is at high level and type II methodology implemented which is at middle level as shown in Figure 13. The equation used in ROI for computing cost effective is: 24 Hrs-Total time- Utilized time) x performance utilization.

Figure 13. ROI using Time factor

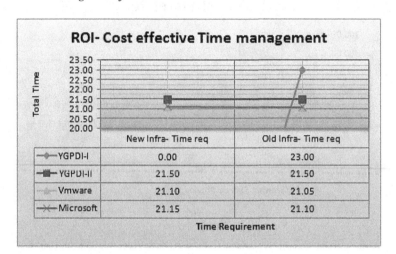

	New Infra- Time req	Old Infra- Time req
YGPDI-I	0.00	23.00
YGPDI-II	21.50	21.50
Vmware	21.10	21.05
Microsoft	21.15	21.10

ROI: Cost Effective With Space Utilization

In Space effective factor, the result obtained is more effective in datacenter service provider i.e. Vmware and Microsoft is 0% compared to space required for 'YGDI' I which is at highest level by 75% and type II at 20% as shown in the Figure 14. The cost compared to space plays vital role as per the geographical location with urban and rural categorization.

Figure 14. ROI using Space factor

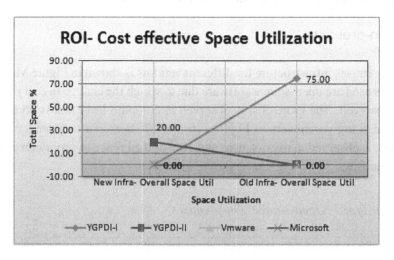

ROI: Cost Effective With Resource Utilization

In Resource effective factor, the result obtained is highly effective in 'YGPDI' I with maximum utilization of old infrasturture, the type II is on high level for new resource utilization along with datacenter service provider i.e. Vmware and Microsoft. But 'YGPDI' I is on bottom level with value 0 for new infrastructure as shown in Figure 15.

Figure 15. ROI using Resource factor

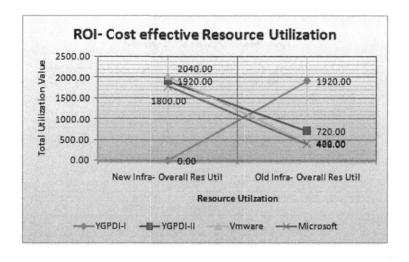

Cloud Infrastructure Solution: Hybrid Cloud

TCO: On-premises

The On-premises infrastructure for different vendors is shown in Figure Most of the software's used are open-source software due to which the change in cost parameter can be observed. The more cost is observed at compute level that is compared to other computing parameters in Figures 16 and 17. Between two vendors 19% of difference is observed in open-source and 10% of difference in proprietary vendors in On-premises.

Figure 16. Type I- Open-source: On-premises

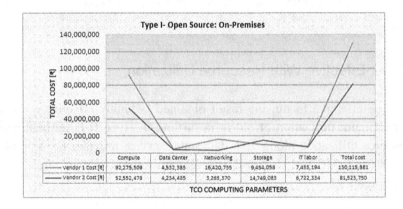

Figure 17. Type II- Proprietary: On-premises

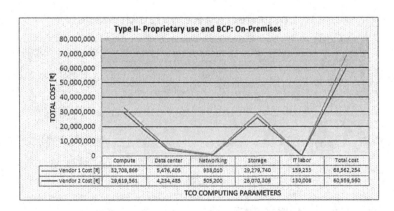

Single Cloud Vendor

The single cloud vendor with parameter such as web direct, one-year reserved VM, and three years reserved are considered for stakeholder or enterprise requirement as per performance and cost computing as observed in Figures 18 and 19. There are minor differences between different cost computing parameters.

Figure 18. Type I- Open-source: Cloud Vendor

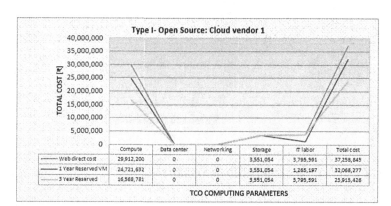

	Compute	Data center	Networking	Storage	IT labor	Total cost
Web direct cost	29,912,200	0	0	3,551,054	3,795,591	37,258,845
1 Year Reserved VM	24,721,632	0	0	3,551,054	1,265,197	32,068,277
3 Year Reserved	16,568,781	0	0	3,551,054	3,795,591	23,915,426

Figure 19. Type II- Proprietary: Cloud Vendor

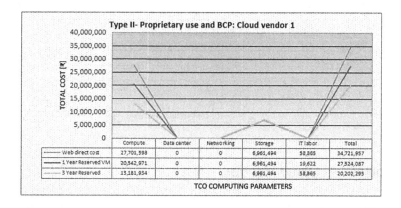

	Compute	Data center	Networking	Storage	IT labor	Total
Web direct cost	27,701,598	0	0	6,961,494	58,865	34,721,957
1 Year Reserved VM	20,542,971	0	0	6,961,494	19,622	27,524,087
3 Year Reserved	13,181,934	0	0	6,961,494	58,865	20,202,293

Cloud Vendor

The cloud vendors play a vital role in cloud infrastructure by allocating resources as per the requirement of the enterprise. There is more cost requirement in compute in open-source and compute with storage in proprietary use that is observed in Figures 20 and 21.

Figure 20. Type I- Open-source: Cloud Vendors

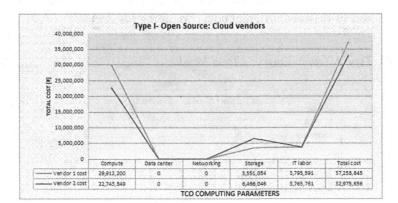

Figure 21. Type II- Proprietary: Cloud Vendors

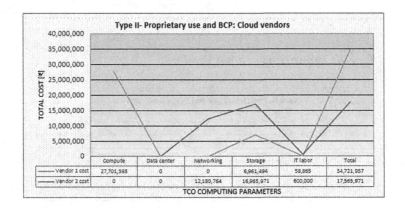

On-premises vs. Cloud Vendor

The TCO difference observed between the On-premise and cloud vendors results that the cost of Compute is more in On-premise and compute with storage is more in proprietary as per observation obtained. The cloud vendors such as vendor 1 and 2 are more effective compare to On-premise vendors that is observed in Figures 22 and 23.

Figure 22. Type I- Open-source: On-premises vs. Cloud Vendors

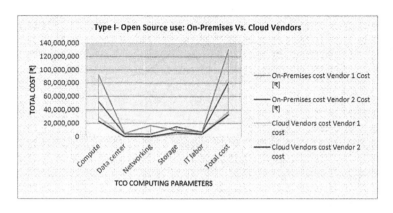

Figure 23. Type II- Proprietary: On-premises vs. Cloud Vendors.

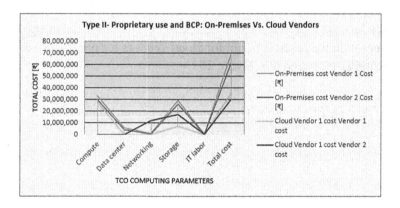

Result Cost Effective Solution

The TCO cost effective solution is obtained using 'YGCCS' is observed is impactful. The 54% cost difference is observed between Cloud vendors and On-premise vendors in open-source category. The important result observed in below Figure is cost effective-ness impact for all TCO computing parameters is high. The model or methodology results to opt for cloud vendors for open-source environment that is observed in Figure 24.

Figure 24. Type I- Open-source: On-premises vs. Cloud Vendors.

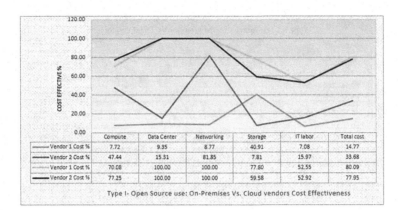

	Compute	Data Center	Networking	Storage	IT labor	Total cost
Vendor 1 Cost %	7.72	9.35	8.77	40.91	7.08	14.77
Vendor 2 Cost %	47.44	15.31	81.85	7.81	15.97	33.68
Vendor 1 Cost %	70.08	100.00	100.00	77.80	52.55	80.09
Vendor 2 Cost %	77.25	100.00	100.00	59.58	52.92	77.95

Type I- Open Source use: On-Premises Vs. Cloud vendors Cost Effectiveness

The observation for cost effective solution using 'YGCCS' in below Figure is impactful. The 22% cost difference is observed between Cloud vendors and On-premise vendors in Proprietary with BCP category. Therefore, the methodology or model comes with the result is to opt for cloud vendors for proprietary using BCP environment that is observed in Figure 25.

Figure 25. Type II- Proprietary: On-premises vs. Cloud Vendors

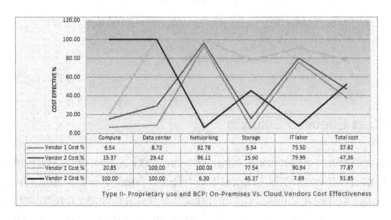

	Compute	Data center	Networking	Storage	IT labor	Total cost
Vendor 1 Cost %	6.54	8.72	92.78	5.54	75.50	37.82
Vendor 2 Cost %	15.37	29.42	96.11	15.90	79.99	47.36
Vendor 1 Cost %	20.85	100.00	100.00	77.54	90.94	77.87
Vendor 2 Cost %	100.00	100.00	6.30	45.27	7.69	51.85

Type II- Proprietary use and BCP: On-Premises Vs. Cloud Vendors Cost Effectiveness

CONCLUSION

Cloud Infrastructure Solution

This chapter covers the results of cost-effective approach using different virtualization and cloud infrastructure models for building and management of educational infrastructure. The results in this chapters are obtained by considering different design consideration and its requirements. This chapter also, covers the percentile results for cost effective measurement of TCO and ROI.

The overall cost-effective solution using 'YGCCS' methodology is impactful by 38% for Cloud vendors compared to On-premise vendors. The cost-effective framework and its implementation is useful in building Cloud infrastructure towards cost-effective solution. The experimental infrastructure is implemented, and an integrated cost-effective solution is achieved for hybrid and multi-cloud. This cloud solution in IT infrastructure will leverage skill required in cluster building of IT resources, infrastructure managing, lab designing and hands on activity through on-premises or off-premises from anywhere. Thus, it provides a roadmap and strategy to adopt a feasible and cost-effective solution in education environment where the infrastructure plays a vital role.

REFERENCES

Al-Shargabi, B., AlJawarneh, S., & Hayajneh, S. M. (2020). A cloudlet based security and trust model for e-government web services. *Journal of Theoretical and Applied Information Technology*, *98*(1), 27–37.

Aljawarneh, S. (Ed.). (2012). *Cloud computing advancements in design, implementation, and technologies*. IGI Global.

Aljawarneh, S., & Malhotra, M. (Eds.). (2017). *Critical Research on Scalability and Security Issues in Virtual Cloud Environments*. IGI Global.

Ana-Ramona, B., & Razvan, B. (2011). A Perspective on the Benefits of Data Virtualization Technology. Informatica Economica, 15.

Anton, B., Rajkumar, B., Lee, Y. C., & Zomaya, A. (2010). *A Taxonomy and Survey of Energy-Efficient Data Centers and Cloud Computing Systems*. Green Cloud Taxonomy.

Apon, Mache, Buyya, & Jin. (2004). Cluster Computing in the Classroom and Integration with Computing Curricula 2001. IEEE Transactions on Education, 47(2).

Avanade Perspective Paper. (2009). *Server Virtualization: A Step Toward Cost Efficiency and Business Agility*. avanade perspective paper server Virtualization.

Barham, P., Dragovic, B., & Fraser, K. (2003). Xen and the art of virtualization. ACM Journal, 37, 164-177.

Behrend, T. S., & Wiebe, E. N. (2011). Cloud computing adoption and usage in community colleges. Behaviour & Information Technology Journal, 30(2), 231-240.

Chehbi-Gamoura, S., Derrouiche, R., Malhotra, M., & Koruca, H. I. (2018, June). Adaptive management approach for more availability of big data business analytics. In *Proceedings of the Fourth International Conference on Engineering & MIS 2018* (pp. 1-8). Academic Press.

Dell Software. (n.d.). *Top 10 Virtualization Automation Tips for Infrastructure and Operations Administrators*. Whitepaper-VirtualAutoTips-InfraOpAdmin-US-KS-23761.

Do More for Less. (2008). *Build a Cost-Effective, Optimized IT Infrastructure*. IBM.

Dong, B., Zheng, Q., Yang, J., Li, H., & Qiao, M. (2009). An E-learning Ecosystem Based on Cloud Computing Infrastructure. *Ninth IEEE International Conference on Advanced Learning Technologies*. doi:10.1109/ICALT.2009.21

Dong, B., Zheng, Q., Yang, J., Li, H., & Qiao, M. (2009). An E-learning Ecosystem Based on Cloud Computing Infrastructure. *2009 Ninth IEEE International Conference on Advanced Learning Technologies*, 125-127.

Esposito, C., Su, X., Aljawarneh, S. A., & Choi, C. (2018). Securing collaborative deep learning in industrial applications within adversarial scenarios. *IEEE Transactions on Industrial Informatics*, *14*(11), 4972–4981.

Gartner Research. (2006-2007). *IT Spending and Staffing Report*. North America 5 ID Number: G00146284.

Ghorpade, Shaikh, & Acharya. (2012). Educational Infrastructure Management: Paravirtualization in the classroom. *Allana Management Journal of Research*.

Ghorpade & Acharya. (2013). Data Mining Performance Parameters of Client Machine Under a Flat Network and Subnetted Network. *2nd National Conference on Data Mining*.

Ghorpade, Ghorpade, Bennur, & Acharya. (2013). Server Virtualization, A Cost Effective and Green Computing Approach Towards Educational Infrastructure Management. *International Conference on Cloud Computing and Computer Science IRAJ*.

Ghorpade, Bennur, & Acharya. (2013). Server Virtualization: A Cost-Effective Approach towards Educational Infrastructure Management. *Checkmate 2013 - 4th Annual International Conference*.

Ghorpade, Bennur, Acharya, & Kamatchi. (2015). Server Virtualization Implementation: An Experimental Study for Cost Effective and Green Computing Approach towards Educational Infrastructure Management. *International Journal of Computer Science Trends and Technology, 3*(6).

Ghorpade, Y. (2013). Data Communication and Computer Network. Suyog Publication.

Greer. (n.d.). *Why Choose VMware Robust and Reliable Foundation.* vmware.com.

ICCS. (2008). Deploying Virtual Infrastructure on Standard Operating Systems. Iccs Whitepaper, IDEAS Custom Consulting Services.

India's Technology Opportunity. (2012). *Transforming work, empowering people.* McKinsey Technology, Media, and Telecom Practice.

IT Value Transformation Road Map Vision, Value, and Virtualization. (2000). IT Process Institute, Advancing the Science of IT Management VMware.

Jain & Pandey. (2013). Role of Cloud Computing in Higher Education. *International Journal of Advanced Research in Computer Science and Software Engineering, 3*(7).

Jaswal, S., & Malhotra, M. (2019, December). A detailed analysis of trust models in cloud environment. In *Proceedings of the Second International Conference on Data Science, E-Learning and Information Systems* (pp. 1-5). Academic Press.

Kalpana, G., Kumar, P. V., Aljawarneh, S., & Krishnaiah, R. V. (2018). Shifted adaption homomorphism encryption for mobile and cloud learning. *Computers & Electrical Engineering, 65*, 178–195.

Khmelevsky, Y., & Voytenko, V. (2010). Cloud computing infrastructure prototype for university education and research. *Proceeding WCCCE Journal '10.* doi:10.1145/1806512.1806524

Kim, K. H., Buyya, R., & Kim, J. (2007). Power Aware Scheduling of Bag-of-Tasks Applications with Deadline Constraints on DVS-enabled Clusters. In *Proc. of 7th IEEE International Symposium on Cluster Computing and the Grid (CCGrid 2007)*.

Kumar, Kommareddy, & Rani. (2013). Effective ways Cloud Computing can contribute To Education success. *Advanced Computing: An International Journal, 4*(4).

Kusnetzky. (2007). *Virtualization and green computing*. ZDNet.

Lee, Y., & Zomaya, A. (2009). Minimizing Energy Consumption for Precedence-Constrained Applications Using Dynamic Voltage Scaling. *Proc. of the 9th IEEE/ACM International Symposium on Cluster Computing and the Grid (CCGrid 2009)*.

Lizcano, D., Lara, J. A., White, B., & Aljawarneh, S. (2020). Blockchain-based approach to create a model of trust in open and ubiquitous higher education. *Journal of Computing in Higher Education, 32*(1), 109–134.

Malhotra, M., & Singh, A. (2019). Role of Agents to Enhance the Security and Scalability in Cloud Environment. In Cloud Security: Concepts, Methodologies, Tools, and Applications (pp. 552-573). IGI Global.

Mohammed, T. A., Ghareeb, A., Al-bayaty, H., & Aljawarneh, S. (2019, December). Big data challenges and achievements: applications on smart cities and energy sector. In *Proceedings of the Second International Conference on Data Science, E-Learning and Information Systems* (pp. 1-5). Academic Press.

Moreno-Vozmediano, R., Montero, R. S., & Llorente, I. M. (2012). IaaS Cloud Architecture: From Virtualized Datacenters to Federated Cloud Infrastructures. *IEEE Explore in Computer, 45*(12), 65-72. doi:10.1109/MC.2012.76

Moreno-Vozmediano, R., Montero, R. S., & Llorente, I. M. (2012). IaaS Cloud Architecture: From Virtualized Datacenters to Federated Cloud Infrastructures. *IEEE Explore in Computer, 45*(12), 65–72.

Mouchili, M. N., Aljawarneh, S., & Tchouati, W. (2018, October). Smart city data analysis. In *Proceedings of the First International Conference on Data Science, E-learning and Information Systems* (pp. 1-6). Academic Press.

Peters, M. (2012). *The Economic and Operational Value of Storage Virtualization*. The HDS Perspective, ESG White Paper, 2012.

Preparing for Successful VDI Implementation. (2014). A Business Perspective, Virtual Bridges.

Richardson & Mahfouz. (n.d.). Aligning business service management to goals: an integrated approach at BMC Software. *Journal of Technology Research.*

Scott & Marshall. (2013). Mastering VMware vSphere 5.5. In *Planning and installing VMware ESXi*. Academic Press.

Singh, A., Juneja, D., & Malhotra, M. (2017). A novel agent based autonomous and service composition framework for cost optimization of resource provisioning in cloud computing. *Journal of King Saud University-Computer and Information Sciences, 29*(1), 19–28.

Truong, H.-L., Pham, T.-V., & Thoai, N. (n.d.). *Cloud Computing for Education and Research in Developing Countries*. IGI Global, doi:10.4018/978-1-4666-0957-0.ch005

Uddin & Rahman. (2011). Implementing Virtualization A six-step guide to virtualization implementation for a more efficient, reliable, and flexible data center. *International Journal of Advanced Computer Science and Applications, 2*(1).

Watfa, Udoh, & Al Abdulsalam. (2015). *An Educational Virtualization Infrastructure*. Springer.

Why operational management in virtualized data centers is critical to delivering service assurance. (2012).,EMC Perspective.

Yadav. (2014). Role of Cloud Computing in Education. *International Journal of Innovative Research in Computer and Communication Engineering, 2*(2).

Yeo, Buyya, Pourreza, & Eskicioglu. (2006). Cluster Computing: High-Performance, High-Availability, and High-Throughput Processing on a Network of Computers. In Handbook of nature. Springer.

Chapter 11
A Study of Security Challenges From a Federeated Cloud Perspective

Prathap R.
https://orcid.org/0000-0003-4736-6811
Vellore Institute of Technology, Vellore, India

Mohanasundaram R.
Vellore Institute of Technology, Vellore, India

ABSTRACT

In the information technology sector, cloud computing plays an important role. Information was externalized in the cloud in the IT sector and part of data as a software. These offer utilities such as storage, software as a service, and application as a service and some web models, such as the deployment models, in four forms. The third-party wanted the data to be outsourced. In this chapter, the authors research and analyze technologies and frameworks for cloud computing. In cloud services, security problems are important. Therefore, the authors discuss safety problems and the concerns found in this chapter.

1. INTRODUCTION

Cloud computing is a new computer technology and it has scalable resources provisioned over the internet providers. Cloud figuring provides resources consuming virtualization. The element of the cloud requires security, which varies the level of deployment model. Protection of data storage, protection of data transmission

DOI: 10.4018/978-1-7998-5040-3.ch011

and safety related to third-party networks are some basic security concerns. We're talking about computing and its models of operation and implementation models in this article. They are some types involving in these technologies. One of the new techniques in business models in computing is federated cloud computing. It reduces the reliability and reduces the cost to an organization (Al-Shargabi et al, 2020; Aljawarneh, 2012; Aljawarneh et al, 2017; Chehbi-Gamoura et al, 2018; Esposito et al, 2018; Jaswal et al, 2019; Kalpana et al, 2018; Lizcano et al, 2020; Malhotra et al, 2019; Mohammed et al, 2019; Mouchili et al, 2018; Singh,2011).

Federated cloud computing is the management of multiple cloud computing services. The main motivation of this article is to address safety problems and challenges in infrastructure and cloud figuring.

Cloud Service Models

Cloud computing as greater flexibility and availability at a lower cost. They are three ways of service representations.

1. **Software as a Service:** Software as a provision is a service to provide a set of application software. Customers use only applications. The application software interacts through the interface. Example: Webmail, Facebook, Twitter, etc.
2. **Platform as a Service:** Platform as a providing is a set of software and advance tools provided by a cloud service provider (CSP) server. Google app engine is one of the most famous service providers. It can reduce the factors involved in a complicated process for buying and organization hardware and software of the policy.
3. **Infrastructure as a Service:** It is enabling on-demand service in which applications can develop and execute in the platform. It is less use of networking components. It is also called utility computing. Customers can pay for the usage of services.

Distribution Models

Distribution models in the cloud can be depending on the requirements.

1. **Public Cloud:** They made the broad industry or public available in a digital cloud. An organization that sells cloud services is owned by a large industry group.
2. **Private Cloud:** Private cloud infrastructure, operated by a particular organization, has been introduced. A certain distance is measured and engaged.

3. **Community Cloud:** This infrastructure shared by every organization and support a specific community. It is defined as managed by a third party or an organization.
4. **Hybrid Cloud:** It is defined as two or more clouds (ex: private, public) that remain inimitable objects. It is also called a load balancing cloud.

Key Characteristics of Cloud Computing

1. **On-Demand Self Services:** On-demand self-service is a service provided by cloud computing vendors. The provision of cloud resources whenever they are required. Cloud users access the service through online. Cloud computing provides resources on-demand when the user wants the services.

2. **Board/ Huge Network Access:** The network capacity is available over the network and accessed standard level. It is available for a wide range of devices (such as pc, tab, and mobile phones, etc.)

Resources Provider

It provides the resources to multiple users using the multi-tenant model. The resources are provided dynamically according to customer demand. (Ex: state or data center).

Some Important Security Issues

- **Secure Data Transfer:** When the data transferring between the network. So, always we check the data are encrypted or authenticated to the cloud. Users must check the data are transferring in a secure channel on the internet.
- **Secure Software Interfaces:** The computer system exchanges the information in the shared boundary. We realize that the interface is being used to communicate with cloud services. The API and interfaces are exposed to a range of security issues related to fairness, compatibility, and privacy.
- **Secure Storing of Data:** The stored data should be securely stored in the cloud platform. Always we check the stored data has been encrypted. We assure that the protection of data being used within the application.

Cloud Federation (Cloud of Cloud)

Also called federated cloud computing, multiple cloud services are used to meet business needs. A common operation is carried out by each service. Cloud federal services aim to balance loads and meet their requirements. Load balancing is defined as divided the amount of work to do between two or more computers. It involves multiple computers to improve the efficiency and performance of the services.

A MODEL OF FEDERATED CLOUD COMPUTING

The entities need computational resources to offer some services. The federated cloud computing provides a platform such as service providers and infrastructure providers. Which provides and compute network and storage resources.

FEATURES OF FEDERATION OF CLOUD

The framework agreement to be supported: The framework should be supported by architecture in the service.

Resources reservation support is an existing feature in use in the federated cloud computing.

Architecture for Federated Cloud

See Figure 1.

Figure 1. Layout of Federated Cloud

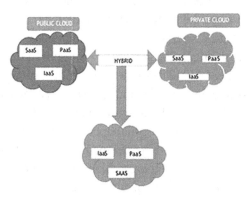

Survey of Cloud and Multi Cloud Computing

Muhil, M., et al (2015), the storage benefactor must ensure that the records provided through the customer are protected, that the information can be asked about and that the after-effects of the matter are also safe and not untrue to the provider. CIA (Confidentiality, Accuracy, and Availability) are the main issues involved in the management of information storage. Nonetheless, due to numerous security issues in a single cloud, companies and consumers settle in "multi-cloud" also called "private clouds" or "inter clouds." Such multi-clouds are protected by different procedures and hidden communication algorithms are one of them.

Sulochana, M., et al (2015) the important aspects of security of cloud computing are quality of service from the service supplier. The most important solution for creativities by providing effective properties and reliable resources as a service. They offer the resources by either pay or pay as you need. Cloud providers gaining complete knowledge of customer data. The security issues of the resource provider side are weak as consider the quality of service we need.

Aizain, Mohammed A., et al (2012) Safety is the biggest issue of cloud computing in multi-cloud settings. The customer has stored sensitive information with the cloud storage company, but sometimes the vendor has no faith. Cloud as a lot of benefits concerning low cost and computer usability. Using cryptographic strategies to encrypt data in the cloud and reduce the risk of the web owner or application. The hash function for data integrity is part of one of the cryptographic techniques. Several protocols are used to monitor multi-clouds. The data of the customer is managed on the cloud provider's virtual machine.

Ghazizadeh, Eghbal, et al (2012) in a cloud environment new level of computing is federated cloud computing. In these methods, we thought about federated identity management it useful feature for user management and single sign-on is also an important feature for the federated cloud environment. Some techniques such as OAUTH, open ID these are the main concept in the federated cloud environment. There are many techniques used against cloud authentication. It arises from the misuse of identity and identity management to point out in this paper.

Bernsmed, Karin, et al (2012) in this paper they say about federated cloud environment provides one or number of cloud services. Customer to enable the storage, processing, and transfer in a public cloud environment. But the federated cloud-enable the individual cloud service provider. In this paper, they use cryptographic encryption techniques. The arithmetic operation performed for the customer side and return into plaintext. They have identified four problems longer chain of trustworthiness, arise legal issues, the third-party initializes the cloud customer and cloud provider.

El Zant, Bassem, et al (2013) In a Federated environment, CSP has a boundless measure of resources because of the way that each CSP can utilize the resources of different CSPs to serve its customers when its particular resources can't do it. A security plan of the cloud that sureties the security of the data ought to be created. This arrangement ought to incorporate the get to controls, Encryption of information honesty, accessibility and classification of the information.

Wen, Zhenyu, Jacek Cala., et al (2014) this article describes a new organization that organizes the measurement for lightweight, compact and secretarial work process-based applications across a single cloud. The issues with encryption are focused on the past, which requires cloud computing to include the Bell-LaPadula model. The least expensive option to break a method over a resource bundle seemed an NP-issue that could be separated over various clouds into a large number of labor processes.

Rekaby, Fayza, et al (2013) A securely shared verification convention for combined communicate cloud is introduced. A federated identity administration component and a forward secure communicate encryption plot utilizing (various leveled character-based encryption) to have the remarkable computerized character for a client, which will handle all the above issues. They are secure and authenticated broadcasting technology to all servers and users.

Altmann, Jörn, et al (2014) This sort of cloud is made out of a private cloud and various interoperable open clouds. The proposed cost model is connected inside a cost minimization calculation for settling on administration position choices in the cloud. We exhibit the workings of our cost model and administration arrangement calculation inside a particular cloud situation. It likewise expands the adaptability of organizations to adjust their IT assets to changes as demand.

Alam, Md Kausar., et al (2013) The information security part of cloud computing, information and data will be imparted to an outsider with no hacks. Each cloud clients need to stay away from untrusted cloud supplier for individual and essential archives, for example, charge/MasterCard subtle elements or medicinal report from programmers or malevolent insiders is the significance. Strong system security is conceivable around the administration conveyance stage Information encryption: for information in travel (especially over wide zone systems), and some of the time put away information, yet it can't be connected to information being used. Get to controls to guarantee that lone approved client's access applications, information, and the preparing environment and is the essential method for securing cloud-based administrations.

Existing Security Models in Cloud Computing

- Broker facilitated Federated Cloud layout. The character illustrations two Clouds, both serving a upright stack of service layer assistances from the operating system and network layer at the top via the middleware or platform layer.
- Expending assignment, or a significant other cloud by the association, a choice is made on each layer to satisfy a service entreaty over limited resources. A key feature of our model is that federation exists between cloud benefactors at matching amenity stack levels.

- Cloud may not be appropriate for all data, e.g. records of employees. Encryption of information before uploading. Specifications for decrypting shared data steps and recording and identification of key issues for individuals. Excluding private clouds, some degree of access needed on a physical server or manage -VMS. Encrypted Connections: Isolate client VMs using client secure shell keys and server passwords Prevent VM dump. Use trust configuration to ensure that certain hypervisors and software configured are enabled.

Trust Third Party

The trusted third party services within the cloud to establishing the trust level and ideas preserves CIA (Confidentiality, integrity, authentication) of data on services. The trusted third party is an entity of communicating between the two parties in the services. They provide end to end security services.

They create a security domain and it will perform a low and high level of CIA. The cryptographic techniques only for the splitting of data. Cloud is a common service platform, requires authorization and authentication of the services.

Creation of Security Domains

A cloud federation provides some set of structure and framework that enables the CIA across different organization.

PROPOSED FRAMEWORK FOR FEDERATED CLOUD COMPUTING

The first solution is to enforce a third party's confidence in the network, storage and computing capacities of external cloud service providers. Most of the security and privacy issues of cloud users mimic traditional non-cloud services. Subcontracting data and services to a public cloud can lead to more accountability for the cloud provider. The customer hereby allots to the contractor the deployment, implementation, and maintenance of the necessary safety measures, which means a greater level of confidence and assurance. Ensuring that the client has and is properly implementing adequate security measures.

Proposed Techniques

Fully homomorphic encryption: Fully homomorphic encryption is an encryption scheme where, for example, arithmetic operations can be performed on the encrypted data and when the encrypted result is decrypted, the right plaintext result can be returned. Encrypt my data before sending it to the cloud.

Analysis of Survey

- We analyzed the cloud federation processes with security and privacy issues. We coming to know about to create efficient techniques to emphasis the process.
- Most important thing is, we need to provide security and privacy for both cloud customer and Cloud providers.
- The key idea of this paper is to create any cryptographic techniques to resolve these problems.
- In the future, we need to develop and define the power efficiency sequence delivered to the cloud consumer.
- Certificate-based authorization is used to reduce software unity.
- Cryptographic techniques are used to protect personal information.
- Privacy and Confidentiality of data can be protected by cryptography (encryption/decryption).s

CONCLUSION

In this paper cloud computing provides how the hybrid cloud is provisioned over the internet. We specify the security issues related to federated cloud computing. We discuss some ideas about hybrid cloud and we provide basics knowledge about service models and deployment models. We noticed that scalability is high in cloud computing. For the future, we plan to develop how to overcome energy efficiency in the cloud computing environment.

REFERENCES

Al-Shargabi, B., AlJawarneh, S., & Hayajneh, S. M. (2020). A cloudlet based security and trust model for e-government web services. *Journal of Theoretical and Applied Information Technology*, *98*(1), 27–37.

Alain, M. A. (2012). Cloud computing security: from single to multi-clouds. *System Science (HICSS), 2012 45th Hawaii International Conference on.*

Alam. (2013). *An approach secret sharing algorithm in cloud computing security over single to multi-clouds.* Academic Press.

Ali, M., Khan, S. U., & Vasilakos, A. V. (2015). Security in cloud computing: Opportunities and challenges. *Information Sciences*, *305*, 357–383. doi:10.1016/j.ins.2015.01.025

Aljawarneh, S. (Ed.). (2012). *Cloud computing advancements in design, implementation, and technologies*. IGI Global.

Aljawarneh, S., & Malhotra, M. (Eds.). (2017). *Critical Research on Scalability and Security Issues in Virtual Cloud Environments*. IGI Global.

Altmann, J., & Kashef, M. M. (2014). Cost model-based service placement in federated hybrid clouds. *Future Generation Computer Systems*, *41*, 79–90. doi:10.1016/j.future.2014.08.014

Ashokkumar, K., Sam, B., Arshadprabhu, R., & Britto. (2015). Baron Sam, and R. Arshadprabhu. "Cloud-based intelligent transport system. *Procedia Computer Science*, *50*, 58–63. doi:10.1016/j.procs.2015.04.061

Bernsmed, K. (2012). Thunder in the Clouds: Security challenges and solutions for federated Clouds. *Cloud Computing Technology and Science (CloudCom), 2012 IEEE 4th International Conference on*. 10.1109/CloudCom.2012.6427547

Chang, V., Kuo, Y.-II., & Ramachandran, M. (2016). Cloud computing adoption framework: A security framework for business clouds. *Future Generation Computer Systems*, *57*, 24–41. doi:10.1016/j.future.2015.09.031

Chehbi-Gamoura, S., Derrouiche, R., Malhotra, M., & Koruca, H. I. (2018, June). Adaptive management approach for more availability of big data business analytics. In *Proceedings of the Fourth International Conference on Engineering & MIS 2018* (pp. 1-8). 10.1145/3234698.3234758

El Zant, B. (2013). Security of cloud federation. In *Cloud Computing and Big Data (CloudCom-Asia), 2013 International Conference on*. IEEE.

Esposito, C., Su, X., Aljawarneh, S. A., & Choi, C. (2018). Securing collaborative deep learning in industrial applications within adversarial scenarios. *IEEE Transactions on Industrial Informatics*, *14*(11), 4972–4981. doi:10.1109/TII.2018.2853676

Flouris, I. (2016). Issues in Complex Event Processing: Status and Prospects in the Big Data Era. *Journal of Systems and Software*.

Ghazizadeh, E., Zamani, M., & Pahang, A. (2012). A survey on security issues of federated identity in cloud computing. In *Cloud Computing Technology and Science (CloudCom), 2012 IEEE 4th International Conference on*. IEEE. 10.1109/CloudCom.2012.6427513

Hashem, I. A. T., Yaqoob, I., Anuar, N. B., Mokhtar, S., Gani, A., & Ullah Khan, S. (2015). The rise of "big data" on cloud computing: Review and open research issues. *Information Systems*, *47*, 98–115. doi:10.1016/j.is.2014.07.006

Jansen, W. A. (2011). Cloud hooks: Security and privacy issues in cloud computing. In *System Sciences (HICSS), 2011 44th Hawaii International Conference on*. IEEE. 10.1109/HICSS.2011.103

Jaswal, S., & Malhotra, M. (2019, December). A detailed analysis of trust models in cloud environment. In *Proceedings of the Second International Conference on Data Science, E-Learning and Information Systems* (pp. 1-5). 10.1145/3368691.3368740

Jeffery, K. (2015). Challenges emerging from future cloud application scenarios. *Procedia Computer Science*, *68*, 227–237. doi:10.1016/j.procs.2015.09.238

Kalpana, G., Kumar, P. V., Aljawarneh, S., & Krishnaiah, R. V. (2018). Shifted adaption homomorphism encryption for mobile and cloud learning. *Computers & Electrical Engineering*, *65*, 178–195. doi:10.1016/j.compeleceng.2017.05.022

Kchaou, H., Kechaou, Z., & Alimi, A. M. (2015). Towards an Offloading Framework based on Big Data Analytics in Mobile Cloud Computing Environments. *Procedia Computer Science*, *53*, 292–297. doi:10.1016/j.procs.2015.07.306

Kim, H., Kang, J., & Park, J. H. (2016). A light-weight secure information transmission and device control scheme in the integration of CPS and cloud computing. *Microprocessors and Microsystems*.

Kong, X. (2015). Cloud-enabled real-time platform for adaptive planning and control in the auction logistics center. *Computers & Industrial Engineering, 84*, 79-90.

Krishna, B. H., Kiran, S., Murali, G., & Reddy, R. P. K. (2016). Security Issues in Service Model of Cloud Computing Environment. *Procedia Computer Science*, *87*, 246–251. doi:10.1016/j.procs.2016.05.156

Le Vinh, T., Bouzefrane, S., Farinone, J.-M., Attar, A., & Kennedy, B. P. (2015). Middleware to integrate mobile devices, sensors, and cloud computing. *Procedia Computer Science*, *52*, 234–243. doi:10.1016/j.procs.2015.05.061

Liu, W., Nishio, T., Shinkuma, R., & Takahashi, T. (2014). Adaptive resource discovery in mobile cloud computing. *Computer Communications*, *50*, 119–129. doi:10.1016/j.comcom.2014.02.006

Lizcano, D., Lara, J. A., White, B., & Aljawarneh, S. (2020). Blockchain-based approach to create a model of trust in open and ubiquitous higher education. *Journal of Computing in Higher Education*, *32*(1), 109–134. doi:10.100712528-019-09209-y

Louis, A. (2016). Healing on the cloud: Secure cloud architecture for medical wireless sensor networks. *Future Generation Computer Systems, 55*, 266–277. doi:10.1016/j.future.2015.01.009

Magalhães, D., Calheiros, R. N., Buyya, R., & Gomes, D. G. (2015). Workload modeling for resource usage analysis and simulation in cloud computing. *Computers & Electrical Engineering, 47*, 69–81. doi:10.1016/j.compeleceng.2015.08.016

Mai, V., & Khalil, I. (2016). Design and implementation of a secure cloud-based billing model for smart meters as an Internet of things using homomorphic cryptography. *Future Generation Computer Systems*.

Malhotra, M., & Singh, A. (2019). Role of Agents to Enhance the Security and Scalability in Cloud Environment. In Cloud Security: Concepts, Methodologies, Tools, and Applications (pp. 552-573). IGI Global. doi:10.4018/978-1-5225-8176-5.ch028

Marston, S., Li, Z., Bandyopadhyay, S., Zhang, J., & Ghalsasi, A. (2011). Cloud computing—The business perspective. *Decision Support Systems, 51*(1), 176–189. doi:10.1016/j.dss.2010.12.006

Mital, M., Pani, A. K., Damodaran, S., & Ramesh, R. (2015). Cloud-based management and control system for smart communities: A practical case study. *Computers in Industry, 74*, 162–172. doi:10.1016/j.compind.2015.06.009

Mohammed, T. A., Ghareeb, A., Al-bayaty, H., & Aljawarneh, S. (2019, December). Big data challenges and achievements: applications on smart cities and energy sector. In *Proceedings of the Second International Conference on Data Science, E-Learning and Information Systems* (pp. 1-5). 10.1145/3368691.3368717

Mouchili, M. N., Aljawarneh, S., & Tchouati, W. (2018, October). Smart city data analysis. In *Proceedings of the First International Conference on Data Science, E-learning and Information Systems* (pp. 1-6). Academic Press.

Moura, J., & Hutchison, D. (2016). Review and analysis of networking challenges in cloud computing. *Journal of Network and Computer Applications, 60*, 113–129. doi:10.1016/j.jnca.2015.11.015

Muhil, M., Krishna, U. H., Kumar, R. K., & Anita, E. A. M. (2015). Securing multi-cloud using secret sharing algorithm. *Procedia Computer Science, 50*, 421–426. doi:10.1016/j.procs.2015.04.011

Rao, R. V., & Selvamani, K. (2015). Data Security Challenges and Its Solutions in Cloud Computing. *Procedia Computer Science, 48*, 204–209. doi:10.1016/j.procs.2015.04.171

Reka, F. (2015). Federated cloud computing security using forward-secure broadcast encryption HIBE. In *2015 11th International Computer Engineering Conference (ICENCO)*. IEEE.

Singh, A., Juneja, D., & Malhotra, M. (2017). A novel agent based autonomous and service composition framework for cost optimization of resource provisioning in cloud computing. *Journal of King Saud University-Computer and Information Sciences, 29*(1), 19–28. doi:10.1016/j.jksuci.2015.09.001

Stanik, A., Koerner, M., & Lymberopoulos, L. (2014). SLA-driven Federated Cloud Networking: Quality of Service for Cloud-based Software-Defined Networks. *Procedia Computer Science, 34*, 655–660. doi:10.1016/j.procs.2014.07.093

Subashini, S., & Kavitha, V. (2011). A survey on security issues in service delivery models of cloud computing. *Journal of Network and Computer Applications, 34*(1), 1–11. doi:10.1016/j.jnca.2010.07.006

Sulochana, M., & Dubey, O. (2015). Preserving Data Confidentiality Using Multi-cloud Architecture. *Procedia Computer Science, 50*, 357–362. doi:10.1016/j.procs.2015.04.035

Tong-rang, F. A. N. (2012). Integration of IoT and DRAGON-lab in a cloud environment. *Journal of China Universities of Posts and Telecommunications, 19*(2), 87–91. doi:10.1016/S1005-8885(11)60250-1

Wang & Mu. (2011). Security issues and countermeasures in cloud computing. In *Proceedings of 2011 IEEE International Conference on Grey Systems and Intelligent Services*. IEEE.

Wen, Z. (2015). Cost-Effective, Reliable, and Secure Workflow Deployment over Federated Clouds. In *2015 IEEE 8th International Conference on Cloud Computing*. IEEE. 10.1109/CLOUD.2015.86

Wen, Z., Cala, J., & Watson, P. (2014). A scalable method for partitioning workflows with security requirements over federated clouds. In *Cloud Computing Technology and Science (CloudCom), 2014 IEEE 6th International Conference on*. IEEE. 10.1109/CloudCom.2014.89

Yang, J. (2016). Multimedia recommendation and transmission system based on a cloud platform. *Future Generation Computer Systems*.

Zissis, D., & Lekkas, D. (2012). Addressing cloud computing security issues. *Future Generation Computer Systems, 28*(3), 583–592. doi:10.1016/j.future.2010.12.006

Section 4
Energy and Scheduling Optimization

Chapter 12

A Decadal Walkthrough on Energy Modelling for Cloud Datacenters

Ahan Chatterjee

https://orcid.org/0000-0001-5217-4457

The Neotia University, India

ABSTRACT

Cloud computing is the growing field in the industry, and every scale industry needs it now. The high scale usage of cloud has resulted in huge power consumption, and this power consumption has led to increase of carbon footprint affecting our mother nature. Thus, we need to optimize the power usage in the cloud servers. Various models are used to tackle this situation, of which one is a model based on link load. It minimized the bit energy consumption of network usage which includes energy efficiency routing and load balancing. Over this, multi-constraint rerouting is also adapted. Other power models which have been adapted are virtualization framework using multi-tenancy-oriented data center. It works by accommodating heterogeneous networks among virtual machines in virtual private cloud. Another strategy that is adopted is cloud partitioning concept using game theory. Other methods that are adopted are load spreading algorithm by shortest path bridging, load balancing by speed scaling, load balancing using graph constraint, and insert ranking method.

DOI: 10.4018/978-1-7998-5040-3.ch012

INTRODUCTION

In a recent study shows that the power consumed by ICT equipment is 8% of the total power consumption and that's a pretty big figure. While it ejects 2-4% of carbon dioxide emission of the total emission in the world. Thus saving energy is necessity of the time. But in parallel network consumption is also increasing exponentially thus but need to be controlled. While in working state there always some nodes which remain in idle state but costs us power consumption, we need to manifest those. Thus we need multiple constraints for high energy efficiency in network. Thus an E2MR algorithm is adapted, which works on load balancing. This power model takes some link between link load and energy consumption and after that energy bit to characterize energy efficiency of the networks. (Jiang et al., 2016)

Implementation of any design directly to hardware costs much higher, thus technique named virtualization is adapted. This technique is used to support the enormous amount of cloud information in data center converting the hardware into cloud infrastructure. Virtual Machines (VM) are units which act as supervisor, between hardware and operating system. VM shifts between optimizing and re-balancing server workloads. Through the modernization of networking the latest technique that is being used is software-defined networking (SDN), and its underlying distributed virtual switch (DVS) (Al-Shargabi et al, 2020; Aljawarneh, 2012; Aljawarneh et al, 2017; Chehbi-Gamoura et al, 2018; Esposito et al, 2018; Jaswal et al, 2019; Kalpana et al, 2018; Lizcano et al, 2020; Malhotra et al, 2019; Mohammed et al, 2019; Mouchili et al, 2018; Singh,2011).

Distributed computer system is adapted to optimize the energy system, here 2 or more computer are arbitrarily connected, the processors are interconnected among. This model thus also called loosely coupled system. A heterogeneous processor system is designed where different processor have different capacities and working capabilities, in this model task is assigned to such a processor in such a way that the execution time of the entire program is being minimized. To maximize the performance through this type of approach is commonly known as load balancing. An algorithm is being developed to form a distributed network and an n-processor distributed system a minimal cost task-processor assignment.

In local load balancing faces a constraint problem while optimizing the energy usage. Thus an algorithm is developed to maintain global load balancing using local adjustment. As in local load balancing large scale load balancing occurs some problem.

To optimize power in cloud system, LAN is also adapted. The incoming jobs are being allocated to different processors in dynamic method. Most of the algorithms which are being designed use difference of workstation speed to allocate the respective jobs. Job delay technique also been adapted to increase the productivity while consuming low power. This LAN method can be applied in scheduler to check the results satisfactory or not.

Public cloud platform is also deployed sometimes to optimize the energy usage. This service model has a huge computational resource to provide service to user. To lower the energy consumption more load can be assigned to a Data Center (DC) to work in that way. In this model load balancing can be achieved by creating dynamic DNS response. (Duan & Yang, 2017)

Public cloud has various nodes in it for working. They are arranged in a distributed computing resource around the world thus breaking the whole into smaller parts make the complex thing a bit simpler

The optimization of energy through Ethernet protocol is being adapted newly to cut down to excessive energy consumption. Thus an algorithm is designed to operate on IEEE shortest bridge path using Ethernet connection is used. This is based on the concept of Virtual LAN (VLAN).

Speed Scaling is also an important method to optimize energy usage over cloud data centers. Thus an algorithm is developed to match the load balancing and speed scaling; there the dispatcher energy is minimized by minimizing the delay experienced in processing a job. In this way the consumption of energy is capped.

The server which is at rest consumes dynamic power thus managing the servers is very much important. Thus a method is proposed in which the load balancing can be distributed in particular subsets of server.

Another algorithm is developed where job is assigned to server just before its deadline. This also lowers power consumption.

Another method which has been used is to route the work in the nearest possible geographically located datacenter to lower power consumption.

Bell proposed a game theory approach to identify the intrusion detection, through failure of nodes which will apparently affect the network performances. Here it's a two player game router and virtual network tester. The aim for network tester is to maximize the trip cost whereas the same for router is to find least cost path.

Viera et al proposed intrusion detection system based on network nodes in cloud computing environment. This method used grid type detection but the major drawback in this methodology is it cannot detect any kind of new attack.

Han et al proposed a method, in which it will detect the potential attacks and it will cluster into 3 different types of sub sections namely high, moderate, and low risk afterward it will be 2 player optimization strategy play in which the attackers are forced to behave as common element and total cost of attacker gets increased in a significant manner, but the major drawback in this case is it's basically designed for independent datacenters it cannot support multiple datacenter.

Ferdousi et al proposed a method in which the datacenters are placed in a disaster management system and the protection policy was dynamic in nature.

DETAILED STUDY

Implementation of the E2MR algorithm to cut down the usage of power needs a robust network topology to manage the traffic load over various nodes and links over the network. The between links and nodes are being measured by random walk process.

Graph theory is being adapted to analyze and propose the power theory model. A power model function is generated to for measuring the link energy, which is basically based on the link node energy consumption. The method says that when the link load is zero then the energy consumption is zero but when it is not equal to zero energy consumption is equal to the sum of basic energy consumption.

In the link power model to calculate allocation energy of traffic flow a network optimization model is also being used. Network criticality parameter is used for load balancing in which it is used to map the linked weights and to calculate the link cost. Network criticality can be measured from a global point of view in which it denotes the robustness of a network. The equation goes as smaller network implies more robust network. Similarly greater network criticality the more unstable the network is.

To find end to end shortest path MCRA algorithm is used. To get better network path we can use the MCRA algorithm to calculate the new path for better and satisfactory results. And energy consumption in a network can be calculated from the paths according to link energy function.

The E2MR2 algorithm proposes a multi constraint path, it's has 2 stages of operation in the first stage it decides the path through which energy consumption will be minimized, according to link weight. And in the next path guarantees the constraint of the requests. Through this E2MR2 algorithm we can raise the energy efficiency of the networks.

Another method to optimize the energy usage is to directly convert the metal data center into cloud environment. For this a network model is being proposed. To cut down the consumption a framework is being designed and this is mainly divided into 2 parts namely static strategies and dynamic strategies. Computing resource assigned is fixed in the static part while on the other hand substrate resource is allowed reconfiguration in dynamic strategies. The implementation is also divided into 2 major parts namely, VM placement and link establishment.

The placement of VM is done in a particular response of tenant. Here the framework is designed in such a manner that it improves the traffic locality. Thus they are being placed in topologically close order. Efforts are made to localize them so that least possible edge switches are used to maintain a smooth flow of data. (Xu et al., 2013)

The second phase or level is based on the link connection. In this level the framework selects appropriate core switches and then it links between the edge switch tier and core switch tier to route the data flow. Here also we use the dynamic strategy implementation for obtaining better results. (Chou et al., 1982)

In a wrapping context it may be said that by implementing this algorithm that no specific hardware server is being dedicated for a particular job. And inter edge flow is maintained by these links and switches gets assigned.

A computational model is being proposed for the consumption of energy, the computational model is based on the distributed system. The computational model is based on and parallel works on probabilistic branch points and fork points.

Every node leads to an edge this edge can be a terminating edge or a fork point. From the each edge it leads to a probabilistic branch point is a probability itself. And when the execution leads to a probabilistic branch point only one output edge is being selected. The common point here is known as probabilistic join point.

The model proposed is dynamic execution model; the modeling is done by semi-Markov process. It is a two phase model a state in the model will represent the execution of the task. And meanwhile the reward structure is designed to model the time behavior.

There are 3 types of programming framework used, programming with no branches, Programs with branches, and program with concurrency. In the first case there are no branch points all. Similarly in the second case have branches in it. And in the third and final case concurrent processing takes place they have nodes in between fork and joint points.

The power consumption can also be reduced by proper implementation of LAN network over the datacenters. There are mainly two kinds of LAN which is used namely, local and schedulable. The local setup is based on information of the workstations which act locally, while on the other hand the schedulable jobs are bound to CPU. By default method the jobs are taken as schedulable in nature over its local counterpart. (Lenhardt et al., 2015)

In a datacenter huge number of jobs comes at a time and to process all these data consumes time, while all the servers when in act some jobs come and have to wait to be processed from here the delay term comes into the game. (Moharir & Shakkottai, 2013)

Introducing the delay factor in a scheduling algorithm reduces the time consumption in job groups and improves response of individual jobs.

The dynamic load balancing technique takes the path of least-loaded approach to work on. In this methodology the job is allocated to the least loaded computer to get it processed in minimal time required. But in threshold based approach the workstation gets triggered the load balancing if the measured load exceeds the limit value.

In this method three types of things occur, the highly loaded computer unloads and dispatches its load to lighter loaded computer this method is known as sender initiated approach. On the other hand the lighter loaded computer itself calls for load from heavily loaded computer and this method is known as receiver initiated approach. And when these two approaches are being combined in a work it's then called symmetrically initiated approach.

Public Cloud platform is also often adapted to cap the power consumption. A large public cloud has more number of presences of nodes in it. In this case we use cloud partitioning to make it in use. Here the load balancing is based on the concept of cloud partitioning concept. The assignment of job is done in three steps. (Hajek, 1990)

First when the job arrives the main controller decides and analyze that does really cloud partition should receive that particular job or not. Then the particular job is being assigned to a particular node by load balancer. If the load status is normal then the cloud partition is being done locally or its then further transferred into other partition.

Cloud Computer Architecture

Cloud Computing is one of the fastest growing sectors in the IT industry in today's world. As every organization is seeking for connected storage place and enough good which can be analyzed to obtain results. Cloud service providers have started to provide integrated framework to support parallel data processing. (Doel et al., 2013)

Deployment Model

All the applications which are being used needs to be deployed in the cloud with the variable requirements, now all the deployment model have their own characteristics which are discussed.

Private Cloud

One organization operates and maintains the entire cloud infrastructure. People outside the organization don't have any access to the resources in the cloud. (Allan et al., 2013)

Public Cloud

This type of cloud infrastructure is made available to the consumer on a subscription basis by the cloud service provider. This enables the consumers to invest a minimal amount in the cloud storage to deploy there system into cloud.

Hybrid Cloud

Hybrid cloud can be a merged form of public cloud and private cloud platform where the cloud provider can support some data of the organization and also provide some service in cloud with exchange of some subscription fees. Here consist different types of clouds of different types, and it allows data/ or application to be transfer from one to other cloud.

Service Model

Cloud Computing provides various models to its consumer in exchange of subscription fees. This provides infrastructure, platform, and software as services. The following models are the models which are being use.

Software as a Service (Saas)

The Saas model provides user not to install any software, physically in their computer system all the required software is there on the cloud. A Saas provides access to both resource and application to its user. (Chen & Li, 2015)

Platform as a Service (Paas)

The Paas Platform provides the consumers as a service based platform. It provides access to the platform that the consumer need to develop to run their own applications.

Infrastructure as a Service (Iaas)

The Iaas Platform provides the consumer a computational infrastructure platform to its user. The consumer has total access over storage in cloud and resources which are available in the cloud both hardware and software on a proprietary basis. (Hui & Chanson, 1999)

ENERGY EFFICIENT SCHEDULING OF VIRTUAL MACHINE

The current scenario is such we need to provide securities to the challenges seen in the contemporary market. Marking and refining the connecting links in the cloud network increases the security and reliability in the system. When one datacenter is down or not in use state, in that state it's called an open space and from there vulnerability can arise. That point becomes the open port through which the attack could be carried out. Underperformance of any datacenter or taking up too much time to respond generally indicates any vulnerability attack. In similar condition if the attacker can overuse or misuse the data assignments in the datacenters it can lead to massive carbon footprints and heating in the system, and too much heating can lead to poor performance even malfunction of device. The game theory is basically examines the strategic decision makings, here users or actors are taken and an optimal solution is being created based on the inputs from the users. In this case these actors are user and a tester. User opts for low cost datacenter with as high as possible security and the job of tester here to maximize the response cost function. This game is being tested and played in Nash Equilibrium strategy, where the selection probabilities is optimal for user and failing to breach is optimal for tester. The vulnerability test for data centre is being done using Method of Successive Weighted Averages (MSWA). (Boel & Van, 1989)

CONCLUSION

The biggest challenge faced while attempting to reduce the data center's electrical consumption is to link data center activities to electrical use. Data center consumption is based on IT and infrastructure loads or when cooling systems remove heat from the data center to keep the temperature optimal. The fuel or energy is used to generate electricity is the most significant factor affecting the year to year changes in CO_2 emissions. The proposed algorithm shows the reduced energy consumption of data center.

In this paper it has some short comings which can be modified and can be treated as future scope of study. One of the key assumption taken in the model is that the information in the workload is well informed but in more practical scenario this is not always maintained thus we have further develop a model which can take the un-informed instructions in the respective datacenters.

REFERENCES

Al-Shargabi, B., AlJawarneh, S., & Hayajneh, S. M. (2020). A cloudlet based security and trust model for e-government web services. *Journal of Theoretical and Applied Information Technology*, 98(1), 27–37.

Aljawarneh, S. (Ed.). (2012). *Cloud computing advancements in design, implementation, and technologies*. IGI Global.

Aljawarneh, S., & Malhotra, M. (Eds.). (2017). *Critical Research on Scalability and Security Issues in Virtual Cloud Environments*. IGI Global.

Allan, D., Farkas, J., & Mansfield, S. (2012). Intelligent load balancing for shortest path bridging. *IEEE Communications Magazine*, *50*(7), 163–167. doi:10.1109/MCOM.2012.6231293

Boel, R. K., & van Schuppen, J. H. (1989). Distributed routing for load balancing. *Proceedings of the IEEE*, *77*(1), 210–221. doi:10.1109/5.21080

Chehbi-Gamoura, S., Derrouiche, R., Malhotra, M., & Koruca, H. I. (2018, June). Adaptive management approach for more availability of big data business analytics. In *Proceedings of the Fourth International Conference on Engineering & MIS 2018* (pp. 1-8). 10.1145/3234698.3234758

Chen, L., & Li, N. (2015). On the interaction between load balancing and speed scaling. *IEEE Journal on Selected Areas in Communications*, *33*(12), 2567–2578. doi:10.1109/JSAC.2015.2482098

Chou, T. C. K., & Abraham, J. A. (1982). Load balancing in distributed systems. *IEEE Transactions on Software Engineering*, *SE-8*(4), 401–412. doi:10.1109/TSE.1982.235574

Doyle, J., Shorten, R., & O'Mahony, D. (2013). Stratus: Load balancing the cloud for carbon emissions control. *IEEE Transactions on Cloud Computing*, *1*(1), 1–1. doi:10.1109/TCC.2013.4

Duan, J., & Yang, Y. (2017). A load balancing and multi-tenancy oriented data center virtualization framework. *IEEE Transactions on Parallel and Distributed Systems*, *28*(8), 2131–2144. doi:10.1109/TPDS.2017.2657633

Esposito, C., Su, X., Aljawarneh, S. A., & Choi, C. (2018). Securing collaborative deep learning in industrial applications within adversarial scenarios. *IEEE Transactions on Industrial Informatics*, *14*(11), 4972–4981. doi:10.1109/TII.2018.2853676

Hajek, B. (1990). Performance of global load balancing by local adjustment. *IEEE Transactions on Information Theory*, *36*(6), 1398–1414. doi:10.1109/18.59935

Hui, C. C., & Chanson, S. T. (1999). Improved strategies for dynamic load balancing. *IEEE Concurrency*, *7*(3), 58–67. doi:10.1109/4434.788780

Jaswal, S., & Malhotra, M. (2019, December). A detailed analysis of trust models in cloud environment. In *Proceedings of the Second International Conference on Data Science, E-Learning and Information Systems* (pp. 1-5). 10.1145/3368691.3368740

Jiang, D., Zhang, P., Lv, Z., & Song, H. (2016). Energy-efficient multi-constraint routing algorithm with load balancing for smart city applications. *IEEE Internet of Things Journal*, *3*(6), 1437–1447. doi:10.1109/JIOT.2016.2613111

Kalpana, G., Kumar, P. V., Aljawarneh, S., & Krishnaiah, R. V. (2018). Shifted adaption homomorphism encryption for mobile and cloud learning. *Computers & Electrical Engineering*, *65*, 178–195. doi:10.1016/j.compeleceng.2017.05.022

Lenhardt, J., Chen, K., & Schiffmann, W. (2015). Energy-efficient web server load balancing. *IEEE Systems Journal*, *11*(2), 878–888. doi:10.1109/JSYST.2015.2465813

Lizcano, D., Lara, J. A., White, B., & Aljawarneh, S. (2020). Blockchain-based approach to create a model of trust in open and ubiquitous higher education. *Journal of Computing in Higher Education*, *32*(1), 109–134. doi:10.100712528-019-09209-y

Malhotra, M., & Singh, A. (2019). Role of Agents to Enhance the Security and Scalability in Cloud Environment. In Cloud Security: Concepts, Methodologies, Tools, and Applications (pp. 552-573). IGI Global. doi:10.4018/978-1-5225-8176-5.ch028

Mohammed, T. A., Ghareeb, A., Al-bayaty, H., & Aljawarneh, S. (2019, December). Big data challenges and achievements: applications on smart cities and energy sector. In *Proceedings of the Second International Conference on Data Science, E-Learning and Information Systems* (pp. 1-5). 10.1145/3368691.3368717

Moharir, S., Sanghavi, S., & Shakkottai, S. (2013, June). Online load balancing under graph constraints. In *Proceedings of the ACM SIGMETRICS/international conference on Measurement and modeling of computer systems* (pp. 363-364). 10.1145/2465529.2465751

Mouchili, M. N., Aljawarneh, S., & Tchouati, W. (2018, October). Smart city data analysis. In *Proceedings of the First International Conference on Data Science, E-learning and Information Systems* (pp. 1-6). Academic Press.

Singh, A., Juneja, D., & Malhotra, M. (2017). A novel agent based autonomous and service composition framework for cost optimization of resource provisioning in cloud computing. *Journal of King Saud University-Computer and Information Sciences*, *29*(1), 19–28. doi:10.1016/j.jksuci.2015.09.001

Xu, G., Pang, J., & Fu, X. (2013). A load balancing model based on cloud partitioning for the public cloud. *Tsinghua Science and Technology*, *18*(1), 34–39. doi:10.1109/TST.2013.6449405

Chapter 13
Migrating Complex Applications From On-Premises to Cloud Interface:
Cloud Migration

Lokesh Pawar
https://orcid.org/0000-0002-1396-6088
Chandigarh University, India

Gaurav Bathla
Chandigarh University, India

ABSTRACT

Migrating applications on the cloud storage from the systems physically available on the premises is a difficult task. There are a lot of research articles providing solutions for the current problem of migration of applications by software industry. The chapter is shedding light on how to migrate the application efficiently using mathematical approach. The dependency of migration is directly proportional to the size of the data and the speed of the network. There are a number of storage options available on cloud for easy accessibility, cache-ability, and consistency. This chapter focuses on difficult migration of an application.

DOI: 10.4018/978-1-7998-5040-3.ch013

I. INTRODUCTION

Cloud Migration is a term utilized for migrating applications on cloud based services. Cloud based services are available in all forms IaaS, SaaS and PaaS. Now a days all sort of industries are switching from their own premises storage to cloud storage for performing day to day routine tasks like Online compilation service, Storage service, Software availability and many more application oriented services are available rather easily available with the help of cloud interface. Although all these application services were already available but with the advent and evolution of cloud based services they are easily available with a better performance. Achieving migration with higher rate of efficiency is a daunting task. There are several approaches to achieve cloud migration easily without losing the performance and efficiency of the already working software and application with the consistency of performance. In near future almost ½ th of the data will be passing through cloud based services. If an organization switches to cloud number of benefits can be availed like Disaster recovery, Security, Lesser Cost etc. Through Testing, we have encountered mistakes and compatibility errors, which we have identified kept a note for future work which we are going to do in migrating applications. Then a migration management framework was proposed for providing the installation automation and configuration validation, which uses templates to simplify the large scale enterprise system installation process and uses policy to validate the configuration and monitor the configuration change (Scandurra, 2015). Why Migration is becoming so prominent in this decade, because it allows new entrepreneurs to invest into business without investing in owing a building hardware software to run the business. No need of purchasing licenses but this depends upon which type of service we are opting out from the 3 available options (Al-Shargabi et al, 2020; Aljawarneh, 2012; Aljawarneh et al, 2017; Chehbi-Gamoura et al, 2018; Esposito et al, 2018; Jaswal et al, 2019; Kalpana et al, 2018; Lizcano et al, 2020; Malhotra et al, 2019; Mohammed et al, 2019; Mouchili et al, 2018; Singh,2011).

Right now we have 3 different scenarios:

- **On premises:** If we opt out for this option then we need to purchase the software, all the infrastructure required for Network, servers, operating system etc. The sole responsibility for running all of these software, hardware is of the owner only.
- **Hosted:** This is somehow similar to the on-premises approach but it is different as compared to the purchase of the hardware and infrastructure, we need to purchase only the licenses for the software and rent the hardware and infrastructure.

- **Cloud:** Need not to purchase anything, we take SaaS from any of the companies available in the market and can easily use the services even without purchasing the licenses. All the responsibilities are of the service provider.

Do not incline towards cloud migration because not all the applications supports efficiently for the cloud migration. Some software are safety critical software, which are not advisable to migrate. Embedded applications are not all benefited from such type of migration. And eventually we find certain application which actually suites the cloud environment so these type of application are highly cloud oriented can be migrated in high spirits of efficient working of the application.

II. MIGRATION APPROACH

A lot of application base from a company can cause problem in migrating complex applications directly to the cloud. A step by step procedure should be followed for migrating applications directly on to the cloud. Cloud Migration without experts help becomes worse and more than 58% business application faces problem when they are migrated from on-premises to private cloud. Almost all giants are providing cloud services, IBM, Amazon and Google.

There are few steps which should be followed in migrating an application:

1. Feasibility Study: There should be a feasibility study for migration of the application. In this process, requirement of migration, selection of the provider, the subroutines to be migrated are recognized.
2. Execution: Migration actually takes place in this process, all the relevant irrelevant data is extracted modified according to use case, architectures are recovered and the transformation at concrete and conceptual level takes place.
3. Evaluation: At this stage deployment testing and validation takes place.

Figure 1. Cloud Migration

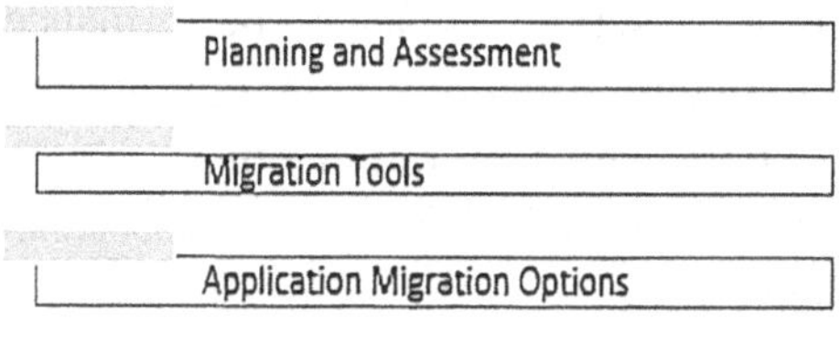

207

Planning Assessment phase comprises of Financial Assessment, Security and Compliance, Functional and Technical assessment. Before starting for cloud migration, cost estimation is required to be discussed and estimated. A vigilant analysis [Pawar, (2015)] is required to check the financial perspective of on-premises center against migrating to a cloud-based infrastructure. Security risks covers Overall risk tolerance Main [Zhao,(2014)] concerns around availability, durability, and confidentiality of your data[Scandurra,(2015)]. Security management can recover the lost data as well. Security managers should be involved at an early age of migration. Depending on the data security can be managed that which data sets are to be moved and which ones to keep on premises. Technical assessment delivers understandability that which application suits more to switched to the cloud interface. The interface may be on premises or out premises depending upon the severity of the security. Sometimes replication of data is also required to make availability which depending upon case to case variability change the requirement for further processing and taking step towards cloud migration.

III. MIGRATION TOOL

Physical and technical limitations becomes a barrier for migration of applications, here the factor of migration tools come to rescue. Migration tools helps to move data through network sites various technological partners.

1. **Unmanaged Migration Tool:** These tools are used only for transferring open-source projects to the developers or we can say only one time deliverables/products/software to the end users which sometimes requires customization at the user end. Unmanaged Migration tools are not suggested for frequent use, change sets are advisable for using unmanaged migration. In a Scenario if data transfer is at small scale unmanaged cloud data transfer tools can be easily used and the application may perform efficiently as well. Glacier CLI can be used for on-premises data and it will transfer the whole dump to the glacier vaults easily. S3 CLI certain commands will directly transfer the data to S3 Buckets available online as cloud interface [Pawar,(2015)]. It may cause a lot of staggering of data and may increase the response time for certain queries which requires quite a large fields to access and process results of a certain query. It may cause very serious impact on performance of the system.

2. **Proposed Cloud Efficient Migration Tool:** Proposed technique utilizes basic functionality of the unmanaged migration tool along with performance checks with google cloud services and amazon cloud services. It outperforms AWS in a few performance issues.

Figure 2. Proposed Architecture

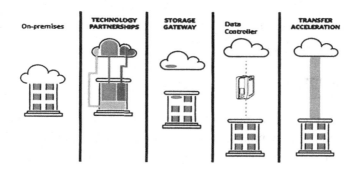

Fig 2 clearly depicts the process of internet support and data migration using Data Controller. Each phase shown in the architectural view has its own algorithms for data processing and converting it into easy transferrable form [Pawar, (2015)]. This data controller keep proper checks on data transfer and movement for transfer acceleration. This approach is ideal for cache data locally in a hybrid model and collect data and ingest into multiple streams data sources. There are a lot of storage options available according to the importance, usage, functionality of the data. Storage facility can be chosen from the list of availability. It can be Cost as one of the concern for the organization it may be cache-ability, latency Consistency Update Frequency etc.

Strategy utilized for migration in CEM tool is Hybrid Migration Technology says about only caching the frequently required data from the cloud. There are a lot of benefits a few are mentioned as: Lower-risk, Part By Part movement of application with proper functionality supported by data controller, deals with all sort of unexpected behavior [Sharma, (2019)].

IV. MIGRATING APPLICATIONS

Few applications which can directly help in application migration they are 1) live migration: without disconnecting a live running application. The memory and network connection of the remote machine/virtual machine [Pawar, (2015)] are copied from the physical device to the cloud. 2) host cloning : It means cloning of the operating system and it is one time migration [Randhawa, (2018)]. 3) For synchronization of data amongst computer storage and cloud file formats data migration is used. 4) For deployment of applications and for running applications which are distributed application containerization is used. 5) Virtual machine disk is used for reading writing on the cloud[Randhawa, (2018)].

V. CHALLENGES IN MIGRATION

Based on the above comparison and analysis, we identified the following challenges that could be research topics in the future.

1. Holistic Approach

There must be a system for migration to be followed, it must be divided into different types. A particular legacy migration strategy must be used and followed. With the help of this approach an organization may not face any difficulty in processing the request of migration.

2. Scalability in IaaS

It becomes a vital bottleneck when number of resources are ideal at one time and there are no resources at the time of requirement. This scenario happens when requirement of resources is uneven so a system is required to manage all abrupt requirements of the resources.

3. Use of Programming Language

If we want to migrate to PaaS, certain programming languages are required. For example, PaaS provides MapReduce programming model which is a simple data-parallel programming model designed for scalability and fault-tolerance.[Scandurra, (2015)]

VI. CONCLUSION

The proposed Migrating tool is under development phase which is going to work for complex application migration. There are few advantages and disadvantages of migration. Validity of the product rests on the shoulder of threat. The threat can be on the basis of result biasness – the tendency of the result to deviate from the actual result. The other threat may arise due to the validity of the tool/application due to the design of the tool. An application has recently transferred using the architectural approach described in the article and it outperformed the current architecture in migration speed and efficiency. Future work is a practical implementation along with comparative results.

REFERENCES

Al-Shargabi, B., AlJawarneh, S., & Hayajneh, S. M. (2020). A cloudlet based security and trust model for e-government web services. *Journal of Theoretical and Applied Information Technology*, *98*(1), 27–37.

Aljawarneh, S. (Ed.). (2012). *Cloud computing advancements in design, implementation, and technologies*. IGI Global.

Aljawarneh, S., & Malhotra, M. (Eds.). (2017). *Critical Research on Scalability and Security Issues in Virtual Cloud Environments*. IGI Global.

Bathla, G. (2013). Minimum Spanning Tree based Protocol for Heterogeneous Wireless Sensor Networks. *i-Manager's Journal of Wireless Communication Networks*, *1*(4), 12-22.

Chehbi-Gamoura, S., Derrouiche, R., Malhotra, M., & Koruca, H. I. (2018, June). Adaptive management approach for more availability of big data business analytics. In *Proceedings of the Fourth International Conference on Engineering & MIS 2018* (pp. 1-8). 10.1145/3234698.3234758

Esposito, C., Su, X., Aljawarneh, S. A., & Choi, C. (2018). Securing collaborative deep learning in industrial applications within adversarial scenarios. *IEEE Transactions on Industrial Informatics*, *14*(11), 4972–4981. doi:10.1109/TII.2018.2853676

Jaswal, S., & Malhotra, M. (2019, December). A detailed analysis of trust models in cloud environment. In *Proceedings of the Second International Conference on Data Science, E-Learning and Information Systems* (pp. 1-5). 10.1145/3368691.3368740

Kalpana, G., Kumar, P. V., Aljawarneh, S., & Krishnaiah, R. V. (2018). Shifted adaption homomorphism encryption for mobile and cloud learning. *Computers & Electrical Engineering*, *65*, 178–195. doi:10.1016/j.compeleceng.2017.05.022

Khan, G. (2011). Energy- efficient Routing Protocol for Homogeneous Wireless Sensor Networks. *International Journal on Cloud Computing: Services and Architecture*, *1*(1), 12-20.

Lizcano, D., Lara, J. A., White, B., & Aljawarneh, S. (2020). Blockchain-based approach to create a model of trust in open and ubiquitous higher education. *Journal of Computing in Higher Education*, *32*(1), 109–134. doi:10.100712528-019-09209-y

Lokesh. (2019). *Smart City IOT: Smart Architectural Solution for Networking, Congestion and Heterogeneity*. IEEE ICICCS.

Lokesh, P. (2012). Design of Simulator for Finding the Delay Distribution in Delay Tolerant Networking. GJCST, 12(14).

Malhotra, M., & Singh, A. (2019). Role of Agents to Enhance the Security and Scalability in Cloud Environment. In Cloud Security: Concepts, Methodologies, Tools, and Applications (pp. 552-573). IGI Global. doi:10.4018/978-1-5225-8176-5.ch028

Mohammed, T. A., Ghareeb, A., Al-bayaty, H., & Aljawarneh, S. (2019, December). Big data challenges and achievements: applications on smart cities and energy sector. In *Proceedings of the Second International Conference on Data Science, E-Learning and Information Systems* (pp. 1-5). 10.1145/3368691.3368717

Mouchili, M. N., Aljawarneh, S., & Tchouati, W. (2018, October). Smart city data analysis. In *Proceedings of the First International Conference on Data Science, E-learning and Information Systems* (pp. 1-6). Academic Press.

Pawar. (2014). Comparing: Routing Protocols on Basis of sleep mode. *International Journal of Modern Research, 4*(7).

Pawar. (2015). Reducing Impact of Flooding In VANETs Due To Distributed Denial. *International Journal of Engineering Science and Computing.*

Pawar. (2015). A Survey on Energy Efficient Clustering Protocols in Heterogeneous Wireless Sensor Networks. *International Journal of Advanced Research in Computer and Communication Engineering, 4*(8).

Pawar. (2015). IBEENISH: Improved Balanced Energy Efficient Network Integrated Super Heterogeneous Protocol for Wireless Sensor Networks. *International Journal of Computer Science and Networking, 4*(4).

Pawar, L. (2017). Optimized Route Selection on the Basis of Discontinuity and Energy Consumption in Delay-Tolerant Networks. Advances in Computer and Computational Sciences, 439-449. doi:10.1007/978-981-10-3770-2_41

Randhawa, R. (2018). Virtual Tier structured Grid based Dynamic Route Adjustment scheme for mobile sink based Wireless Sensor Networks (VTGDRA). *International Journal of Applied Engineering Research: IJAER, 13*(7), 4702–4707.

Scandurra, P. (2015). *Challenges and Assessment in Migrating IT Legacy Applications to the Cloud.* MESOCA. doi:10.1109/MESOCA.2015.7328120

Sharma.(2019). An Intelligent Genetic Base Algorithm for Optimal Virtual Machine Migration in Cloud Computing. *IJRTE, 8*(1).

Singh, A., Juneja, D., & Malhotra, M. (2017). A novel agent based autonomous and service composition framework for cost optimization of resource provisioning in cloud computing. *Journal of King Saud University-Computer and Information Sciences*, 29(1), 19–28. doi:10.1016/j.jksuci.2015.09.001

Suri & Pawar. (2012). Stochastic Simulator For Estimating Delay in DTN Environment. *IJETAE*, 2(8), 183-189.

Zhao, J. F. (2014). *Strategies and Methods for Cloud Migration*. IJAC. doi:10.100711633-014-0776-7

Chapter 14
Future of Business Intelligence in Cloud Computing

Krishan Tuli
Chandigarh University, India

ABSTRACT

Cloud business intelligence can solve numerous management issues that are faced by many businesses. If it is used in a correct manner, it can substitute seamless utilization of crucial information in the growth of business. In the self-hosted environment, business intelligence will face resource crisis situation on the never-ending expansion of warehouses and OLAP's demands on the primary network. Today, cloud computing has instigated optimism for the prospects of future business intelligence. But thing to focus here is, how will business intelligence be implemented on cloud platform, and further, how will the traffic be managed and what will the demand profile look like? Moreover, in today's world, data generated on a daily basis from many different sources are numerous and valuable information for making effective decisions. This chapter focuses and tries to attempt these questions related to taking business intelligence to the cloud.

INTRODUCTION

Cloud Computing, in today's world is the very important service now a days. Cloud computing is delivering the computational services to the users which includes storage, networking, databases, software, platform, analytics and intelligence over the internet on a faster, flexible rates. Cloud offers the flexible resources on a very economical scale and on a very fast innovation. This service is available on pay as you go model which means user has to pay only for the service he is using. This will

DOI: 10.4018/978-1-7998-5040-3.ch014

help the user to lower down the operating cost and runs the infrastructure on a more efficient way and help in business scale changes (Krishna et al, 2018). There are many other benefits of using cloud as a model on internet. Using cloud as a service model is not only cost effective but it gives uninterrupted speed on as per the demand. The other benefit of using cloud service is its ability to scale elastically that means to deliver the accurate amount of services provided to the user when it is needed. So with this benefit, it will increase the productivity of on-site datacenters by not spending much time on hardware - software setups and many other time consuming IT things which make the team to spend more time on achieving important business goals. Lastly the biggest service of cloud is the performance and security, which keeps on upgrading on a regular basis (NIST, 2011). Below Figure 1 will brief about the types of cloud computing. Public cloud delivers there services of resources like storage, servers etc on to the internet and it is owned by the third party. Private cloud is those types of cloud computing which are operated by the private network only and lastly the hybrid computing which is a mixture of both public as well as private cloud. It allows data and applications to be shared among each other so that they can exchange the information as and when required. By doing this, a hybrid cloud will give your businesses a greater flexibility and more deployment which will further help in optimizing existing user's infrastructure (Ali et al, 2019, Al-Shargabi et al, 2020; Aljawarneh, 2012; Aljawarneh et al, 2017; Chehbi-Gamoura et al, 2018; Esposito et al, 2018; Jaswal et al, 2019; Kalpana et al, 2018; Lizcano et al, 2020; Malhotra et al, 2019; Mohammed et al, 2019; Mouchili et al, 2018; Singh,2011).

Further, cloud computing comes in four more broad categories that is Infrastructure as a Service which is abbreviated as IaaS, Platform as a Service abbreviated as

Figure 1. Types of Cloud Computing

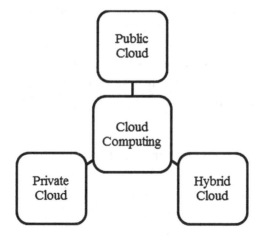

Figure 2. Types of Cloud Service Model

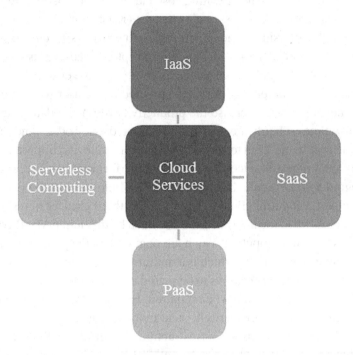

PaaS, Server-less computing and lastly Software as a Service abbreviated as SaaS (Pardeep et al, 2018). Figure 2, shows the various categories of cloud computing.

Information technology industry faces lot of ethical issues related to infrastructures and other software. So providing the correct resource to the right person is one of the important challenge and need of business intelligence service provided by cloud (Soltanshahi et al, 2019). As the technology is growing at a rapid speed, so the demand and desire of emergent technologies is also increased. The superlative performance in technology can only be measured in terms of customer satisfaction. In terms of cloud computing scenarios, two important perspectives are there, consumer and service providers. Consumers are the users of cloud services which are provided by the cloud providers. Business Intelligence and cloud computing always moves parallelly considering the technical understandings but BI require large storage production as compare to cloud.

WHAT IS BUSINESS INTELLIGENCE?

BI contains the strategies and technology which are used by the various enterprises for the analysis of data in business information. With the help of technological data storage, OLAP, Data Mining and other data warehouse technologies combines the both internal and external data to come up with the confined decisions. Operational decisions may be the product pricing and on the other hand strategic decisions could be the goals and other important development directions (Demchenko et al, 2011).

Figure 3. Business Intelligence

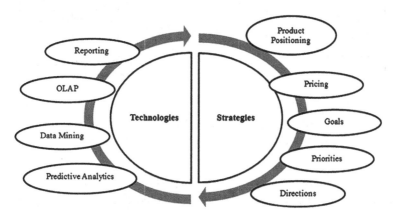

BUSINESS INTELLIGENCE FRAMEWORK

Business intelligence framework is a framework which helps in the stream less connection between the multiple elements of business like authorization, visualization, riles of organizations and other KPI's. This helps in the implementation of business intelligence plans at a faster and easier way (NIST, 2011). The framework of BI helps in structuring the improvement process in Business Intelligence. On the priority, it will implement business intelligence strategically model in cost effective manner. Many years of research had made this strategically model to develop this framework which is of high quality and at a reasonable price.

Business intelligence frameworks have all the information related to any organizational role and in the same form which is required by them. In other words we can say that, all the relevant information whosoever needs will be available effortlessly and at a given point of time and that information will be at current time, more interactive and at a faster time. So users are no longer need to struggle with various complex files and with their file structures (Krishna et al, 2018). They just need to click and just look for the right report or the particular dashboard designed for.

There are various key points of this framework

Figure 4. Business Intelligence Framework

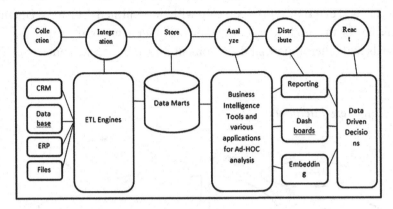

- There are many possibilities of reusability due to object oriented.
- It is very user friendly and very easy to access due to the standardized experience.
- It is highly flexible, if it is made for the particular organizational roles.
- It can be easily access in a portable devices like smartphones, tablets etc.

Broadly speaking, frameworks are not only concerned with the data layers of the data warehouse and its architecture but they are concerned with the presentation layer of business intelligence that more over concentrates on the authorization. Because in that layer, one can get lot of efficiency and uncountable reports in the form of pie charts, graphs and tables.

Business Intelligence consists of various other layers also. Each component of its layer has own purpose and following are the various components BI is made up of.

A Business intelligence framework consist of following components

1. Data Collection: The first and very important step in creating or developing a stable architecture will start for gathering information from various sources depending on the requirement of the company such as CRM, Databases, ERP's and other related files or application programming interfaces. In today's technology of business intelligence various tools offers fast and easy to access data connectors to make this process easy to use by using ETL engines. These ETL engines enables a communication between various scattered departments and other systems that otherwise could not be possible. For a successful business prospective, this is a very crucial element in maintaining and developing a successful decision making without any errors and with the increased productivity.

Figure 5. Detailed Business Intelligence Architecture

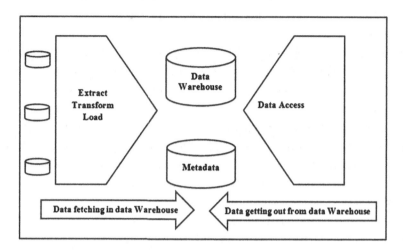

2. Data Integration: When data is scattered at different location then next step is to extract the data and load on to the data warehouse. This technique is called ETL process. The full form of ETL is called Extract-Transform-Load. In today's technology, as the data is generated in a huge amount hence it is also going to increase the overload on the IT industries. ETL comes as a service to answer these complex problems. The process of ETL is shown in the figure 6 below.

Figure 6. Data Integration

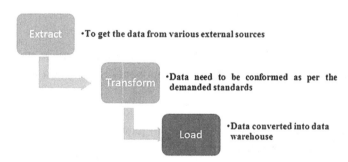

3. Data Storage: Both the terms that's business intelligence concept and data warehousing, both the terms are used interchangeably but there is certain other difference between these two. Basically business intelligence is used for decision support system and data warehousing is used for the data storage system. In business intelligence data is collected from the data warehousing

for analysis purpose and in data warehousing data is collected from various different sources and further organizes it for the efficient used of business intelligence.

4. Data Analysis: In this step of data analysis, the focus is on the analysis of data and how it is handled, process and helped in managing the various steps of data warehouse. There is a global need of successful analysis of data for empowering the businesses of all sizes to grow and gain profit with the help of various business intelligence tools. So when it comes to the various ad hoc analyses, it enables the flexibility in performing the analysis and helping in answers the critical questions of business in an accurate and effective manner. Data warehouse has always works behind the process and creates the overall architecture of business intelligence possible.

5. Distribution of data: Distribution of data is one of the very crucial process when it comes to the sharing of data and information and providing the same to the stakeholders to obtain a maintained business development model. Distribution of data is performed in three ways:
   a. Dashboards
   b. Embedded
   c. Reporting through automated emails

6. Reactions insights: This is the final stage of business intelligence architecture where the power of BI is expounds is creating the data driven decisions. Without data warehousing and business intelligence this stage would not be possible and business crucial decisions would not be possible.

BUSINESS INTELLIGENCE AND OLAP

Business Intelligence and OLAP architecture makes a complex structure in the multi-layer environment. There are few components of business intelligence and OLAP architecture

- The user interface layer in business intelligence comprising of dashboards for various graphical interfaces reports.
- The layer for various data analytics are comprising of what and if scenarios, depending on the data models, queries and reports.
- The layer that is used for storing the OLAP's which are formed in the multi-layered dimensions are extracting the data from data warehouses.
- The layer of data integration for the purpose of organizing and grouping from the various data warehouses for the data extraction is done before the OLAP cubes are formulated.

- The data layer in business intelligence always comprises of data warehouses.
- The layer that is used for acquiring data from the number of business processing, decision support system and other transactional databases which are used by various other functions of different organisations.
- The data layer in business intelligence and OLAP comprises of various infrastructure components and other resources like data storage, networking and data processing methods.

So the key feature in business intelligence and OLAP architecture is the OLAP cubes, which is a multi-dimensional structure formed in the shape of matrix. The complex structure of data view is OLAP cubes in which data views are running in the simultaneous queries on the various tables and data is fetched from various data warehouses. In the typical OLAP applications, the various queries that are attached with this are typically fetch 10-12 times more data as compare to the traditional one. OLAP application may use various multiple OLAP cubes that are stored in the form of very complex hierarchy of matrix and all the data have been organized in a tabular format. It has been defined that all the data cubes are stored in a data marts in the data warehouses attached to it. Each one of the matrix is classified by its own classification and they comprise of different data map sets. The matrix is in the form of nest like structure due to its inter relationship between each other and the resultant of this structure looks like a hierarchical structure. The main dashboard operator can easily change and modify the both the variables that is primary as well as secondary which further directs the queries to fetch the data from various different queries from the data warehouses. So the nutshell is that the OLAP cubes can be changed dynamically and they are very flexible as per the need of our business requirement. In the below figure 7, it shows the framework of BI and OLAP

BENEFITS OF BUSINESS INTELLIGENCE IN CLOUD

In today's technological world, the business intelligence in cloud computing is gaining lot of popularity among various businesses and further businesses are getting the benefits from various data analytics. Businesses now days need a quality of data driven by exact and accurate data. The software as a service provider severed as the key interface to the entire business user's community so the cloud Business intelligence is the main concept of delivering this service of BI capabilities. Following are the main benefits of business intelligence in cloud computing.

1. Cost efficiency: The key point in the cloud computing is its cost efficiency which works on the concept of pay as per you go model. So companies don't

Figure 7. OLAP and Business Intelligence Framework

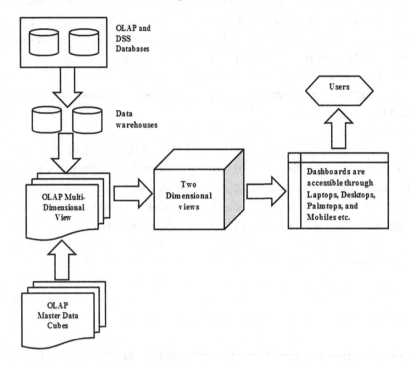

need to make a budget for the large purchases and to create a large infrastructure of its business intelligence.

2. Scalability and flexibility: cloud Business Intelligence has a greater flexibility to modify quickly and to give the access to the new data sources which are used by various analytics models. Also the resources in cloud can scale in and out easily which can support the various users simultaneously.

3. Enhanced sharing of data: All the cloud applications share the data remotely and it also enable the cross location of data at a faster rates.

4. Reliability: Reliability can be improved through the use of various multiple sites which also provide the reality of various data elements for the data storage and the resources that need to be spread to the number of users.

5. No capital expenditure: Reduction in the total cost of expenditure is the very key factor and the main benefit in the cloud model. In cloud models, companies only pay for those resources which are actually used by them.

CONCLUSION

Cloud computing is the very crucial part in the future of business intelligence and it also served as a number of various advantages in terms of data sharing, cost effectiveness, flexibility and scalability of resources, the reliability of resource availability etc. cloud computing has potentially provides the new life to the business intelligence and OLAP architecture. Cloud's services that are software as a service, platform as a service and infrastructure as a service cloud models provides these services to the various BI's and OLAP frameworks. May be these services are provided by various different providers but they have to depend on the various business arrangements. So cloud computing is providing the routing for various search engines which can effectively make the load pattern on the resources. Nutshell, we can say is Business intelligence and OLAP framework is a demanding framework and it has a multilayered architecture with the multi-dimensional matrix which represents the relationship between various matrix variables. The size of OLAP queries are around 10 times larger than the data bases of various other query data bases. So if the business intelligence and OLAP framework servers to thousands of users on cloud, it is essential to make the parallel processing of resources and moreover cloud also offers sufficient amount of power and capacity to the various resources.

REFERENCES

Al-Shargabi, B., AlJawarneh, S., & Hayajneh, S. M. (2020). A cloudlet based security and trust model for e-government web services. *Journal of Theoretical and Applied Information Technology*, *98*(1), 27–37.

Ali, S. A., Affan, M., & Alam, M. (2019). A Study of Efficient Energy Management Techniques for Cloud Computing Environment. *2019 9th International Conference on Cloud Computing, Data Science & Engineering (Confluence)*, 13-18. 10.1109/CONFLUENCE.2019.8776977

Aljawarneh, S. (Ed.). (2012). *Cloud computing advancements in design, implementation, and technologies*. IGI Global.

Aljawarneh, S., & Malhotra, M. (Eds.). (2017). *Critical Research on Scalability and Security Issues in Virtual Cloud Environments*. IGI Global.

Bakshi, K. (2012). Considerations for big data: Architecture and approach. *IEEE Aerospace Conference*, 1-7. 10.1109/AERO.2012.6187357

Banerjee, S., Mandal, R., & Biswas, U. (2018). An Approach Towards Amelioration of an Efficient VM Allocation Policy in Cloud Computing Domain. *Wireless Personal Communications*, *98*(2), 1799–1820. doi:10.100711277-017-4946-0

Barthwal, V., Rauthan, M., & Verma, R. (2019). Virtual Machines Placement Using Predicted Utilization of Physical Machine in Cloud Datacenter. In *International Conference on Advances in Engineering Science Management & Technology (ICAESMT)*. Uttaranchal University.

Basu, S., Kannayaram, G., Ramasubbareddy, S., & Venkatasubbaiah, C. (2019). Improved Genetic Algorithm for Monitoring of Virtual Machines in Cloud Environment. In *Smart Intelligent Computing and Applications* (Vol. 105, pp. 319–326). Springer. doi:10.1007/978-981-13-1927-3_34

Bhattacherjee, S., Das, R., Khatua, S., & Roy, S. (2019). Energy-efficient migration techniques for cloud environment: A step toward green computing. *The Journal of Supercomputing*, 1–29. doi:10.100711227-019-02801-0

Chaudhrani, V., Acharya, P., & Chudasama, V. (2018). Energy Aware Computing Resource Allocation Using PSO in Cloud. In *Information and Communication Technology for Intelligent Systems* (pp. 511–519). Springer.

Chehbi-Gamoura, S., Derrouiche, R., Malhotra, M., & Koruca, H. I. (2018, June). Adaptive management approach for more availability of big data business analytics. In *Proceedings of the Fourth International Conference on Engineering & MIS 2018* (pp. 1-8). 10.1145/3234698.3234758

Convery, N. (2010). *Cloud computing toolkit: guidance for outsourcing information storage to the Cloud, Department of Information Studies, Aberystwyth University*. Archives and Records Association.

Das, J., Dasgupta, A., Ghosh, S. K., & Buyya, R. (2019). A Learning Technique for VM Allocation to Resolve Geospatial Queries. In *Recent Findings in Intelligent Computing Techniques* (pp. 577–584). Springer. doi:10.1007/978-981-10-8639-7_61

Demchenko, Y., & Laat, C. D. (2011). Defining generic architecture for Cloud infrastructure as a service model. *The International Symposium on Grids and Clouds and the Open Grid Forum Academia*, 2–10.

Esposito, C., Su, X., Aljawarneh, S. A., & Choi, C. (2018). Securing collaborative deep learning in industrial applications within adversarial scenarios. *IEEE Transactions on Industrial Informatics*, *14*(11), 4972–4981. doi:10.1109/TII.2018.2853676

Han, G., Que, W., Jia, G., & Zhang, W. (2018). Resource-utilization-aware energy efficient server consolidation algorithm for green computing in IIOT. *Journal of Network and Computer Applications, 103*, 205–214. doi:10.1016/j.jnca.2017.07.011

Jana, B., Chakraborty, M., & Mandal, T. (2019). A task scheduling technique based on particle swarm optimization algorithm in cloud environment. In Soft Computing: Theories and Applications. Springer. doi:10.1007/978-981-13-0589-4_49

Jaswal, S., & Malhotra, M. (2019, December). A detailed analysis of trust models in cloud environment. In *Proceedings of the Second International Conference on Data Science, E-Learning and Information Systems* (pp. 1-5). 10.1145/3368691.3368740

Kalpana, G., Kumar, P. V., Aljawarneh, S., & Krishnaiah, R. V. (2018). Shifted adaption homomorphism encryption for mobile and cloud learning. *Computers & Electrical Engineering, 65*, 178–195. doi:10.1016/j.compeleceng.2017.05.022

Kaur, S., & Kaur, K. (2019). Enhancing Reliability of Cloud Services Using Mechanism of Dynamic Replication and Migration of Data. *International Journal of Applied Engineering Research: IJAER, 14*(8), 1976–1983.

Krishnadoes, P., & Jacob, P, (2018). OCSA: task scheduling algorithm in the cloud computing environment. *International Journal of Intelligent Engineering & Systems, 11*(3), 271-279.

Kurdi, H. A., Alismail, S. M., & Hassan, M. M. (2018). LACE: A Locust-Inspired Scheduling Algorithm to Reduce Energy Consumption in Cloud Datacenters. *IEEE Access: Practical Innovations, Open Solutions, 6*, 35435–35448. doi:10.1109/ACCESS.2018.2839028

Latiff, M. S. A., Madni, S. H. H., & Abdullahi, M. (2018). Fault tolerance aware scheduling technique for cloud computing environment using dynamic clustering algorithm. *Neural Computing & Applications, 29*(1), 279–293. doi:10.100700521-016-2448-8

LD, D. B., & Krishna, P. V. (2013). Honey bee behavior inspired load balancing of tasks in cloud computing environments. *Applied Soft Computing, 13*(5), 2292–2303. doi:10.1016/j.asoc.2013.01.025

Li, C., Liao, X., & Jin, H. (2019). Enhancing application performance via DAG-driven scheduling in task parallelism for cloud center. *Peer-to-Peer Networking and Applications, 12*(2), 381–391. doi:10.100712083-017-0576-2

Li, J., Jia, Y., Liu, L., & Wo, T. (2013). CyberLiveApp: A secure sharing and migration approach for live virtual desktop applications in a Cloud environment. *Future Generation Computer Systems*, 29(1), 330–340. doi:10.1016/j.future.2011.08.001

Li, J., Li, B., Wo, T., Hu, C., Huai, J., Liu, L., & Lam, K. (2012). CyberGuarder: A virtualization security assurance architecture for green Cloud computing. *Future Generation Computer Systems*, 28(2), 379–390. doi:10.1016/j.future.2011.04.012

Lizcano, D., Lara, J. A., White, B., & Aljawarneh, S. (2020). Blockchain-based approach to create a model of trust in open and ubiquitous higher education. *Journal of Computing in Higher Education*, 32(1), 109–134. doi:10.100712528-019-09209-y

Malhotra, M., & Singh, A. (2019). Role of Agents to Enhance the Security and Scalability in Cloud Environment. In Cloud Security: Concepts, Methodologies, Tools, and Applications (pp. 552-573). IGI Global. doi:10.4018/978-1-5225-8176-5.ch028

Mishra, S. K., Sahoo, B., & Jena, S. K. (2019). A Secure VM Consolidation in Cloud Using Learning Automata. In *Recent Findings in Intelligent Computing Techniques* (pp. 617–623). Springer. doi:10.1007/978-981-10-8639-7_65

Moges, F. F., & Abebe, S. L. (2019). Energy-aware VM placement algorithms for the OpenStack Neat consolidation framework. *Journal of Cloud Computing*, 8(1), 2–12. doi:10.118613677-019-0126-y

Mohamad, Z., Mahmoud, A. A., Nik, W. N. S. W., Mohamed, M. A., & Deris, M. M. (2018). A Genetic Algorithm for Optimal Job Scheduling and Load Balancing in Cloud Computing. *IACSIT International Journal of Engineering and Technology*, 7(3), 290–294.

Mohammed, T. A., Ghareeb, A., Al-bayaty, H., & Aljawarneh, S. (2019, December). Big data challenges and achievements: applications on smart cities and energy sector. In *Proceedings of the Second International Conference on Data Science, E-Learning and Information Systems* (pp. 1-5). 10.1145/3368691.3368717

Mouchili, M. N., Aljawarneh, S., & Tchouati, W. (2018, October). Smart city data analysis. In *Proceedings of the First International Conference on Data Science, E-learning and Information Systems* (pp. 1-6). Academic Press.

NIST. (2011). *US Government Cloud computing technology roadmap*. Special Publication 500-293, Cloud Computing Program, National Institute of Standards and Technology (NIST), US Department of Commerce.

Pradeep, K., & Jacob, T. P. (2018). A hybrid approaches for task scheduling using the cuckoo and harmony search in cloud computing environment. *Wireless Personal Communications*, *101*(4), 2287–2311. doi:10.100711277-018-5816-0

Ragmani, A., El Omri, A., Abghour, N., Moussaid, K., & Rida, M. (2018). A performed load balancing algorithm for public Cloud computing using ant colony optimization. *Recent Patents on Computer Science*, *11*(3), 179–195. doi:10.2174/2213275911666180903124609

Singh, A., Juneja, D., & Malhotra, M. (2017). A novel agent based autonomous and service composition framework for cost optimization of resource provisioning in cloud computing. *Journal of King Saud University-Computer and Information Sciences*, *29*(1), 19–28. doi:10.1016/j.jksuci.2015.09.001

Soltanshahi, M., Asemi, R., & Shafiei, N. (2019). Energy-aware virtual machines allocation by krill herd algorithm in cloud data centers. *Heliyon, 5*(7).

Thiam, C., & Thiam, F. (2019). Energy Efficient Cloud Data Center Using Dynamic Virtual Machine Consolidation Algorithm. In *International Conference on Business Information Systems*. Springer. 10.1007/978-3-030-20485-3_40

Witanto, J∙N., Lim, H., & Atiquzzaman, M. (2018). Adaptive selection of dynamic VM consolidation algorithm using neural network for cloud resource management. *Future Generation Computer Systems*, *87*, 35–42. doi:10.1016/j.future.2018.04.075

Xiao, X., & Li, Z. (2019). Chemical Reaction Multi-Objective Optimization for Cloud Task DAG Scheduling. *IEEE Access: Practical Innovations, Open Solutions*, *7*, 102598–102605. doi:10.1109/ACCESS.2019.2926500

Compilation of References

Abbadi, I. M. (2013). A framework for establishing trust in Cloud Provenance. *International Journal of Information Security*, *11*(2), 111–128. doi:10.100710207-012-0179-0

Abbadi, I. M., & Alawneh, M. (2012). A framework for establishing trust in the cloud. *Computers & Electrical Engineering*, *38*(5), 1073–1087. doi:10.1016/j.compeleceng.2012.06.006

Adamson, D., Dyke, G., Jang, H., & Rosé, C. P. (2014). Towards an agile approach to adapting dynamic collaboration support to student needs. *International Journal of Artificial Intelligence in Education*, *24*(1), 92–124. doi:10.100740593-013-0012-6

Agaoglu, M. (2016). Predicting instructor performance using data mining techniques in higher education. *IEEE Access: Practical Innovations, Open Solutions*, *4*, 2379–2387. doi:10.1109/ACCESS.2016.2568756

Alain, M. A. (2012). Cloud computing security: from single to multi-clouds. *System Science (HICSS), 2012 45th Hawaii International Conference on.*

Alam. (2013). *An approach secret sharing algorithm in cloud computing security over single to multi-clouds.* Academic Press.

Alba, E., & Dorronsoro, B. (2005). The exploration/exploitation tradeoff in dynamic cellular genetic algorithms. *IEEE Transactions on Evolutionary Computation*, *9*(2), 126–142. doi:10.1109/TEVC.2005.843751

Aleem, S. H. A., Zobaa, A. F., Balci, M. E., & Ismael, S. M. (2019). Harmonic overloading minimization of frequency-dependent components in harmonics polluted distribution systems using harris hawks optimization algorithm. *IEEE Access: Practical Innovations, Open Solutions*, *7*, 100824–100837. doi:10.1109/ACCESS.2019.2930831

Ali, S. A., Affan, M., & Alam, M. (2019). A Study of Efficient Energy Management Techniques for Cloud Computing Environment. *2019 9th International Conference on Cloud Computing, Data Science & Engineering (Confluence)*, 13-18. 10.1109/CONFLUENCE.2019.8776977

Ali, M., Khan, S. U., & Vasilakos, A. V. (2015). Security in cloud computing: Opportunities and challenges. *Information Sciences*, *305*, 357–383. doi:10.1016/j.ins.2015.01.025

Compilation of References

Aljawarneh, S. (Ed.). (2012). *Cloud computing advancements in design, implementation, and technologies*. IGI Global.

Aljawarneh, S., & Malhotra, M. (Eds.). (2017). *Critical Research on Scalability and Security Issues in Virtual Cloud Environments*. IGI Global.

Allan, D., Farkas, J., & Mansfield, S. (2012). Intelligent load balancing for shortest path bridging. *IEEE Communications Magazine, 50*(7), 163–167. doi:10.1109/MCOM.2012.6231293

Almezeini, N., & Hafez, A. (2017). Task scheduling in cloud computing using lion optimization algorithm. *Algorithms, 5*, 7.

Alshamaila, Y., Papagiannidis, S., & Li, F. (2013). Cloud computing adoption by SMEs in the northeast of England: A multi-perspective framework. *Journal of Enterprise Information Management, 26*(3), 250–275. doi:10.1108/17410391311325225

Al-Shargabi, B., Al-Jawarneh, S., & Hayajneh, S. M. (2020). A cloudlet based security and trust model for e-government web services. *Journal of Theoretical and Applied Information Technology, 98*(1), 27–37.

Altmann, J., & Kashef, M. M. (2014). Cost model-based service placement in federated hybrid clouds. *Future Generation Computer Systems, 41*, 79–90. doi:10.1016/j.future.2014.08.014

Ana-Ramona, B., & Razvan, B. (2011). A Perspective on the Benefits of Data Virtualization Technology. Informatica Economica, 15.

Anton, B., Rajkumar, B., Lee, Y. C., & Zomaya, A. (2010). *A Taxonomy and Survey of Energy-Efficient Data Centers and Cloud Computing Systems*. Green Cloud Taxonomy.

Apon, Mache, Buyya, & Jin. (2004). Cluster Computing in the Classroom and Integration with Computing Curricula 2001. IEEE Transactions on Education, 47(2).

Arlitt, M. F., & Williamson, C. L. (1997). Internet web servers: Workload characterization and performance implications. *IEEE/ACM Transactions on Networking, 5*(5), 631–645. doi:10.1109/90.649565

Asha, N., & Rao, G. R. (2013). A Review on Various Resource Allocation Strategies in Cloud Computing. *International Journal of Emerging Technology and Advanced Engineering, 3*(7).

Ashokkumar, K., Sam, B., Arshadprabhu, R., & Britto. (2015). Baron Sam, and R. Arshadprabhu. "Cloud-based intelligent transport system. *Procedia Computer Science, 50*, 58–63. doi:10.1016/j.procs.2015.04.061

Aslanpour, M. S., Ghobaei-Arani, M., & Toosi, A. N. (2017). Auto-scaling web applications in clouds: A cost-aware approach. *Journal of Network and Computer Applications, 95*, 26–41. doi:10.1016/j.jnca.2017.07.012

Avanade Perspective Paper. (2009). *Server Virtualization: A Step Toward Cost Efficiency and Business Agility*. avanade perspective paper server Virtualization.

Baars, H., & Kemper, H. G. (2010, July). Business intelligence in the cloud? In PACIS (p. 145). Academic Press.

Baars, H., & Kemper, H. G. (2008). Management support with structured and unstructured data—An integrated business intelligence framework. *Information Systems Management*, 25(2), 132–148. doi:10.1080/10580530801941058

Babić, I. D. (2017). Machine learning methods in predicting the student academic motivation. *Croatian Operational Research Review*, 8(2), 443–461. doi:10.17535/crorr.2017.0028

Babikir, H. A., Abd Elaziz, M., Elsheikh, A. H., Showaib, E. A., Elhadary, M., Wu, D., & Liu, Y. (2019). Noise prediction of axial piston pump based on different valve materials using a modified artificial neural network model. *Alexandria Engineering Journal*, 58(3), 1077–1087. doi:10.1016/j.aej.2019.09.010

Baker, R. S. (2016). Stupid Tutoring Systems Intelligent Humans. *International Journal of Artificial Intelligence in Education*, 26(2), 600–614. doi:10.100740593-016-0105-0

Bakshi, K. (2012). Considerations for big data: Architecture and approach. *IEEE Aerospace Conference*, 1-7. 10.1109/AERO.2012.6187357

Banerjee, S., Mandal, R., & Biswas, U. (2018). An Approach Towards Amelioration of an Efficient VM Allocation Policy in Cloud Computing Domain. *Wireless Personal Communications*, 98(2), 1799–1820. doi:10.100711277-017-4946-0

Bao, X., Jia, H., & Lang, C. (2019). A novel hybrid harris hawks optimization for color image multilevel thresholding segmentation. *IEEE Access: Practical Innovations, Open Solutions*, 7, 76529–76546. doi:10.1109/ACCESS.2019.2921545

Barham, P., Dragovic, B., & Fraser, K. (2003). Xen and the art of virtualization. ACM Journal, 37, 164-177.

Barthwal, V., Rauthan, M., & Verma, R. (2019). Virtual Machines Placement Using Predicted Utilization of Physical Machine in Cloud Datacenter. In *International Conference on Advances in Engineering Science Management & Technology (ICAESMT)*. Uttaranchal University.

Basu, S., Kannayaram, G., Ramasubbareddy, S., & Venkatasubbaiah, C. (2019). Improved Genetic Algorithm for Monitoring of Virtual Machines in Cloud Environment. In *Smart Intelligent Computing and Applications* (Vol. 105, pp. 319–326). Springer. doi:10.1007/978-981-13-1927-3_34

Bathla, G. (2013). Minimum Spanning Tree based Protocol for Heterogeneous Wireless Sensor Networks. *i-Manager's Journal of Wireless Communication Networks*, 1(4), 12-22.

Bazi, G., El Khoury, J., & Srour, F. J. (2017). Integrating Data Collection Optimization into Pavement Management Systems. *Business & Information Systems Engineering*, 59(3), 135–146. doi:10.100712599-017-0466-4

Behrend, T. S., & Wiebe, E. N. (2011). Cloud computing adoption and usage in community colleges. Behaviour & Information Technology Journal, 30(2), 231-240.

Berkowitz, J. (2009). *Cloud Computing (Part 1): Advantages, Types and Challenges.* CRM Mastery Weblog. http://crmweblog.crmmastery.com/2009/11/cloud-computing-part1-advantages-types-and-challenges

Berkowitz, J. (2009). *Cloud Computing (Part 1): Advantages, Types and Challenges.* CRM Mastery Weblog.

Bernsmed, K. (2012). Thunder in the Clouds: Security challenges and solutions for federated Clouds. *Cloud Computing Technology and Science (CloudCom), 2012 IEEE 4th International Conference on.* 10.1109/CloudCom.2012.6427547

Berson, A., & Dubov, L. (2007). *Master data management and customer data integration for a global enterprise.* McGraw-Hill, Inc.

Bhattacherjee, S., Das, R., Khatua, S., & Roy, S. (2019). Energy-efficient migration techniques for cloud environment: A step toward green computing. *The Journal of Supercomputing, 1–29.* doi:10.100711227-019-02801-0

Bhavani, B. H., & Guruprasad, H. S. (2014). Resource provisioning techniques in cloud computing environment: A survey. *International Journal of Research in Computer and Communication Technology, 3*(3), 395–401.

Birst. (2010). *Why Cloud BI? The 9 Substantial Benefits of Software-as-a Service Business Intelligence.* Birst, Inc.

Birst. (2010). *Why Cloud BI? The 9 Substantial Benefits of Software-as-aService Business Intelligence.* Birst, Inc.

Boel, R. K., & van Schuppen, J. H. (1989). Distributed routing for load balancing. *Proceedings of the IEEE, 77*(1), 210–221. doi:10.1109/5.21080

Bohn, R. B., Messina, J., Liu, F., Tong, J., & Mao, J. (2011, July). NIST cloud computing reference architecture. In *2011 IEEE World Congress on Services* (pp. 594-596). IEEE. 10.1109/SERVICES.2011.105

Buyya, R., Ranjan, R., & Calheiros, R. N. (2009, June). Modeling and simulation of scalable Cloud computing environments and the CloudSim toolkit: Challenges and opportunities. In *2009 international conference on high performance computing & simulation* (pp. 1-11). IEEE.

Calheiros, R. N., Ranjan, R., Beloglazov, A., De Rose, C. A., & Buyya, R. (2011). CloudSim: A toolkit for modeling and simulation of cloud computing environments and evaluation of resource provisioning algorithms. *Software, Practice & Experience, 41*(1), 23–50. doi:10.1002pe.995

Cardellini, V., Casalicchio, E., Grassi, V., & Presti, F. L. (2007, July). Flow-based service selection for web service composition supporting multiple qos classes. In *IEEE International Conference on Web Services (ICWS 2007)* (pp. 743-750). IEEE. 10.1109/ICWS.2007.91

Carroll, M., Van Der Merwe, A., & Kotze, P. (2011, August). Secure cloud computing: Benefits, risks and controls. In *2011 Information Security for South Africa* (pp. 1-9). IEEE.

Catteddu, D. (2009, December). Cloud Computing: benefits, risks and recommendations for information security. In *Iberic Web Application Security Conference* (pp. 17-17). Springer.

Chamodrakas, I., Batis, D., & Martakos, D. (2010). Supplier selection in electronic marketplaces using satisficing and fuzzy AHP. *Expert Systems with Applications, 37*(1), 490–498. doi:10.1016/j.eswa.2009.05.043

Chandrashekar, D. P. (2015). *Robust and fault-tolerant scheduling for scientific workflows in cloud computing environments* (Doctoral dissertation).

Chandrawat, R. K., Kumar, R., Garg, B. P., Dhiman, G., & Kumar, S. (2017). An analysis of modeling and optimization production cost through fuzzy linear programming problem with symmetric and right angle triangular fuzzy number. In *Proceedings of Sixth International Conference on Soft Computing for Problem Solving* (pp. 197-211). Springer. 10.1007/978-981-10-3322-3_18

Chang, V., Kuo, Y.-H., & Ramachandran, M. (2016). Cloud computing adoption framework: A security framework for business clouds. *Future Generation Computer Systems, 57*, 24–41. doi:10.1016/j.future.2015.09.031

Chaudhrani, V., Acharya, P., & Chudasama, V. (2018). Energy Aware Computing Resource Allocation Using PSO in Cloud. In *Information and Communication Technology for Intelligent Systems* (pp. 511–519). Springer.

Chehbi Gamoura, S. (2019). A Cloud-Based Approach for Cross-Management of Disaster Plans: Managing Risk in Networked Enterprises. In Emergency and Disaster Management: Concepts, Methodologies, Tools, and Applications (pp. 857-881). IGI Global.

Chehbi-Gamoura, S., Derrouiche, R., Malhotra, M., & Koruca, H. I. (2018, June). Adaptive management approach for more availability of big data business analytics. In *Proceedings of the Fourth International Conference on Engineering & MIS 2018* (pp. 1-8). 10.1145/3234698.3234758

Chehbi-Gamoura, S., Derrouiche, R., Malhotra, M., & Koruca, H. I. (2018, June). Adaptive management approach for more availability of big data business analytics. In *Proceedings of the Fourth International Conference on Engineering & MIS 2018* (pp. 1-8). Academic Press.

Chehbi-Gamoura, S., & Derrouiche, R. (2017). Big valuable data in supply chain: Deep analysis of current trends and coming potential. In *Collaboration in a Data-Rich World* (pp. 230–241). Springer. doi:10.1007/978-3-319-65151-4_22

Chehbi-Gamoura, S., Derrouiche, R., Damand, D., & Barth, M. (2020). Insights from big Data Analytics in supply chain management: An all-inclusive literature review using the SCOR model. *Production Planning and Control, 31*(5), 355–382. doi:10.1080/09537287.2019.1639839

Chehbi-Gamoura, S., Derrouiche, R., Damand, D., Kucharavy, D., & Barth, M. (2020). Cross-management of risks in big data-driven industries by the use of fuzzy cognitive maps. *Logistique & Management, 28*(2), 155–166. doi:10.1080/12507970.2019.1686437

Chen, H., Jiao, S., Wang, M., Heidari, A. A., & Zhao, X. (2020). Parameters identification of photovoltaic cells and modules using diversification-enriched Harris hawks optimization with chaotic drifts. *Journal of Cleaner Production, 244,* 118778. doi:10.1016/j.jclepro.2019.118778

Chen, L., & Li, N. (2015). On the interaction between load balancing and speed scaling. *IEEE Journal on Selected Areas in Communications, 33*(12), 2567–2578. doi:10.1109/JSAC.2015.2482098

Choi, Y., & Lim, Y. (2016). Optimization approach for resource allocation on cloud computing for iot. *International Journal of Distributed Sensor Networks, 12*(3), 3479247. doi:10.1155/2016/3479247

Chou, T. C. K., & Abraham, J. A. (1982). Load balancing in distributed systems. *IEEE Transactions on Software Engineering, SE-8*(4), 401–412. doi:10.1109/TSE.1982.235574

Convery, N. (2010). *Cloud computing toolkit: guidance for outsourcing information storage to the Cloud, Department of Information Studies, Aberystwyth University.* Archives and Records Association.

Coursaris, C. K., van Osch, W., & Sung, J. (2013). *A "cloud lifestyle": The diffusion of cloud computing applications and the effect of demographic and lifestyle clusters.* Paper presented at the 2013 46th Hawaii International Conference on System Sciences.

Cruz, N. D., Schiefelbein, P., Anderson, K., Hallock, P., & Barden, D. (2010). ORM and MDM/MMS: integration in an enterprise level conceptual data model. In R. Meersman, T. Dillon, & P. Herrero, In *Proceeding of OTM Confederated International Conferences On the Move to Meaningful Internet Systems* (pp. 457-463). Rhodes, Greece: Springer International Publishing.

Das, J., Dasgupta, A., Ghosh, S. K., & Buyya, R. (2019). A Learning Technique for VM Allocation to Resolve Geospatial Queries. In *Recent Findings in Intelligent Computing Techniques* (pp. 577–584). Springer. doi:10.1007/978-981-10-8639-7_61

Datactics. (2016). Retrieved 05 22, 2017, from https://www.datactics.com/

Dell Software. (n.d.). *Top 10 Virtualization Automation Tips for Infrastructure and Operations Administrators.* Whitepaper-VirtualAutoTips-InfraOpAdmin-US-KS-23761.

Demchenko, Y., & Laat, C. D. (2011). Defining generic architecture for Cloud infrastructure as a service model. *The International Symposium on Grids and Clouds and the Open Grid Forum Academia,* 2–10.

Dhiman, G. (2019). *Multi-objective metaheuristic approaches for data clustering in engineering application (s)* (Doctoral dissertation).

Dhiman, G. (2019). *Multi-objective Metaheuristic Approaches for Data Clustering in Engineering Application (s)* (Doctoral dissertation).

Dhiman, G. (2019b). *Multi-objective Metaheuristic Approaches for Data Clustering in Engineering Application (s)* (Doctoral dissertation).

Dhiman, G., & Kaur, A. (2017, December). Spotted hyena optimizer for solving engineering design problems. In *2017 international conference on machine learning and data science (MLDS)* (pp. 114-119). IEEE.

Dhiman, G. (2019). ESA: A hybrid bio-inspired metaheuristic optimization approach for engineering problems. *Engineering with Computers*, 1–31. doi:10.100700366-019-00826-w

Dhiman, G. (2020). MOSHEPO: A hybrid multi-objective approach to solve economic load dispatch and micro grid problems. *Applied Intelligence*, *50*(1), 119–137. doi:10.100710489-019-01522-4

Dhiman, G., & Kaur, A. (2018). Optimizing the design of airfoil and optical buffer problems using spotted hyena optimizer. *Designs*, *2*(3), 28. doi:10.3390/designs2030028

Dhiman, G., & Kaur, A. (2019). A hybrid algorithm based on particle swarm and spotted hyena optimizer for global optimization. In *Soft Computing for Problem Solving* (pp. 599–615). Springer. doi:10.1007/978-981-13-1592-3_47

Dhiman, G., & Kaur, A. (2019). Stoa: A bio-inspired based optimization algorithm for industrial engineering problems. *Engineering Applications of Artificial Intelligence*, *82*, 148–174. doi:10.1016/j.engappai.2019.03.021

Dhiman, G., & Kumar, V. (2017). Spotted hyena optimizer: A novel bio-inspired based metaheuristic technique for engineering applications. *Advances in Engineering Software*, *114*, 48–70. doi:10.1016/j.advengsoft.2017.05.014

Dhiman, G., & Kumar, V. (2018). Emperor penguin optimizer: A bio-inspired algorithm for engineering problems. *Knowledge-Based Systems*, *159*, 20–50. doi:10.1016/j.knosys.2018.06.001

Dhiman, G., & Kumar, V. (2018). Multi-objective spotted hyena optimizer: A multi-objective optimization algorithm for engineering problems. *Knowledge-Based Systems*, *150*, 175–197. doi:10.1016/j.knosys.2018.03.011

Dhiman, G., & Kumar, V. (2019). KnRVEA: A hybrid evolutionary algorithm based on knee points and reference vector adaptation strategies for many-objective optimization. *Applied Intelligence*, *49*(7), 2434–2460. doi:10.100710489-018-1365-1

Dhiman, G., & Kumar, V. (2019). Seagull optimization algorithm: Theory and its applications for large-scale industrial engineering problems. *Knowledge-Based Systems*, *165*, 169–196. doi:10.1016/j.knosys.2018.11.024

Dhiman, G., & Kumar, V. (2019). Spotted hyena optimizer for solving complex and non-linear constrained engineering problems. In *Harmony search and nature inspired optimization algorithms* (pp. 857–867). Springer. doi:10.1007/978-981-13-0761-4_81

Dhiman, G., Soni, M., Pandey, H. M., Slowik, A., & Kaur, H. (2020). A novel hybrid hypervolume indicator and reference vector adaptation strategies based evolutionary algorithm for many-objective optimization. *Engineering with Computers*, 1–19. doi:10.100700366-020-00986-0

Di, S., & Wang, C. L. (2012). Error-tolerant resource allocation and payment minimization for cloud system. *IEEE Transactions on Parallel and Distributed Systems, 24*(6), 1097–1106. doi:10.1109/TPDS.2012.309

Do More for Less. (2008). *Build a Cost-Effective, Optimized IT Infrastructure.* IBM.

Dong, B., Zheng, Q., Yang, J., Li, H., & Qiao, M. (2009). An E-learning Ecosystem Based on Cloud Computing Infrastructure. *Ninth IEEE International Conference on Advanced Learning Technologies.* doi:10.1109/ICALT.2009.21

Dong, B., Zheng, Q., Yang, J., Li, H., & Qiao, M. (2009). An E-learning Ecosystem Based on Cloud Computing Infrastructure. *2009 Ninth IEEE International Conference on Advanced Learning Technologies,* 125-127.

Dorigo, M., Birattari, M., & Stutzle, T. (2006). Ant colony optimization. *IEEE Computational Intelligence Magazine, 1*(4), 28–39. doi:10.1109/CI-M.2006.248054

Doyle, J., Shorten, R., & O'Mahony, D. (2013). Stratus: Load balancing the cloud for carbon emissions control. *IEEE Transactions on Cloud Computing, 1*(1), 1–1. doi:10.1109/TCC.2013.4

Dregvaite, G., & Damasevicius, R. (2015). Integrating Multiple Analytics Techniques in a Custom Moodle Report Information and Software Technologies. 21st International Conference, ICIST 2015 (CVLA), *538,* 115—126.

Duan, J., & Yang, Y. (2017). A load balancing and multi-tenancy oriented data center virtualization framework. *IEEE Transactions on Parallel and Distributed Systems, 28*(8), 2131–2144. doi:10.1109/TPDS.2017.2657633

Dubey, V. K., & Menascé, D. A. (2010, July). Utility-based optimal service selection for business processes in service oriented architectures. In *2010 IEEE International Conference on Web Services* (pp. 542-550). IEEE. 10.1109/ICWS.2010.33

Du, H., Wu, X., & Zhuang, J. (2006, September). Small-world optimization algorithm for function optimization. In *International conference on natural computation* (pp. 264-273). Springer. 10.1007/11881223_33

Eirinaki, M., & Vazirgiannis, M. (2003). Web mining for web personalization. *ACM Transactions on Internet Technology, 3*(1), 1–27. doi:10.1145/643477.643478

El Zant, B. (2013). Security of cloud federation. In *Cloud Computing and Big Data (CloudCom-Asia), 2013 International Conference on.* IEEE.

Elkadeem, M. R., Abd Elaziz, M., Ullah, Z., Wang, S., & Sharshir, S. W. (2019). Optimal planning of renewable energy-integrated distribution system considering uncertainties. *IEEE Access: Practical Innovations, Open Solutions, 7,* 164887–164907. doi:10.1109/ACCESS.2019.2947308

Elkahky, A. M., Song, Y., & He, X. (2015, May). A multi-view deep learning approach for cross domain user modeling in recommendation systems. In *Proceedings of the 24th International Conference on World Wide Web* (pp. 278-288). International World Wide Web Conferences Steering Committee. 10.1145/2736277.2741667

Erol, O. K., & Eksin, I. (2006). A new optimization method: Big bang–big crunch. *Advances in Engineering Software, 37*(2), 106–111. doi:10.1016/j.advengsoft.2005.04.005

Esposito, C., Su, X., Aljawarneh, S. A., & Choi, C. (2018). Securing collaborative deep learning in industrial applications within adversarial scenarios. *IEEE Transactions on Industrial Informatics, 14*(11), 4972–4981. doi:10.1109/TII.2018.2853676

Ewees, A. A., & Abd Elaziz, M. (2020). Performance analysis of chaotic multi-verse harris hawks optimization: A case study on solving engineering problems. *Engineering Applications of Artificial Intelligence, 88*, 103370. doi:10.1016/j.engappai.2019.103370

Fan, W., Li, J., Ma, S., Tang, N., & Yu, W. (2010). Towards certain fixes with editing rules and master data. *Proceedings of the VLDB Endowment International Conference on Very Large Data Bases, 3*(1-2), 173–184. doi:10.14778/1920841.1920867

Fauche, H., & Latapie, P. (2007). *Un exemple de décisionnel de très grande volumétrie: le SID de l'UNEDIC*. UNIDEC.

Figl, K. (2017). Comprehension of procedural visual business process models. *Business & Information Systems Engineering, 59*(1), 41–67. doi:10.100712599-016-0460-2

Firdhous, Ghazali, & Hassan. (2011). *Trust and Trust Management in Cloud Computing - A Survey*. Inter Networks Research group, University Utara Malaysia, Technical Report.

Fisher, C. W., Chengalur-Smith, I., & Ballou, D. P. (2003). The impact of experience and time on the use of data quality information in decision making. *Information Systems Research, 14*(2), 170–188. doi:10.1287/isre.14.2.170.16017

Flouris, I. (2016). Issues in Complex Event Processing: Status and Prospects in the Big Data Era. *Journal of Systems and Software*.

Formato, R. A. (2009). Central force optimization: A new deterministic gradient-like optimization metaheuristic. *Opsearch, 46*(1), 25–51. doi:10.100712597-009-0003-4

Forsati, R., Meybodi, M. R., & Rahbar, A. (2009, May). An efficient algorithm for web recommendation systems. In *2009 IEEE/ACS International Conference on Computer Systems and Applications* (pp. 579-586). IEEE. 10.1109/AICCSA.2009.5069385

Furukawa, T., Mori, K., Arino, K., Hayashi, K., & Shirakawa, N. (2015). Identifying the evolutionary process of emerging technologies: A chronological network analysis of World Wide Web conference sessions. *Technological Forecasting and Social Change, 91*, 280–294. doi:10.1016/j.techfore.2014.03.013

Garg, M., & Malhotra, M. (2017). Retrieval of Images on the Basis of Content: A Survey. *International Journal of Engineering Development and Research*, *5*, 757–760.

Garg, M., Malhotra, M., & Singh, H. (2018). Statistical Feature Based Image Classification and Retrieval Using Trained Neural Classifiers. *International Journal of Applied Engineering Research: IJAER*, *13*(8), 5766–5771.

Garg, M., Malhotra, M., & Singh, H. (2018). Statistical Feature Based Image Classificationand Retrieval Using Trained Neural Classifiers. *International Journal of Applied Engineering Research: IJAER*, *13*(8), 5766–5771.

Garg, M., Malhotra, M., & Singh, H. (2019). A Novel CBIR-Based System using Texture Fused LBP Variants and GLCM Features. *International Journal of Innovative Technology and Exploring Engineering*, *9*(2), 1247–1257.

Garg, M., Malhotra, M., & Singh, H. (2019). Comparison of deep learning techniques on content-based image retrieval. *Modern Physics Letters A*, *34*, 1950285. doi:10.1142/S0217732319502857

Garg, M., Singh, H., & Malhotra, M. (2019). Fuzzy-NN approach with statistical features for description and classification of efficient image retrieval. *Modern Physics Letters A*, *34*(3), 1950022. doi:10.1142/S0217732319500226

Gartner Research. (2006-2007). *IT Spending and Staffing Report*. North America 5 ID Number: G00146284.

Gartner. (2018). *IT Spending Forecast, 3Q18 Update: Ride the Innovation Wave*. Orlando, FL: Gartner.

Gerrikagoitia, J. K., Castander, I., Rebón, F., & Alzua-Sorzabal, A. (2015). New trends of Intelligent E-Marketing based on Web Mining for e-shops. *Procedia: Social and Behavioral Sciences*, *175*(1), 75–83. doi:10.1016/j.sbspro.2015.01.1176

Ghazizadeh, E., Zamani, M., & Pahang, A. (2012). A survey on security issues of federated identity in cloud computing. In *Cloud Computing Technology and Science (CloudCom), 2012 IEEE 4th International Conference on*. IEEE. 10.1109/CloudCom.2012.6427513

Ghilic-Micu, B., Stoica, M., & Mircea, M. (2008). A framework for measuring the impact of BI solution. *TC, 1*, 3.

Ghilic-Micu, B., Mircea, M., & Stoica, M. (2011). Main aspects of the adoption of cloud solutions in managing service-oriented organizations-the case of higher education. Academy of Economic Studies. *Ecological Informatics*, *11*(1), 27.

Ghorpade & Acharya. (2013). Data Mining Performance Parameters of Client Machine Under a Flat Network and Subnetted Network. *2nd National Conference on Data Mining*.

Ghorpade, Bennur, & Acharya. (2013). Server Virtualization: A Cost-Effective Approach towards Educational Infrastructure Management. *Checkmate 2013 - 4th Annual International Conference*.

Ghorpade, Bennur, Acharya, & Kamatchi. (2015). Server Virtualization Implementation: An Experimental Study for Cost Effective and Green Computing Approach towards Educational Infrastructure Management. *International Journal of Computer Science Trends and Technology, 3*(6).

Ghorpade, Ghorpade, Bennur, & Acharya. (2013). Server Virtualization, A Cost Effective and Green Computing Approach Towards Educational Infrastructure Management. *International Conference on Cloud Computing and Computer Science IRAJ.*

Ghorpade, Shaikh, & Acharya. (2012). Educational Infrastructure Management: Paravirtualization in the classroom. *Allana Management Journal of Research.*

Ghorpade, Y. (2013). Data Communication and Computer Network. Suyog Publication.

Golilarz, N. A., Gao, H., & Demirel, H. (2019). Satellite image de-noising with harris hawks meta heuristic optimization algorithm and improved adaptive generalized gaussian distribution threshold function. *IEEE Access: Practical Innovations, Open Solutions, 7*, 57459–57468. doi:10.1109/ACCESS.2019.2914101

Goyal, T., Singh, A., & Agrawal, A. (2012). Cloudsim: Simulator for cloud computing infrastructure and modeling. *Procedia Engineering, 38*, 3566–3572.

Graupner, S., Basu, S., & Singhal, S. (2011, March). Business operating environment for service Clouds. In *2011 Annual SRII Global Conference* (pp. 1-10). IEEE.

Greer. (n.d.). *Why Choose VMware Robust and Reliable Foundation.* vmware.com.

Grossman, R.L. (2009). The Case for Cloud computing. *IT Professionals, 11*(2), 23-27.

Guo, L., Zhao, S., Shen, S., & Jiang, C. (2012). Task scheduling optimization in cloud computing based on heuristic algorithm. *Journal of Networks, 7*(3), 547.

Guo, Q., Sun, D., Chang, G., Sun, L., & Wang, X. (n.d.). Modeling and evaluation of trust in cloud computing environments. *Third International Conference on Advanced Computer Control*, 112-116.

Gupta, A., Xu, W., Ruiz-Juri, N., & Perrine, K. (2016). A workload aware model of computational resource selection for big data applications In *Big Data (Big Data), IEEE International Conference on* (pp. 2243-2250). IEEE.

Gupta, P., & Ghrera, S. P. (2016). Power and fault aware reliable resource allocation for cloud infrastructure. *Procedia Computer Science, 78*, 457–463. doi:10.1016/j.procs.2016.02.088

Gurjar, Y. S., & Rathore, V. S. (2013). Cloud business intelligence–is what business need today. *International Journal of Recent Technology and Engineering, 1*(6), 81–86.

Hajek, B. (1990). Performance of global load balancing by local adjustment. *IEEE Transactions on Information Theory, 36*(6), 1398–1414. doi:10.1109/18.59935

Han, G., Que, W., Jia, G., & Zhang, W. (2018). Resource-utilization-aware energy efficient server consolidation algorithm for green computing in IIOT. *Journal of Network and Computer Applications*, *103*, 205–214. doi:10.1016/j.jnca.2017.07.011

Han, W., Borges, J., Neumayer, P., Ding, Y., Riedel, T., & Beigl, M. (2017). Interestingness Classification of Association Rules for Master Data. In *Industrial Conference on Data Mining* (pp. 237-245). Springer. 10.1007/978-3-319-62701-4_18

Hashem, I. A. T., Yaqoob, I., Anuar, N. B., Mokhtar, S., Gani, A., & Ullah Khan, S. (2015). The rise of "big data" on cloud computing: Review and open research issues. *Information Systems*, *47*, 98–115. doi:10.1016/j.is.2014.07.006

Hatamlou, A. (2013). Black hole: A new heuristic optimization approach for data clustering. *Information Sciences*, *222*, 175–184. doi:10.1016/j.ins.2012.08.023

Heidari, A. A., Mirjalili, S., Faris, H., Aljarah, I., Mafarja, M., & Chen, H. (2019). Harris hawks optimization: Algorithm and applications. *Future Generation Computer Systems*, *97*, 849–872. doi:10.1016/j.future.2019.02.028

Heilig, L., Lalla-Ruiz, E., Voß, S., & Buyya, R. (2018). Metaheuristics in cloud computing. *Software, Practice & Experience*, *48*(10), 1729–1733. doi:10.1002pe.2628

Hesabian, N., Haj, H., & Javadi, S. (2015). Optimal scheduling in cloud computing environment using the bee algorithm. *Int J Comput Netw Commun Secur*, *3*, 253–258.

Hui, C. C., & Chanson, S. T. (1999). Improved strategies for dynamic load balancing. *IEEE Concurrency*, *7*(3), 58–67. doi:10.1109/4434.788780

Ibrahim, E., El-Bahnasawy, N. A., & Omara, F. A. (2016, March). Task scheduling algorithm in cloud computing environment based on cloud pricing models. In *2016 World Symposium on Computer Applications & Research (WSCAR)* (pp. 65-71). IEEE. 10.1109/WSCAR.2016.20

Ibrahim, E., El-Bahnasawy, N. A., & Omara, F. A. (2017). Load Balancing Scheduling Algorithm in Cloud Computing System with Cloud Pricing Comparative Study. *Menoufia Journal of Electronic Engineering Research*, *26*(1), 129–152.

ICCS. (2008). Deploying Virtual Infrastructure on Standard Operating Systems. Iccs Whitepaper, IDEAS Custom Consulting Services.

India's Technology Opportunity. (2012). *Transforming work, empowering people.* McKinsey Technology, Media, and Telecom Practice.

In, J., Bradley, R., Bichescu, B. C., & Autry, C. W. (2018). Supply chain information governance: Toward a conceptual framework. *International Journal of Logistics Management*.

ISACA. (2009). *Cloud Computing: Business Benefits With Security, Governance and Assurance Perspectives*. ISACA.

Isinkaye, F. O., Folajimi, Y. O., & Ojokoh, B. A. (2015). Recommendation systems: Principles, methods and evaluation. *Egyptian Informatics Journal, 16*(3), 261–273. doi:10.1016/j.eij.2015.06.005

IT Value Transformation Road Map Vision, Value, and Virtualization. (2000). IT Process Institute, Advancing the Science of IT Management VMware.

Jain & Pandey. (2013). Role of Cloud Computing in Higher Education. *International Journal of Advanced Research in Computer Science and Software Engineering, 3*(7).

Jain, G. P., Gurupur, V. P., Schroeder, J. L., & Faulkenberry, E. D. (2014). Artificial intelligence-based student learning evaluation: A concept map-based approach for analyzing a student's understanding of a topic. *IEEE Transactions on Learning Technologies, 7*(3), 267–279.

Jana, B., Chakraborty, M., & Mandal, T. (2019). A task scheduling technique based on particle swarm optimization algorithm in cloud environment. In Soft Computing: Theories and Applications. Springer. doi:10.1007/978-981-13-0589-4_49

Jansen, W. A. (2011). Cloud hooks: Security and privacy issues in cloud computing. In *System Sciences (HICSS), 2011 44th Hawaii International Conference on*. IEEE. 10.1109/HICSS.2011.103

Jaswal, S., & Malhotra, M. (2019, December). A detailed analysis of trust models in cloud environment. In *Proceedings of the Second International Conference on Data Science, E-Learning and Information Systems* (pp. 1-5). 10.1145/3368691.3368740

Jaswal, S., & Malhotra, M. (2019, December). A detailed analysis of trust models in cloud environment. In *Proceedings of the Second International Conference on Data Science, E-Learning and Information Systems* (pp. 1-5). Academic Press.

Jeffery, K. (2015). Challenges emerging from future cloud application scenarios. *Procedia Computer Science, 68*, 227–237. doi:10.1016/j.procs.2015.09.238

Jeong, J. H., Woo, J. H., & Park, J. (2020). Machine Learning Methodology for Management of Shipbuilding Master Data. *International Journal of Naval Architecture and Ocean Engineering, 12*, 428–439. doi:10.1016/j.ijnaoe.2020.03.005

Jeschike, M., Jeschke, S., Pfeiffer, O., Reinhard, R., & Richter, T. (2007). Equipping virtual laboratories with intelligent training scenarios. *AACE Journal, 15*(4), 413–436.

Jia, F., Gao, R., Lamming, R., & Wilding, R. (2016). Adaptation of supply management towards a hybrid culture: the case of a Japanese automaker. *Supply Chain Management: An International Journal, 1*(45-62), 21.

Jia, H., Lang, C., Oliva, D., Song, W., & Peng, X. (2019). Dynamic harris hawks optimization with mutation mechanism for satellite image segmentation. *Remote Sensing, 11*(12), 1421. doi:10.3390/rs11121421

Jiang, D., Zhang, P., Lv, Z., & Song, H. (2016). Energy-efficient multi-constraint routing algorithm with load balancing for smart city applications. *IEEE Internet of Things Journal, 3*(6), 1437–1447. doi:10.1109/JIOT.2016.2613111

Jung, R., & Lehrer, C. (2017). Guidelines for Education in Business and Information Systems Engineering at Tertiary Institutions. *Business & Information Systems Engineering, 59*(3), 189–203. doi:10.100712599-017-0473-5

Kache, F., & Seuring, S. (2017). Challenges and opportunities of digital information at the intersection of Big Data Analytics and supply chain management. *International Journal of Operations & Production Management, 37*(1), 10–36. doi:10.1108/IJOPM-02-2015-0078

Kalpana, G., Kumar, P. V., Aljawarneh, S., & Krishnaiah, R. V. (2018). Shifted adaption homomorphism encryption for mobile and cloud learning. *Computers & Electrical Engineering, 65*, 178–195. doi:10.1016/j.compeleceng.2017.05.022

Kalra, M., & Singh, S. (2015). A review of metaheuristic scheduling techniques in cloud computing. *Egyptian Informatics Journal, 16*(3), 275-295.

Kalz, M., van Bruggen, J., Giesbers, B., Waterink, W., Eshuis, J., & Koper, R. (2008). A model for new linkages for prior learning assessment. *Campus-Wide Information Systems, 25*(4), 233–243. doi:10.1108/10650740810900676

Kamble, S. S., & Gunasekaran, A. (2020). Big data-driven supply chain performance measurement system: A review and framework for implementation. *International Journal of Production Research, 58*(1), 65–86. doi:10.1080/00207543.2019.1630770

Kao, Chen, & Sun. (2010). Using an e-Learning system with integrated concept maps to improve conceptual understanding. *International Journal of Instructional Media, 37*(2), 151–153.

Kaur, A., & Dhiman, G. (2019). A review on search-based tools and techniques to identify bad code smells in object-oriented systems. In *Harmony search and nature inspired optimization algorithms* (pp. 909–921). Springer. doi:10.1007/978-981-13-0761-4_86

Kaur, S., Awasthi, L. K., Sangal, A. L., & Dhiman, G. (2020). Tunicate Swarm Algorithm: A new bio-inspired based metaheuristic paradigm for global optimization. *Engineering Applications of Artificial Intelligence, 90*, 103541. doi:10.1016/j.engappai.2020.103541

Kaur, S., & Kaur, K. (2019). Enhancing Reliability of Cloud Services Using Mechanism of Dynamic Replication and Migration of Data. *International Journal of Applied Engineering Research: IJAER, 14*(8), 1976–1983.

Kaveh, A., & Khayatazad, M. (2012). A new meta-heuristic method: Ray optimization. *Computers & Structures, 112*, 283–294. doi:10.1016/j.compstruc.2012.09.003

Kaveh, A., & Talatahari, S. (2010). A novel heuristic optimization method: Charged system search. *Acta Mechanica, 213*(3), 267–289. doi:10.100700707-009-0270-4

Kchaou, H., Kechaou, Z., & Alimi, A. M. (2015). Towards an Offloading Framework based on Big Data Analytics in Mobile Cloud Computing Environments. *Procedia Computer Science, 53,* 292–297. doi:10.1016/j.procs.2015.07.306

Kennedy, J., & Eberhart, R. (1995, November). Particle swarm optimization. In *Proceedings of ICNN'95-International Conference on Neural Networks* (Vol. 4, pp. 1942-1948). IEEE. 10.1109/ICNN.1995.488968

Khan, G. (2011). Energy-efficient Routing Protocol for Homogeneous Wireless Sensor Networks. *International Journal on Cloud Computing: Services and Architecture, 1*(1), 12-20.

Khan, K. M., & Malluhi, Q. (2010). Establishing trust in cloud computing. *IT Professional, 12*(5), 20–27. doi:10.1109/MITP.2010.128

Khan, M. A., & Salah, K. (2018). IoT security: Review, blockchain solutions, and open challenges. *Future Generation Computer Systems, 82,* 395–411. doi:10.1016/j.future.2017.11.022

Khmelevsky, Y., & Voytenko, V. (2010). Cloud computing infrastructure prototype for university education and research. *Proceeding WCCCE Journal '10.* doi:10.1145/1806512.1806524

Kim, H., Kang, J., & Park, J. H. (2016). A light-weight secure information transmission and device control scheme in the integration of CPS and cloud computing. *Microprocessors and Microsystems.*

Kim, K. H., Buyya, R., & Kim, J. (2007). Power Aware Scheduling of Bag-of-Tasks Applications with Deadline Constraints on DVS-enabled Clusters. In *Proc. of 7th IEEE International Symposium on Cluster Computing and the Grid (CCGrid 2007).*

Kimpan, W., & Kruekaew, B. (2016, August). Heuristic task scheduling with artificial bee colony algorithm for virtual machines. In *2016 Joint 8th International Conference on Soft Computing and Intelligent Systems (SCIS) and 17th International Symposium on Advanced Intelligent Systems (ISIS)* (pp. 281-286). IEEE. 10.1109/SCIS-ISIS.2016.0067

Kirkpatrick, S., Gelatt, C. D., & Vecchi, M. P. (1983). Optimization by simulated annealing. *Science, 220*(4598), 671-680.

Knight, D. (2009). *Why Cloud vs. Premise is the Wrong Question.* Cisco Systems Inc.

Knolmayer, G. F., & Röthlin, M. (2006). Quality of material master data and its effect on the usefulness of distributed ERP systems. *International Conference on Conceptual Modeling,* 362-371. 10.1007/11908883_43

Ko, R., Jagadpramana, P., Mowbray, M., Pearson, S., Kirchberg, M., Liang, Q., & Lee, B. S. (2011), Trust cloud: a framework for accountability and trust in cloud computing. *World Congress on services,* 584-588.

Kong, X. (2015). Cloud-enabled real-time platform for adaptive planning and control in the auction logistics center. *Computers & Industrial Engineering, 84,* 79-90.

Korol, T., & Korodi, A. (2010). Predicting bankruptcy with the use of macroeconomic variables. *Economic Computation and Economic Cybernetics Studies and Research, 44*(1), 201–221.

Krishna Reddy, V., & Reddy, L. S. (2011). Security architecture of Cloud Computing. *International Journal of Engineering Science and Technology, 3*(9), 7149–7155.

Krishna, B. H., Kiran, S., Murali, G., & Reddy, R. P. K. (2016). Security Issues in Service Model of Cloud Computing Environment. *Procedia Computer Science, 87*, 246–251. doi:10.1016/j.procs.2016.05.156

Krishnadoes, P., & Jacob, P, (2018). OCSA: task scheduling algorithm in the cloud computing environment. *International Journal of Intelligent Engineering & Systems, 11*(3), 271-279.

Kruekaew, B., & Kimpan, W. (2014, March). Virtual machine scheduling management on cloud computing using artificial bee colony. In *Proceedings of the International MultiConference of engineers and computer scientists* (*Vol. 1*, pp. 12-14). Academic Press.

Kucharavy, D., Damand, D., Chehbi-Gamoura, S., Barth, M., & Mornay, S. (2020). Warehouse of the future: The concept of contradiction mapping. *Logistique & Management, 28*(1), 48–56. doi:10.1080/12507970.2019.1686436

Kumar, Kommareddy, & Rani. (2013). Effective ways Cloud Computing can contribute To Education success. *Advanced Computing: An International Journal, 4*(4).

Kumar, A., Kumar, D., & Jarial, S. K. (2017). A review on artificial bee colony algorithms and their applications to data clustering. *Cybernetics and Information Technologies, 17*(3), 3–28. doi:10.1515/cait-2017-0027

Kumar, A., & Singh, R. K. (2017). A study on web structure mining. *International Research Journal of Engineering and Technology, 4*(1), 715–720.

Kurdi, H. A., Alismail, S. M., & Hassan, M. M. (2018). LACE: A Locust-Inspired Scheduling Algorithm to Reduce Energy Consumption in Cloud Datacenters. *IEEE Access: Practical Innovations, Open Solutions, 6*, 35435–35448. doi:10.1109/ACCESS.2018.2839028

Kusnetzky. (2007). *Virtualization and green computing.* ZDNet.

Latiff, M. S. A., Madni, S. H. H., & Abdullahi, M. (2018). Fault tolerance aware scheduling technique for cloud computing environment using dynamic clustering algorithm. *Neural Computing & Applications, 29*(1), 279–293. doi:10.100700521-016-2448-8

LD, D. B., & Krishna, P. V. (2013). Honey bee behavior inspired load balancing of tasks in cloud computing environments. *Applied Soft Computing, 13*(5), 2292–2303. doi:10.1016/j.asoc.2013.01.025

Le Vinh, T., Bouzefrane, S., Farinone, J.-M., Attar, A., & Kennedy, B. P. (2015). Middleware to integrate mobile devices, sensors, and cloud computing. *Procedia Computer Science, 52*, 234–243. doi:10.1016/j.procs.2015.05.061

Lee, Y., & Zomaya, A. (2009). Minimizing Energy Consumption for Precedence-Constrained Applications Using Dynamic Voltage Scaling. *Proc. of the 9th IEEE/ACM International Symposium on Cluster Computing and the Grid (CCGrid 2009).*

Lenhardt, J., Chen, K., & Schiffmann, W. (2015). Energy-efficient web server load balancing. *IEEE Systems Journal, 11*(2), 878–888. doi:10.1109/JSYST.2015.2465813

Li, H., Spence, C., Armstrong, R., Godfrey, R., Schneider, R., Smith, J., & White, J. (2010). *Intel Cloud Computing Taxonomy and Ecosystem Analysis.* Printed in USA 0210. KC/KC/PDF, 1-4.

Li, B. H., Zhang, L., Wang, S. L., Tao, F., Cao, J. W., Jiang, X. D., ... Chai, X. D. (2010). Cloud manufacturing: A new service-oriented networked manufacturing model. *Jisuanji Jicheng Zhizao Xitong, 16*(1), 1–7.

Li, C., Liao, X., & Jin, H. (2019). Enhancing application performance via DAG-driven scheduling in task parallelism for cloud center. *Peer-to-Peer Networking and Applications, 12*(2), 381–391. doi:10.100712083-017-0576-2

Lieberman, H. (1995). Letizia: An agent that assists web browsing. *IJCAI (United States), 1995*(1), 924–929.

Li, H., Sedayao, J., Hahn-Steichen, J., Jimison, E., Spence, C., & Chahal, S. (2009). Developing an enterprise cloud computing strategy. *Korea Information Processing Society Review, 16*(2), 4–16.

Li, J., Jia, Y., Liu, L., & Wo, T. (2013). CyberLiveApp: A secure sharing and migration approach for live virtual desktop applications in a Cloud environment. *Future Generation Computer Systems, 29*(1), 330–340. doi:10.1016/j.future.2011.08.001

Li, J., Li, B., Wo, T., Hu, C., Huai, J., Liu, L., & Lam, K. (2012). CyberGuarder: A virtualization security assurance architecture for green Cloud computing. *Future Generation Computer Systems, 28*(2), 379–390. doi:10.1016/j.future.2011.04.012

Linthicum, D. S. (2009). *Moving to Cloud Computing Step-by-Step.* The Linthicum Group.

Li, S. S., & Karahanna, E. (2015). Online recommendation systems in a B2C E-commerce context: A review and future directions. *Journal of the Association for Information Systems, 16*(2), 72–107. doi:10.17705/1jais.00389

Liu, W., Nishio, T., Shinkuma, R., & Takahashi, T. (2014). Adaptive resource discovery in mobile cloud computing. *Computer Communications, 50*, 119–129. doi:10.1016/j.comcom.2014.02.006

Lizcano, D., Lara, J. A., White, B., & Aljawarneh, S. (2020). Blockchain-based approach to create a model of trust in open and ubiquitous higher education. *Journal of Computing in Higher Education, 32*(1), 109–134. doi:10.100712528-019-09209-y

Lokesh, P. (2012). Design of Simulator for Finding the Delay Distribution in Delay Tolerant Networking. GJCST, 12(14).

Lokesh. (2019). *Smart City IOT: Smart Architectural Solution for Networking, Congestion and Heterogeneity.* IEEE ICICCS.

Louis, A. (2016). Healing on the cloud: Secure cloud architecture for medical wireless sensor networks. *Future Generation Computer Systems, 55,* 266–277. doi:10.1016/j.future.2015.01.009

Lozano, M., & García-Martínez, C. (2010). Hybrid metaheuristics with evolutionary algorithms specializing in intensification and diversification: Overview and progress report. *Computers & Operations Research, 37*(3), 481–497. doi:10.1016/j.cor.2009.02.010

Madni, S. H. H., Abd Latiff, M. S., Abdullahi, M., Abdulhamid, S. I. M., & Usman, M. J. (2017). Performance comparison of heuristic algorithms for task scheduling in IaaS cloud computing environment. *PLoS One, 12*(5), e0176321. doi:10.1371/journal.pone.0176321 PMID:28467505

Magalhães, D., Calheiros, R. N., Buyya, R., & Gomes, D. G. (2015). Workload modeling for resource usage analysis and simulation in cloud computing. *Computers & Electrical Engineering, 47,* 69–81. doi:10.1016/j.compeleceng.2015.08.016

Maguluri, S. T., Srikant, R., & Ying, L. (2014). Heavy traffic optimal resource allocation algorithms for cloud computing clusters. *Performance Evaluation, 81,* 20–39. doi:10.1016/j.peva.2014.08.002

Mai, V., & Khalil, I. (2016). Design and implementation of a secure cloud-based billing model for smart meters as an Internet of things using homomorphic cryptography. *Future Generation Computer Systems.*

Malcolm, D. (2009). *The five defining characteristics of cloud computing.* ZDNet.

Malhotra, M., & Singh, A. (2019). Role of Agents to Enhance the Security and Scalability in Cloud Environment. In Cloud Security: Concepts, Methodologies, Tools, and Applications (pp. 552-573). IGI Global.

Malhotra, M., & Singh, A. (2019). Role of Agents to Enhance the Security and Scalability in Cloud Environment. In Cloud Security: Concepts, Methodologies, Tools, and Applications (pp. 552-573). IGI Global. doi:10.4018/978-1-5225-8176-5.ch028

Malik, Z. K., & Fyfe, C. (2012). Review of web personalization. *Journal of Emerging Technologies in Web Intelligence, 4*(3), 285–296. doi:10.4304/jetwi.4.3.285-296

Manuel, P. (2013). A trust model of cloud computing based on the quality of service. *Annals of Operations Research, 2013,* 1–12.

Marodin, G. A., Tortorella, G. L., Frank, A. G., & Godinho Filho, M. (2017). The moderating effect of Lean supply chain management on the impact of Lean shop floor practices on quality and inventory. *Supply Chain Management: An International Journal, 6*(473-485), 22.

Marston, S., Li, Z., Bandyopadhyay, S., Zhang, J., & Ghalsasi, A. (2011). Cloud computing-The Business Perspective. *Decision Support Systems, 51*(1), 176–189. doi:10.1016/j.dss.2010.12.006

Masdari, M., ValiKardan, S., Shahi, Z., & Azar, S. I. (2016). Towards workflow scheduling in cloud computing: A comprehensive analysis. *Journal of Network and Computer Applications*, *66*, 64–82. doi:10.1016/j.jnca.2016.01.018

McKnight, W. (2005). Introducing the Data Warehouse Appliance, Part I. *DMReview*.

Mehmi, Verma, & Sangal. (2017). Simulation modeling of cloud computing for smart grid using CloudSim. *J. Electr. Syst. Inf. Technol.*, *4*(1), 159–172.

Mell, P., & Grance, T. (2011). *The NIST definition of cloud computing*. NIST.

Menascé, D. A., Casalicchio, E., & Dubey, V. (2010). On optimal service selection in service oriented architectures. *Performance Evaluation*, *67*(8), 659–675. doi:10.1016/j.peva.2009.07.001

Meriton, R., Bhandal, R., Graham, G., & Brown, A. (2020). An examination of the generative mechanisms of value in big data-enabled supply chain management research. *International Journal of Production Research*, 1–28. doi:10.1080/00207543.2020.1832273

Miller, B. N., Ried, J. T., & Konstan, J. A. (2003). GroupLens for Usenet: Experiences in applying collaborative filtering to a social information system. In *From Usenet to CoWebs* (pp. 206–231). Springer. doi:10.1007/978-1-4471-0057-7_10

Mingprasert, S., & Masuchun, R. (2017, February). Adaptive artificial bee colony algorithm for solving the capacitated vehicle routing problem. In *2017 9th International Conference on Knowledge and Smart Technology (KST)* (pp. 23-27). IEEE. 10.1109/KST.2017.7886072

Mircea, M., Ghilic-Micu, B., & Stoica, M. (2011). Combining business intelligence with cloud computing to delivery agility in actual economy. *Journal of Economic Computation and Economic Cybernetics Studies*, *45*(1), 39–54.

Mishra, S. K., Sahoo, B., & Jena, S. K. (2019). A Secure VM Consolidation in Cloud Using Learning Automata. In *Recent Findings in Intelligent Computing Techniques* (pp. 617–623). Springer. doi:10.1007/978-981-10-8639-7_65

Mital, M., Pani, A. K., Damodaran, S., & Ramesh, R. (2015). Cloud-based management and control system for smart communities: A practical case study. *Computers in Industry*, *74*, 162–172. doi:10.1016/j.compind.2015.06.009

MKLab. (2016). https://staruml.io/

Moges, F. F., & Abebe, S. L. (2019). Energy-aware VM placement algorithms for the OpenStack Neat consolidation framework. *Journal of Cloud Computing*, *8*(1), 2–12. doi:10.118613677-019-0126-y

Mohamad, Z., Mahmoud, A. A., Nik, W. N. S. W., Mohamed, M. A., & Deris, M. M. (2018). A Genetic Algorithm for Optimal Job Scheduling and Load Balancing in Cloud Computing. *IACSIT International Journal of Engineering and Technology*, *7*(3), 290–294.

Mohammed, T. A., Ghareeb, A., Al-bayaty, H., & Aljawarneh, S. (2019, December). Big data challenges and achievements: applications on smart cities and energy sector. In *Proceedings of the Second International Conference on Data Science, E-Learning and Information Systems* (pp. 1-5). 10.1145/3368691.3368717

Mohammed, T. A., Ghareeb, A., Al-bayaty, H., & Aljawarneh, S. (2019, December). Big data challenges and achievements: applications on smart cities and energy sector. In *Proceedings of the Second International Conference on Data Science, E-Learning and Information Systems* (pp. 1-5). Academic Press.

Moharir, S., Sanghavi, S., & Shakkottai, S. (2013, June). Online load balancing under graph constraints. In *Proceedings of the ACM SIGMETRICS/international conference on Measurement and modeling of computer systems* (pp. 363-364). 10.1145/2465529.2465751

Monsef, M., & Gidado, N. (2011). *Trust and privacy concern in Cloud, European cup.* IT Security for the Next Generation.

Moreno-Vozmediano, R., Montero, R. S., & Llorente, I. M. (2012). IaaS Cloud Architecture: From Virtualized Datacenters to Federated Cloud Infrastructures. *IEEE Explore in Computer, 45*(12), 65-72. doi:10.1109/MC.2012.76

Moreno-Vozmediano, R., Montero, R. S., & Llorente, I. M. (2012). IaaS Cloud Architecture: From Virtualized Datacenters to Federated Cloud Infrastructures. *IEEE Explore in Computer, 45*(12), 65–72.

Mouchili, M. N., Aljawarneh, S., & Tchouati, W. (2018, October). Smart city data analysis. In *Proceedings of the First International Conference on Data Science, E-learning and Information Systems* (pp. 1-6). Academic Press.

Moura, J., & Hutchison, D. (2016). Review and analysis of networking challenges in cloud computing. *Journal of Network and Computer Applications, 60*, 113–129. doi:10.1016/j.jnca.2015.11.015

Muhil, M., Krishna, U. H., Kumar, R. K., & Anita, E. A. M. (2015). Securing multi-cloud using secret sharing algorithm. *Procedia Computer Science, 50*, 421–426. doi:10.1016/j.procs.2015.04.011

Myung, S. (2015). Master Data Management in PLM for the Enterprise Scope. In *Proceeding of IFIP International Conference on Product Lifecycle Management* (pp. 771-779). Doha, Qatar: Springer International Publishing.

Myung, S. (2016). Innovation Strategy for Engineering Plant Product Lifecycle Management based on Master Data Management, Project Management and Quality Management. *Korean Journal of Computational Design and Engineering, 21*(2), 170–176. doi:10.7315/CADCAM.2016.170

Neelima, G., & Rodda, S. (2015). An overview on web usage mining. In *Emerging ICT for Bridging the Future-Proceedings of the 49th Annual Convention of the Computer Society of India CSI* Volume 2 (pp. 647-655). Springer.

NIST. (2011). *US Government Cloud computing technology roadmap*. Special Publication 500-293, Cloud Computing Program, National Institute of Standards and Technology (NIST), US Department of Commerce.

Onyango & Omwenga. (2016). Using Cloud computing in Higher Education: A Strategy to address trust issues in adoption of Cloud services in Kenyan public and private universities. *International Journal of Applied Information Systems, 11*(7).

Otto, B., Hüner, K. M., & Österle, H. (2012). Toward a functional reference model for master data quality management. *Journal of Information Systems and e-Business Management*, 395-425.

Otto, B. (2012). How to design the master data architecture: Findings from a case study at Bosch. *International Journal of Information Management, 32*(4), 337–346. doi:10.1016/j.ijinfomgt.2011.11.018

Oussous, A., Benjelloun, F. Z., Lahcen, A. A., & Belfkih, S. (2018). Big Data technologies: A survey. *Journal of King Saud University-Computer and Information Sciences, 30*(4), 431–448. doi:10.1016/j.jksuci.2017.06.001

Palocsay, S. W., & Stevens, S. P. (2008). A study of the effectiveness of web-based homework in teaching undergraduate business statistics. *Decision Sciences Journal of Innovative Education, 6*(2), 213–232. doi:10.1111/j.1540-4609.2008.00167.x

Park, E., & Kim, K. J. (2014). An integrated adoption model of mobile cloud services: Exploration of key determinants and extension of technology acceptance model. *Telematics and Informatics, 31*(3), 376–385. doi:10.1016/j.tele.2013.11.008

Patel, R., & Patel, S. (2013). Survey on resource allocation strategies in cloud computing. *International Journal of Engineering Research & Technology (Ahmedabad), 2*(2), 1–5.

Pavlou, P. A. (2003). Consumer acceptance of electronic commerce: Integrating trust and risk with the technology acceptance model. *International Journal of Electronic Commerce, 7*(3), 101–134. doi:10.1080/10864415.2003.11044275

Pawar, L. (2017). Optimized Route Selection on the Basis of Discontinuity and Energy Consumption in Delay-Tolerant Networks. Advances in Computer and Computational Sciences, 439-449. doi:10.1007/978-981-10-3770-2_41

Pawar. (2014). Comparing: Routing Protocols on Basis of sleep mode. *International Journal of Modern Research, 4*(7).

Pawar. (2015). A Survey on Energy Efficient Clustering Protocols in Heterogeneous Wireless Sensor Networks. *International Journal of Advanced Research in Computer and Communication Engineering, 4*(8).

Pawar. (2015). IBEENISH: Improved Balanced Energy Efficient Network Integrated Super Heterogeneous Protocol for Wireless Sensor Networks. *International Journal of Computer Science and Networking, 4*(4).

Pawar. (2015). Reducing Impact of Flooding In VANETs Due To Distributed Denial. *International Journal of Engineering Science and Computing.*

Pazzani, M. J., & Billsus, D. (2007). Content-based recommendation systems. In *The adaptive web* (pp. 325–341). Springer. doi:10.1007/978-3-540-72079-9_10

Perez, S., Massey-Allard, J., Butler, D., Ives, J., Bonn, D., Yee, N., & Roll, I. (2017). Identifying productive inquiry in virtual labs using sequence mining. In E. André, R. Baker, X. Hu, M. M. T. Rodrigo, & B. du Boulay (Eds.), Artificial intelligence in education. Academic Press.

Peters, M. (2012). *The Economic and Operational Value of Storage Virtualization.* The HDS Perspective, ESG White Paper, 2012.

Pradeep, K., & Jacob, T. P. (2018). A hybrid approaches for task scheduling using the cuckoo and harmony search in cloud computing environment. *Wireless Personal Communications, 101*(4), 2287–2311. doi:10.100711277-018-5816-0

Pramod, N., Muppalla, A. K., & Srinivasa, K. (2013). Limitations and challenges in cloud-based applications development. In Z. Mahmood & S. Saeed (Eds.), *Software Engineering Frameworks for the Cloud Computing Paradigm* (pp. 55–75). Springer. doi:10.1007/978-1-4471-5031-2_3

Preparing for Successful VDI Implementation. (2014). A Business Perspective, Virtual Bridges.

Puzey, M., & Latham, S. (2016). Enabling operational excellence through the effective management of master data. *APPEA Journal, 56*(2), 575–575. doi:10.1071/AJ15081

Quynh, N. L. T., Heales, J., & Xu, D. (2014). *Examining significant factors and risks affecting the willingness to adopt a cloud-based CRM.* Paper presented at the 1st International Conference on HCI in Business, Crete, Greece. 10.1007/978-3-319-07293-7_4

Ragmani, A., El Omri, A., Abghour, N., Moussaid, K., & Rida, M. (2018). A performed load balancing algorithm for public Cloud computing using ant colony optimization. *Recent Patents on Computer Science, 11*(3), 179–195. doi:10.2174/2213275911666180903124609

Randhawa, R. (2018). Virtual Tier structured Grid based Dynamic Route Adjustment scheme for mobile sink based Wireless Sensor Networks (VTGDRA). *International Journal of Applied Engineering Research: IJAER, 13*(7), 4702–4707.

Rao, R. V., & Selvamani, K. (2015). Data Security Challenges and Its Solutions in Cloud Computing. *Procedia Computer Science, 48*, 204–209. doi:10.1016/j.procs.2015.04.171

Rashedi, E., Nezamabadi-Pour, H., & Saryazdi, S. (2009). GSA: A gravitational search algorithm. *Information Sciences, 179*(13), 2232–2248. doi:10.1016/j.ins.2009.03.004

Rehman, Z., Hussain, F. K., & Hussain, O. K. (2011, June). Towards multi-criteria cloud service selection. In *2011 Fifth International Conference on Innovative Mobile and Internet Services in Ubiquitous Computing* (pp. 44-48). IEEE.

Reka, F. (2015). Federated cloud computing security using forward-secure broadcast encryption HIBE. In *2015 11th International Computer Engineering Conference (ICENCO)*. IEEE.

Richardson & Mahfouz. (n.d.). Aligning business service management to goals: an integrated approach at BMC Software. *Journal of Technology Research.*

Rivas, B., Merino, J., Caballero, I., Serrano, M., & Piattini, M. (2017). Towards a service architecture for master data exchange based on ISO 8000 with support to process large datasets. *Computer Standards & Interfaces, 54,* 94–104. doi:10.1016/j.csi.2016.10.004

Sachdeva, K. (2011), *Cloud computing: Security Risk Analysis and Recommendations* (Master Thesis). University of Texas, Austin, TX.

Sajjad, H. (2013). Cloud computing technology: Security and Trust challenges. *International Journal of Security, Privacy and Trust Management, 2*(5).

Sarathy, R., & Muralidhar, K. (2002). The security of confidential numerical data in databases. *Information Systems Research, 13*(4), 389-403.

Sareen, P., Kumar, P., & Singh, T. D. (2015). Resource Allocation Strategies in Cloud Computing. *International Journal of Computer Science & Communication Networks, 5*(6), 358–365.

SAS. (2016). *SAS MDM*. Retrieved 05 22, 2017, from https://www.sas.com/fr_fr/software/data-management/master-data-management.html

Sato, H., Kanai, A., & Tanimoto, S. (2010). A cloud trust model in a security-aware cloud. *10th IEEE/ IPSJ International Symposium on the application and the internet, IEEE,* 121-124.

Scandurra, P. (2015). *Challenges and Assessment in Migrating IT Legacy Applications to the Cloud*. MESOCA. doi:10.1109/MESOCA.2015.7328120

Schurr, P. H., & Ozanne, J. L. (1985). Influences on exchange processes: Buyers' preconceptions of a seller's trustworthiness and bargaining toughness. *The Journal of Consumer Research, 4*(11), 939–953. doi:10.1086/209028

Schyff, K. (2014). Higher education cloud computing in South Africa: Towards understanding trust and adoption issues. *SACJ, 55,* 40–54.

Scott & Marshall. (2013). Mastering VMware vSphere 5.5. In *Planning and installing VMware ESXi*. Academic Press.

Shardanand, U., & Maes, P. (1995, May). Social information filtering: algorithms for automating" word of mouth". In Chi (Vol. 95, pp. 210-217). ACM.

Sharma.(2019). An Intelligent Genetic Base Algorithm for Optimal Virtual Machine Migration in Cloud Computing. *IJRTE, 8*(1).

Sharma, S., Mahajan, S., & Rana, V. (2019). A semantic framework for ecommerce search engine optimization. *International Journal of Information Technology, 11*(1), 31–36. doi:10.100741870-018-0232-y

Sheetal, A. P., & Ravindranath, K. (2019). Priority based resource allocation and scheduling using artificial bee colony (ABC) optimization for cloud computing systems. *International Journal of Innovative Technology and Exploring Engineering*, *8*(6), 39–44.

Sidhu, H. S. (2014). Comparative analysis of scheduling algorithms of Cloudsim in cloud computing. *International Journal of Computers and Applications*, *975*, 8887.

Sidhu, J., & Singh, S. (2014). Compliance based trustworthiness calculation mechanism in a cloud environment. *Procedia Computer Science*, *37*, 439–446. doi:10.1016/j.procs.2014.08.066

Silvola, R., Jaaskelainen, O., Kropsu-Vehkapera, H., & Haapasalo, H. (2011). Managing one master data–challenges and preconditions. *Industrial Management & Data Systems*, *111*(1), 146–162. doi:10.1108/02635571111099776

Singh, A., Juneja, D., & Malhotra, M. (2017). A novel agent based autonomous and service composition framework for cost optimization of resource provisioning in cloud computing. *Journal of King Saud University-Computer and Information Sciences*, *29*(1), 19–28. doi:10.1016/j.jksuci.2015.09.001

Singh, P., & Dhiman, G. (2017, December). A fuzzy-LP approach in time series forecasting. In *International Conference on Pattern Recognition and Machine Intelligence* (pp. 243-253). Springer. 10.1007/978-3-319-69900-4_31

Singh, P., & Dhiman, G. (2018). A hybrid fuzzy time series forecasting model based on granular computing and bio-inspired optimization approaches. *Journal of Computational Science*, *27*, 370–385. doi:10.1016/j.jocs.2018.05.008

Singh, P., & Dhiman, G. (2018). Uncertainty representation using fuzzy-entropy approach: Special application in remotely sensed high-resolution satellite images (RSHRSIs). *Applied Soft Computing*, *72*, 121–139. doi:10.1016/j.asoc.2018.07.038

Singh, P., Dhiman, G., & Kaur, A. (2018). A quantum approach for time series data based on graph and Schrödinger equations methods. *Modern Physics Letters A*, *33*(35), 1850208. doi:10.1142/S0217732318502085

Singh, P., Rabadiya, K., & Dhiman, G. (2018). A four-way decision-making system for the Indian summer monsoon rainfall. *Modern Physics Letters B*, *32*(25), 1850304. doi:10.1142/S0217984918503049

Smith, B., & Linden, G. (2017). Two decades of recommender systems at Amazon. com. *IEEE Internet Computing*, *21*(3), 12–18. doi:10.1109/MIC.2017.72

Smith, H. A., & McKeen, J. D. (2008). Developments in practice XXX: master data management: salvation or snake oil? *Communications of the Association for Information Systems*, *23*(1), 4. doi:10.17705/1CAIS.02304

Soleimanian, F., & Hashemi, S. (2012). Security Challenges in Cloud computing with more emphasis on Trust and Privacy. *International Journal of Scientific and Technology Research*, *1*(6), 49–54.

Soltanshahi, M., Asemi, R., & Shafiei, N. (2019). Energy-aware virtual machines allocation by krill herd algorithm in cloud data centers. *Heliyon, 5*(7).

Song, Y., Sun, Y., & Shi, W. (2011). A two-tiered on-demand resource allocation mechanism for VM-based data centers. *IEEE Transactions on Services Computing, 6*(1), 116–129. doi:10.1109/TSC.2011.41

Spruit, M., & Pietzka, K. (2015). MD3M: The master data management maturity model. *Computers in Human Behavior, 51*, 1068–1076. doi:10.1016/j.chb.2014.09.030

Sridhar, S. (2016). *A study on various software models as inclusive technology for sustainable solutions*. Academic Press.

Sridhar, S. (n.d.). *A Study On Various Programming Languages to Keep Pace with Innovation*. Academic Press.

Sridhar, S. (2016). Cloud computing made easy. *International Journal of Innovative Technology and Research, 4*(2), 2875–2906.

Stanik, A., Koerner, M., & Lymberopoulos, L. (2014). SLA-driven Federated Cloud Networking: Quality of Service for Cloud-based Software-Defined Networks. *Procedia Computer Science, 34*, 655–660. doi:10.1016/j.procs.2014.07.093

Student, U. G. (2015). Dynamic resource allocation scheme in cloud computing. *Procedia Computer Science, 47*, 30–36. doi:10.1016/j.procs.2015.03.180

Subashini, S., & Kavitha, V. (2010). A survey on security issues in service delivery models of cloud computing. *Network and Computer Applications, 34*, 1–11.

Subashini, S., & Kavitha, V. (2011). A survey on security issues in service delivery models of cloud computing. *Journal of Network and Computer Applications, 34*(1), 1–11. doi:10.1016/j.jnca.2010.07.006

Sulochana, M., & Dubey, O. (2015). Preserving Data Confidentiality Using Multi-cloud Architecture. *Procedia Computer Science, 50*, 357–362. doi:10.1016/j.procs.2015.04.035

Suri & Pawar. (2012). Stochastic Simulator For Estimating Delay in DTN Environment. *IJETAE, 2*(8), 183-189.

Thiam, C., & Thiam, F. (2019). Energy Efficient Cloud Data Center Using Dynamic Virtual Machine Consolidation Algorithm. In *International Conference on Business Information Systems*. Springer. 10.1007/978-3-030-20485-3_40

Tong-rang, F. A. N. (2012). Integration of IoT and DRAGON-lab in a cloud environment. *Journal of China Universities of Posts and Telecommunications, 19*(2), 87–91. doi:10.1016/S1005-8885(11)60250-1

Trummer, I., Leymann, F., Mietzner, R., & Binder, W. (2010, November). Cost-optimal outsourcing of applications into the clouds. In *2010 IEEE Second International Conference on Cloud Computing Technology and Science* (pp. 135-142). IEEE. 10.1109/CloudCom.2010.64

Truong, H.-L., Pham, T.-V., & Thoai, N. (n.d.). *Cloud Computing for Education and Research in Developing Countries.* IGI Global, doi:10.4018/978-1-4666-0957-0.ch005

Uddin & Rahman. (2011). Implementing Virtualization A six-step guide to virtualization implementation for a more efficient, reliable, and flexible data center. *International Journal of Advanced Computer Science and Applications, 2*(1).

Upadhye, G., & Dange, T. (2014, July). Cloud resource allocation as non-preemptive approach. In *Second International Conference on Current Trends In Engineering and Technology-ICCTET 2014* (pp. 352-356). IEEE. 10.1109/ICCTET.2014.6966314

Veeramallu, G. (2014). Dynamically Allocating the Resources Using Virtual Machines. *International Journal of Computer Science and Information Technologies, 5*(3), 4646-4648.

Verizon. (2009). *Start Packing. You're Moving to the Cloud – and We Can Help.* Verizon Business.

Verma, A., & Kaushal, S. (2011). Cloud computing security issues and challenges: A survey. Paper presented at the International Conference on Advances in Computing and Communications, Kochi, India. 10.1007/978-3-642-22726-4_46

Verma, S., Kaur, S., Dhiman, G., & Kaur, A. (2018, December). Design of a novel energy efficient routing framework for wireless nanosensor networks. In *2018 First International Conference on Secure Cyber Computing and Communication (ICSCCC)* (pp. 532-536). IEEE. 10.1109/ICSCCC.2018.8703308

Vilminko-Heikkinen, R., & Pekkola, S. (2019). Changes in roles, responsibilities and ownership in organizing master data management. *International Journal of Information Management, 47*, 76–87. doi:10.1016/j.ijinfomgt.2018.12.017

Vilminko-Heikkinen, R., Vilminko-Heikkinen, R., Pekkola, S., & Pekkola, S. (2017). Master data management and its organizational implementation: An ethnographical study within the public sector. *Journal of Enterprise Information Management, 30*(3), 454–475. doi:10.1108/JEIM-07-2015-0070

Wang & Mu. (2011). Security issues and countermeasures in cloud computing. In *Proceedings of 2011 IEEE International Conference on Grey Systems and Intelligent Services.* IEEE.

Wang, C., Ren, K., Lou, W., & Li, J. (2010). *Towards publicly auditable secure cloud data storage services* (Vol. 24). IEEE.

Wang, W., Jiang, Y., & Wu, W. (2016). Multiagent-based resource allocation for energy minimization in cloud computing systems. *IEEE Transactions on Systems, Man, and Cybernetics. Systems, 47*(2), 205–220. doi:10.1109/TSMC.2016.2523910

Watfa, Udoh, & Al Abdulsalam. (2015). *An Educational Virtualization Infrastructure.* Springer.

Watson, H. J., & McGivern, M. (2016). Getting started with business-driven data governance. *Business Intelligence Journal, 21*(1), 4–7.

Wen, Z. (2015). Cost-Effective, Reliable, and Secure Workflow Deployment over Federated Clouds. In *2015 IEEE 8th International Conference on Cloud Computing*. IEEE. 10.1109/CLOUD.2015.86

Wen, Z., Cala, J., & Watson, P. (2014). A scalable method for partitioning workflows with security requirements over federated clouds. In *Cloud Computing Technology and Science (CloudCom), 2014 IEEE 6th International Conference on*. IEEE. 10.1109/CloudCom.2014.89

Weng, C. F., & Wang, K. (2012, August). Dynamic resource allocation for MMOGs in cloud computing environments. In *2012 8th International Wireless Communications and Mobile Computing Conference (IWCMC)* (pp. 142-146). IEEE. 10.1109/IWCMC.2012.6314192

Why operational management in virtualized data centers is critical to delivering service assurance. (2012).,EMC Perspective.

Witanto, J. N., Lim, H., & Atiquzzaman, M. (2018). Adaptive selection of dynamic VM consolidation algorithm using neural network for cloud resource management. *Future Generation Computer Systems, 87*, 35–42. doi:10.1016/j.future.2018.04.075

Wolpert, D. H., & Macready, W. G. (1997). No free lunch theorems for optimization. *IEEE Transactions on Evolutionary Computation, 1*(1), 67–82. doi:10.1109/4235.585893

Wu, K. J., Liao, C. J., Tseng, M. L., Lim, M. K., Hu, J., & Tan, K. (2017). Toward sustainability: Using big data to explore the decisive attributes of supply chain risks and uncertainties. *Journal of Cleaner Production, 142*, 663–676. doi:10.1016/j.jclepro.2016.04.040

Xiao, X., & Li, Z. (2019). Chemical Reaction Multi-Objective Optimization for Cloud Task DAG Scheduling. *IEEE Access: Practical Innovations, Open Solutions, 7*, 102598–102605. doi:10.1109/ACCESS.2019.2926500

Xiao, Z., Song, W., & Chen, Q. (2012). Dynamic resource allocation using virtual machines for cloud computing environment. *IEEE Transactions on Parallel and Distributed Systems, 24*(6), 1107–1117. doi:10.1109/TPDS.2012.283

Xiong, J., Yu, G., & Zhang, X. (2017). Research on Governance Structure of Big Data of Civil Aviation. *Journal of Computer and Communications, 5*(05), 112–118. doi:10.4236/jcc.2017.55009

Xu, G., Pang, J., & Fu, X. (2013). A load balancing model based on cloud partitioning for the public cloud. *Tsinghua Science and Technology, 18*(1), 34–39. doi:10.1109/TST.2013.6449405

Yadav. (2014). Role of Cloud Computing in Education. *International Journal of Innovative Research in Computer and Communication Engineering, 2*(2).

Yang, C., Lan, S., Wang, L., Shen, W., & Huang, G. G. (2020). Big Data Driven Edge-Cloud Collaboration Architecture for Cloud Manufacturing: A Software Defined Perspective. *IEEE Access: Practical Innovations, Open Solutions, 8*, 45938–45950. doi:10.1109/ACCESS.2020.2977846

Yang, C., Shen, W., & Wang, X. (2018). The internet of things in manufacturing: Key issues and potential applications. *IEEE Systems, Man, and Cybernetics Magazine, 4*(1), 6–15. doi:10.1109/MSMC.2017.2702391

Yang, J. (2016). Multimedia recommendation and transmission system based on a cloud platform. *Future Generation Computer Systems.*

Yan, Z., Wang, J., & Li, G. (2014). A collective neurodynamic optimization approach to bound-constrained nonconvex optimization. *Neural Networks, 55*, 20–29. doi:10.1016/j.neunet.2014.03.006 PMID:24705545

Yeo, Buyya, Pourreza, & Eskicioglu. (2006). Cluster Computing: High-Performance, High-Availability, and High-Throughput Processing on a Network of Computers. In Handbook of nature. Springer.

Zech, P. (2011). Risk-based Security Testing in Cloud Computing Environments. *Fourth IEEE International Conference on Software Testing Verification and Validation*, 411-414. 10.1109/ICST.2011.23

Zhao, C., Ren, L., Zhang, Z., & Meng, Z. (2020). Master data management for manufacturing big data: A method of evaluation for data network. *Journal of the World Wide Web: Internet and Web Information Systems, 23*(2), 1407–1421. doi:10.100711280-019-00707-8

Zhao, J. F. (2014). *Strategies and Methods for Cloud Migration.* IJAC. doi:10.100711633-014-0776-7

Zhou, M., Zhang, R., Xie, W., Qian, W., & Zhou, A. (2010). Security and privacy in Cloud Computing: A Survey. *Sixth International Conference on Semantics, Knowledge, and Grids, IEEE-2010.* 10.1109/SKG.2010.19

Zissis, D., & Lekkas, D. (2012). Addressing Cloud computing security issues. *Future Generation Computer Systems, 28*(3), 583–592. doi:10.1016/j.future.2010.12.006

About the Contributors

Shadi Aljawarneh is ACM Senior member and a full professor, Software Engineering, at Jordan University of Science and Technology. He holds a BSc degree in Computer Science from Jordan Yarmouk University, a MSc degree in Information Technology from Western Sydney University and a PhD in Software Engineering from Northumbria University-England. Aljawarneh has presented at and been on the organizing committees for a number of international conferences and is a board member of the International Community for ACM, Jordan ACM Chapter, ACS, and others. A number of his papers have been selected as "Best Papers" in conferences and journals.

Manisha Malhotra is working as a professor at Chandigarh University, India. She has credible record of various degrees like Ph.D (Computer Science & Applications), MCA (With Distinction), BSC (Computer Science). She has published more than 20 research papers in various National / International Conferences, International Journal having indexed with Sci, Elsevier, Scopus, ACM. Dr. Malhotra is the members of various professional bodies like IEEE, CSI, IAENG. She also has the members of editorial boards of various journals. She has been awarded as Young Faculty & outstanding researcher award in the field of Cloud Computing. Dr. Malhotra research area includes Cloud Computing, Agent Technology, and Information Retrieval.

* * *

Gaurav Bathla is working as Associate Professor in department of Computer Science & Engineering. He is having more than 12 years of teaching experience with more than 30 research papers. His research area includes Wireless Sensor Networks, Algorithms Design, etc.

Ahan Chatterjee is an Engineering Student, in the Department of Computer Science and Engineering, The Neotia University, Sarisha. His research interests are in the areas of Machine Learning, Deep Learning, Applied Data Analytics in Healthcare, and Financial Market fields. Besides, he is a member of the International Association of Engineers (IAENG), Hong Kong. He has worked in several organizations namely, CSIR-CDRI, GoOffer Hyperlocal Pvt. Ltd., Research Guruji, and Daten & Wissen Pvt. Ltd as mainly Research Intern and Data Science Intern. He has contributed research papers in reputed journals at home and abroad, and also in edited books in different domains of computer science and data analytics published by Springer, IGI Global. Moreover, he has presented papers in 6 International Conferences and holds 1 Best Paper Award in an International Conference.

Gaurav Dhiman received his Ph.D. in Computer Engineering from Thapar Institute of Engineering & Technology, Patiala. He has completed his Master Degree of Computer Applications from Thapar Institute of Engineering & Technology, Patiala. He is currently working as an Assistant Professor with the Department of Computer Science, Government Bikram College of Commerce, Patiala. He was selected as an outstanding reviewer from Knowledge- Based Systems (Elsevier). He has published more than 25 peer-review research papers (indexed in SCI-SCIE). He is also in editorial board member of Artificial Intelligence Evolution journal. His research interest includes Single-, Multi-, Many-objectives optimization (Bio-inspired, Evolutionary and Quantum), Soft computing (Type-1 and Type-2 fuzzy sets), Power systems, and Change detection using remotely sensed high-resolution satellite data. His research articles can be found in Knowledge-Based Systems (Elsevier), Advances in Engineering Software (Elsevier), Applied Intelligence (Springer), Journal of Computational Science (Elsevier), Engineering with Computers (Springer), Applied Soft Computing (Elsevier), Engineering Applications of Artificial Intelligence (Elsevier), and so on.

Samia Chehbi Gamoura is an Associate Professor in the Business School EM Strasbourg at Strasbourg University and a research center HUMANIS. She is providing lectures in Artificial Intelligence, Big Data analytics, project management, and information systems. She is a Data Scientist and senior specialist in Artificial Intelligence and Machine Learning with full experience of 14 years in worldwide companies as IT Project Director. She received her Ph.D. in management, information systems and Artificial Intelligence from the Economics and Management Faculty of Lumière Lyon II University, France, in 2007.

Meenakshi Garg received her Master Degree of Technology from KSOU and Mater of Computer Applications from MDU. She also qualified the National Eligibility Test conducted by University Grant Commission, India. She is currently working as an Assistant Professor with the Department of Computer Science, Government

Bikram College of Commerce, Patiala. She has published more than 10 peer-review research papers. Her research interest includes Single-, Multi-, Many-objectives optimization (Bio-inspired, Evolutionary and Quantum), Soft computing (Type-1 and Type-2 fuzzy sets), Power systems, and Change detection using remotely sensed high-resolution satellite data.

Yogesh Madhukar Ghorpade currently working with Hitachi Vantara as an Senior Technical Consultant with competency and capability team Hyderabad, India. Previously worked with Dell technologies as an Advisor within Learning Design & Development in Dell Technologies Education Services (DTES) Bangalore, India. He has more than 14 years of experience in content: research, strategy, design, development, and delivery. He has mentored and managed content development and training delivery team with coordinating with subject matter expert, leaders/ management and other stakeholders. He has primary expertise on the domain such as networking, data-center, SDDC, storage infrastructure, cloud infrastructure, cloud infrastructure services, hybrid cloud, and multi-cloud. My other domain expertise includes data science and information security. He hold M.C.A, PGDCS, PGDM, M. Phil, and Ph. D. He has submitted my Ph. D thesis titled "Cost-Effective Approaches Using Virtualization Infrastructure Model in Educational Infrastructure Management". He has earned more than 12 industry certifications, which include CCNA, ITIL-OSA, VCP6-NSX, CISv2, CISv3, ISMv4, AWS-Solution Architect, SysOps. I have also published more than ten international technical papers, Two ISBN published books and worked on Research projects. Books titled: 1. "Information Security and Audit", Success Publications, 2014. 2. "Data Communication and Computer Networks", Suyog Publication, 2013.

R Kamatchi Iyer is working as a Director, PGDM, ISME School of Management & Entrepreneur entrepreneurship, Mumbai. She completed her Ph.D., thesis titled "Security issues of Web services in a Service Oriented Architecture" with Mother Teresa Women's University, Kodaikanal. She completed her MCA from Baradidasan University and M.Phil., in Computer Science from Alagappa University. She has 15 years of teaching experience with various courses. She has co-authored 5 books and presented more than 35 papers in National and International conference. She has got 15 International journal publications. She has conducted various sessions on the topics of Service modeling, Customer Relationship Management, Internet Security, Current IT trends in various students and faculty forums. She is the approved guide for M.phil. and Ph.d., programmes with Madurai Kamaraj University, Prist University, Bharathiar University, JJTU University. 7 students completed their M.Phil. dissertation under her guidance and two students are pursuing their doctoral research. She is in the editorial board of various peer reviewed journals and books.

Shivani Jaswal is working as an Assistant Professor in University Institute of Computing, Chandigarh University. Currently she is pursuing PhD in the field of Cloud Computing.

R. Kamatchi is working as a Director, PGDM, ISME School of Management & Entrepreneur entrepreneurship, Mumbai. She completed her Ph.D., thesis titled "Security issues of Web services in a Service Oriented Architecture" with Mother Teresa Women's University, Kodaikanal. She completed her MCA from Baradidasan University and M.Phil., in Computer Science from Alagappa University. She has 15 years of teaching experience with various courses. She has co-authored 5 books and presented more than 35 papers in National and International conference. She has got 15 International journal publications. She has conducted various sessions on the topics of Service modeling, Customer Relationship Management, Internet Security, Current IT trends in various students and faculty forums. She is the approved guide for M.phil. and Ph.d., programmes with Madurai Kamaraj University, Prist University, Bharathiar University, JJTU University. 7 students completed their M.Phil. dissertation under her guidance and two students are pursuing their doctoral research . She is in the editorial board of various peer reviewed journals and books.

Amandeep Kaur received her Ph.D. in Computer Engineering from Thapar Institute of Engineering & Technology, Patiala. She has completed his Master Degree in Engineering from GNDU, Amritsar. She is currently working as an Assistant Professor with the Department of Computer Science, SGGSWU, Punjab. Her research interest includes Single-, Multi-, Many-objectives optimization (Bio-inspired, Evolutionary and Quantum), Soft computing (Type-1 and Type-2 fuzzy sets), Power systems, and Change detection using remotely sensed high-resolution satellite data. Her research articles can be found in Knowledge-Based Systems (Elsevier), Advances in Engineering Software (Elsevier), Applied Intelligence (Springer), Journal of Computational Science (Elsevier), Engineering with Computers (Springer), Applied Soft Computing (Elsevier), Engineering Applications of Artificial Intelligence (Elsevier), and so on.

Harjeet Kaur received her B.tech degree from Kukshetra university, Haryana and M.tech degree from Thapar university, Patiala. Presently, She is working as assistant Professor in the Department of Computer Science & Engineering, Chandigarh University, Gharuan Mohali, Punjab, India.

Inderbir Kaur is working as an Assistant Professor in GSSDGS Khalsa College, Patiala. She has experience of more than 8 years. She has published various research papers in National / International Journals/ Conferences.

Anustup Mukherjee Student of Chandigarh university and Present computer vision engineer at Dark Horse INC USA, former Lead AI Engineer at Omdena, worked with 3 + companies in AI development, Holding Patent and Research on AI ,Former Intern at IIT Patna and Researcher at IIT Bombay.

Lokesh Pawar is a professor in Computer Science and Engineering wing and also the founder member of Technical Training Team at Chandigarh University, Mohali, Punjab. He is a recipient of Outstanding Faculty Research Award in 2016, 2017 and 2018. The author's current interest is in the field of Cloud Computing, WSN, Delay tolerant Networks. He has published more than 50 research papers in these areas. He holds two Indian Patents in Hardware Security and easy learning of programming language. He has written several books on delay tolerant networks, route prediction in vanet, Data Structures and on testing your skills in C language.

Prathap R. is currently pursuing his Ph.D. at Vellore Institute of Technology, India. He is working as Assistant Professor (Junior) in the School of Computer Science and Engineering, Vellore Institute of Technology. His research area includes Cloud Computing, Information Security and BlockChain Technologies.

Parneet Rangi Randhawa is an associate professor in the Department of Commerce at DAV College, Sector 10, Chandigarh. The primary area of specialization is marketing Research. She has authored books on marketing research. She has credit of publications in various Journals on topics pertaining to economics and marketing.

Mohanasundaram Ranganathan is an associate professor in the School of computer science and engineering at Vellore Institute of Technology, India and is active in research. He has published several papers in computer science engineering streams in various top reputed journals. He has been guiding several students from various specialization in their research works.

Sunny Sharma is working as an Associate Professor in University of Jammu. He has 3 years of experience. He has published 4 papers is SCI, Scopus. Currently he is doing doctorate of philosophy. His area of interest is Web semantic, web personalization.

Pooja Thakur is working as an Assistant Professor in University Institute of Computing, Chandigarh University. She has more than 6 years of experience.

Krishan Tuli is working as an Assistant Professor in university Institute of Computing, Chandigarh University. He has a decade of experience in computer applications. He has published various research papers in National / International Journals/ Conferences.

Index

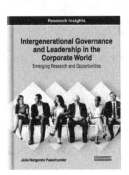

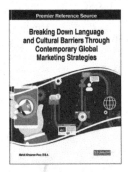
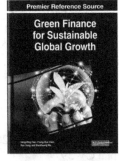

Ensure Quality Research is Introduced to the Academic Community

Become an IGI Global Reviewer for Authored Book Projects

Premier Reference Source
Emerging GIS Applications for Emergency and Disaster Management

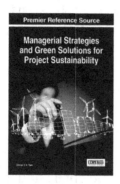
Premier Reference Source
Managerial Strategies and Green Solutions for Project Sustainability

Premier Reference Source
Comparative Approaches to Using R and Python for Statistical Data Analysis

Premier Reference Source
Solutions for High-Touch Communications in a High-Tech World

The overall success of an authored book project is dependent on quality and timely reviews.

In this competitive age of scholarly publishing, constructive and timely feedback significantly expedites the turnaround time of manuscripts from submission to acceptance, allowing the publication and discovery of forward-thinking research at a much more expeditious rate. Several IGI Global authored book projects are currently seeking highly-qualified experts in the field to fill vacancies on their respective editorial review boards:

Applications and Inquiries may be sent to:
development@igi-global.com

Applicants must have a doctorate (or an equivalent degree) as well as publishing and reviewing experience. Reviewers are asked to complete the open-ended evaluation questions with as much detail as possible in a timely, collegial, and constructive manner. All reviewers' tenures run for one-year terms on the editorial review boards and are expected to complete at least three reviews per term. Upon successful completion of this term, reviewers can be considered for an additional term.

If you have a colleague that may be interested in this opportunity, we encourage you to share this information with them.